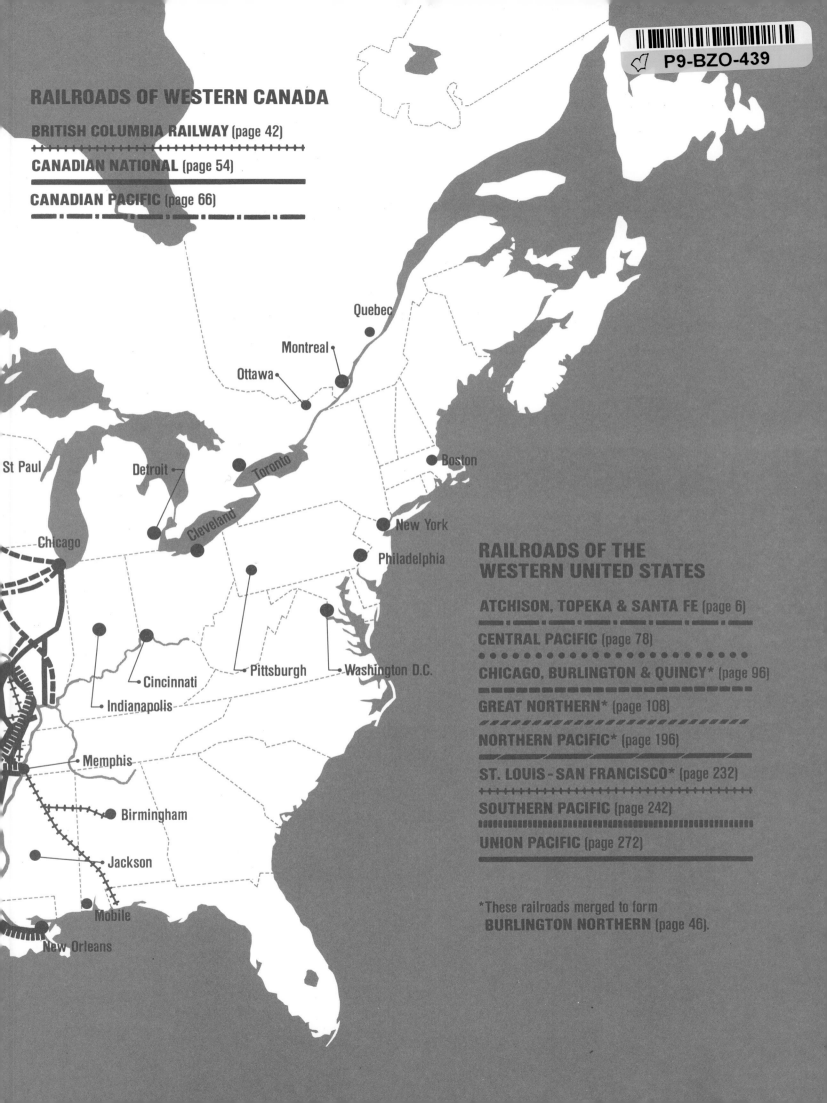

RAILROADS OF WESTERN CANADA

BRITISH COLUMBIA RAILWAY (page 42)

CANADIAN NATIONAL (page 54)

CANADIAN PACIFIC (page 66)

St Paul

Detroit

Chicago

Cleveland

Quebec

Montreal

Ottawa

Toronto

Boston

New York

Philadelphia

Cincinnati

Indianapolis

Pittsburgh

Washington D.C.

Memphis

Birmingham

Jackson

Mobile

New Orleans

RAILROADS OF THE WESTERN UNITED STATES

ATCHISON, TOPEKA & SANTA FE (page 6)

CENTRAL PACIFIC (page 78)

CHICAGO, BURLINGTON & QUINCY* (page 96)

GREAT NORTHERN* (page 108)

NORTHERN PACIFIC* (page 196)

ST. LOUIS – SAN FRANCISCO* (page 232)

SOUTHERN PACIFIC (page 242)

UNION PACIFIC (page 272)

*These railroads merged to form
BURLINGTON NORTHERN (page 46).

THE GREAT RAILROADS
OF NORTH AMERICA

THE GREAT RAILROADS
OF NORTH AMERICA

Bill Yenne, General Editor

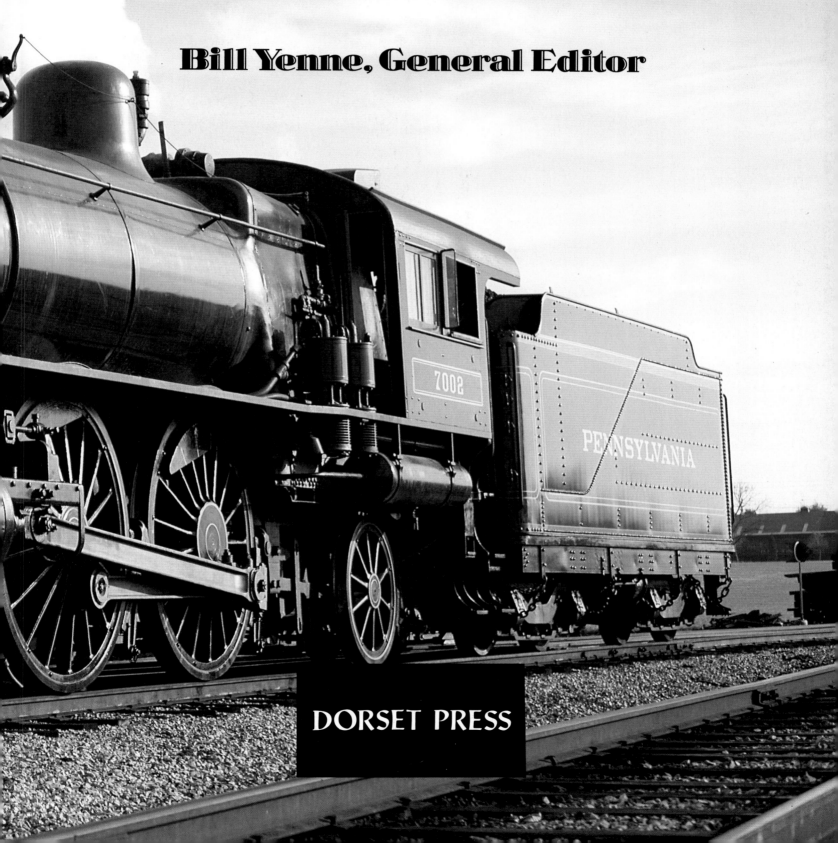

DORSET PRESS

PICTURE CREDITS

All photos originated from the railroad companies whose equipment and facilities are depicted, with the following exception:

AGS Picture Archives: 8 (bottom), 10-11, 24 (top), 116 (bottom), 158, 172 (top), 191, 198 (top), 200-201, 206 (top), 218-219, 282

Albany Institute of History and Art, McKinney Library: 170-171, 173 (top), 174, 175, 181, 186, 187

ALCO Historical Photos: 182-182 (bottom), 184 (top), 188-189 (bottom), 192-193 (both), 279 (bottom)

©American Graphic Systems: 19 (bottom), 166, 270 (top)

Amtrak: 194

The Association of American Railroads: 102-103, 141, 145, 168-169, 190 (bottom), 239 (top), 245 (bottom)

Baltimore & Ohio Railroad Museum: 24-25 (bottom), 26-27, 30 (both), 36-37 (all)

The Bancroft Library, University of California, Berkeley: 14 (top), 254 (bottom)

HL Broadbelt: 32-33 (bottom), 94-95 (top), 124-125 (bottom), 216 (top), 228 (top), 228-229 (bottom)

Charles A Brown: 31, 33 (top), 40-41, 189 (top)

California State Railroad Museum: 216 (bottom), 217, 220-221 (top), 221 (bottom), 224, 225 (top), 226, 227 (both), 230 (bottom)

Electro-Motive Division, General Motors Corporation: 104 (bottom), 160

General Electric: 225 (bottom), 230 (top)

©Golden Spike Productions: 34-35 (all), 38-39 (all), 51 (bottom), 106, 107, 130 (top), 134, 210-211, 240 (top), 241 (top)

Gulf Oil Company: 172 (bottom)

©Nils Huxtable/Steamscenes: 2-3, 7, 21 (top), 47, 51 (top), 55, 71, 195, 222-223, 231, 273, 277, 284-285 (bottom)

Library of Congress Collection: 83

National Railway Historical Society: 249

New York Central Historical Society, Inc, Purinton Collection: 178- 179 (bottom), 182 (top), 184-185 (bottom)

New York Historical Society: 176-177 (both), 179 (top), 180

PHMC Railroad Museum of Pennsylvania: 229 (top)

Pullman Company: 151 (bottom), 220 (bottom)

Vic F Reyna: 242 (top), 243

©Ron Ruhoff's Photomusical Adventures: 280-281

Seaver Center for Western History Research, Natural History Museum of Los Angeles County: 15 (top), 16 (top), 17 (both)

Smithsonian Institution: 96-97 (both), 98-99 (all), 100-101 (all), 110, 114, 116-117 (top), 119 (top), 140, 142, 143, 146-147 (both), 148-149, 150, 152-153 (all), 154-155 (all), 156-157 (both), 164, 196-197, 202 (bottom), 204 (top), 205 (top), 208- 209 (bottom), 214 (bottom), 232-233, 234, 235, 236-237, 238- 239 (bottom)

Southern Pacific Company: 78-79, 80-81 (all), 82 (both), 84-85 (all), 86-87, 88-89 (all)

Stevens Institute of Technology: 214 (top)

Stan F Styles: 72 (bottom)

Jack Swanberg: 190 (top)

Union Pacific Railroad Museum Collection: 274, 275 (both), 276 (both)

This edition published by
Dorset Press,
a division of Marboro Books Corp.,
by arrangement with Brompton Books Corporation.

Produced by Brompton Books Corporation
15 Sherwood Place
Greenwich, CT 06830

ISBN 0-88029-783-2

Printed in Slovenia

Designed by Tom Debolski

Captioned by Annie McGarry and Lynne Piade

Page 1: Eastbound Santa Fe passenger train, the Grand Canyon, races through Cajon Pass, where the main line crosses the coast range of mountains.
Pages 2-3: An E2 4-4-2 Atlantic passenger engine. The original No 7002, an E3, attained 127.1 mph with the Pennsylvania Special in 1905.

CONTENTS

THE ATCHISON, TOPEKA & SANTA FE

Edited by Pamela Berkman

*F*or years recognized as one of the greatest railroads in the United States, the Atchison, Topeka & Santa Fe had its beginnings in a dusty trail that snaked its way across the plains and through the mountains of the southwestern United States. At one end of the trail was Independence, Missouri. At the other rested Santa Fe, an exotic city nestling in the remoteness of the great American desert. As the United States began its westward expansion, the Santa Fe Trail became a major trade thoroughfare.

The first successful attempt to carry on overland trade with Santa Fe was a small expedition from Missouri organized and led by Captain William Becknell in 1821, shortly after Mexico gained its freedom. So successful was Captain Becknell's first trip that a larger expedition was formed the next year, and a new and shorter route to Santa Fe was pioneered and mapped.

Both routes departed southwesterly from Council Grove, Kansas, and intersected the Arkansas River near Great Bend, following the river to a point just east of Dodge City. Here the trails diverged, one branch heading south and west across the plains to Las Vegas, and the other, more generally used, following the Arkansas River to La Junta and turning south over the Raton Pass to Las Vegas. After Becknell's second caravan, commerce over the Santa Fe Trail expanded by leaps and bounds.

As trade expanded and navigation of the Missouri River extended westward, so too, the outfitting points for the caravans moved further west, to Kansas City and Independence. Normal practice was for the adventurous trader to load his provisions and trade goods and strike out alone for Council Grove, a rendezvous point on the route to Santa Fe.

It was in full recognition of this ever-increasing commerce that the soon-to-be-railroad builders, mindful of the tremendous potential, cast longing glances in the direction of Santa Fe.

The early Santa Fe was the vision of Cyrus Kurtz Holliday, a Pennsylvanian who traveled to what is now Kansas in 1854 and laid the foundations of the Santa Fe before the Civil War. Holliday wanted to build a railroad from Topeka to Santa Fe, New Mexico to serve the entire region between those communities. He secured a charter in 1859 for his railroad—which he and his fellow investors modestly called the Atchison & Topeka Railroad—and gave himself the title of president.

Holliday believed Kansas would soon be settled and developed into a great region of agriculture and commerce. His dream did not appear realistic at the time because Kansas was then so wild and unsettled. However, Holliday realized that when settlers came to farm the fertile, cheap lands, the territory would grow rapidly.

Beyond Kansas lay the fabled city of Santa Fe, once part of the Spanish empire, but seized in 1846 for the United States during its war with Mexico. In Holliday's time, it was already a bustling center of trade and farming, and Holliday wanted to replace the wagons that lumbered along the old pack-and-cattle Santa Fe Trail with locomotives and freight cars.

Holliday set about to build his railroad but was unable to attract investors until 1863, when Congress came to his rescue. In an effort to keep Kansas in the Union during the Civil War, Congress granted the Santa Fe three million acres of land, in alternate sections, to help finance and spur construction, just as it had helped the Union Pacific and Central Pacific lines build the transcontinental railroad. Congress, however, put one major stipulation on the land grants: the Santa Fe would have to reach the Colorado border within 10 years to take title to the lands that they had been granted.

Previous page: *The familiar Santa Fe logo accompanies this westbound locomotive going through the snow-covered high desert between Mojave and Tehachapi, California, delivering freight over that well-worn path so many Santa Fe trains have travelled over the last century.*

Above: *Original No. 5 was built for the Santa Fe Railway by the Taunton Locomotive Works in 1870. It had four drive wheels and was named* Thomas Sherlock.

Left: *A construction scene from the 1850s.*

Above, right: *Cyrus Kurtz Holliday, father of the Santa Fe Railroad.*

Right: *The Santa Fe station in El Paso, Texas.*

Like other western railroads, the Santa Fe found it difficult to raise adequate financing during the Civil War years. Yet Holliday remained optimistic, and eventually, bolstered by support from the federal government, the Santa Fe's stockholders met and changed the name of the line to the Atchison, Topeka & Santa Fe Railway (ATSF).

Construction got under way in the fall of 1868, after local newspapers advertised for 500 men to work on the fledgling rail lines at the rate of $1.75 a day. During ground-breaking ceremonies, Holliday predicted that the Santa Fe would one day reach the Pacific and the Gulf of Mexico. His prediction came true within the next quarter century.

By 1869, the Santa Fe was operating 28 miles of track, and by 1871 track gangs had reached the notorious Dodge City, where arguments were often settled with guns. Dodge City and other cattle towns along the Kansas frontier were important to the Santa Fe, as they served as railheads for the large herds of the Longhorn cattle driven up from Texas via the Old Chisolm Trail. Until then the Kansas Pacific Railroad had enjoyed a monopoly on the cattle trade to Chicago. Now the Santa Fe wanted to cross Kansas south of Abilene to take some of Kansas Pacific's business.

In the early 1870s, these towns also served as major shipping points for buffalo hides. The enormous buffalo herds of the great plains were especially bountiful in Kansas, but with the coming of the railroads they were doomed. Buffalo coats and robes were highly fashionable in the eastern United States and Europe, and so much money could be made in hides

that professional hunters undertook a wholesale slaughter of buffalo.

The Santa Fe track gangs continued working westward until they reached the Colorado border late in 1872, well ahead of the deadline set by Congress. Like other western railroad employees, Santa Fe track gangs consisted of Civil War veterans—mostly Irish—and local farm boys who drove teams of horses and mules.

The men did not have the best working conditions. In summer, the gangs labored under a

Left: *This Currier & Ives print depicts one of the perils faced by early railroads—prairie fires.*

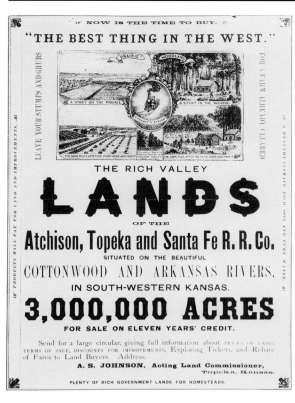

hot, pounding sun, and in winter they faced freezing rain and snow. They lived in construction camps, slept in sheds built of scrap lumber and existed on harsh food such as beans, salt pork, bread and sorghum. For meat they ate buffalo slaughtered by professional hunters hired by the railroad. Construction camps followed the railhead as it moved westward. With the camps came gamblers and prostitutes who set up shop in makeshift tents.

It was cattle drivers, the cowboys of the frontier—not the Indians—who were the worst threat to the workmen. The drivers and the railroad workers did not mix easily in the dance halls and saloons, often arguing and fighting, sometimes to the death.

As track construction progressed westward, the Santa Fe discovered that Kansas did not have enough people. Without people to farm the land and without towns to generate business, there could be no freight and no passenger service. So the Santa Fe set about to bring settlers to the region, opening a land development department to publish booklets and pamphlets to lure new settlers. In Europe,

Left: Promotionals like this lured farmers westward, and thus built business for the Santa Fe.

Below: Wells Fargo raced the Santa Fe across the plains.

Right: A vintage Santa Fe 4-4-0 and passenger train on the Canyon Diablo bridge.

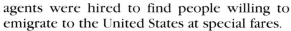

agents were hired to find people willing to emigrate to the United States at special fares.

Santa Fe's immigration program got off to a shaky start. Kansas suffered through several grasshopper plagues in the late 1870s and through two serious droughts in 1879 and 1880. The crops withered and thousands of farm animals perished. The grasshoppers became so dense on the prairies that the farmers could not work their horse teams. The Santa Fe trains were slowed, and finally brought to a shuddering halt, when the smashed grasshoppers grew too slippery to allow traction. As thousands of people fled Kansas for other sections of the country with fewer grasshoppers and more water, the Santa Fe was plunged into the red.

Eventually, the grasshoppers disappeared and the rains returned, enabling the Santa Fe to recover financially and continue its westward expansion.

The Santa Fe reached the Colorado-Kansas border in 1872, one year ahead of the 10-year deadline set by Congress to claim title to the land grants. Continued progress also set the stage for a showdown with another competitor, the Denver & Rio Grande Railroad (D&RG), which had grand expansion plans of its own in Colorado.

William Jackson Palmer, a former Union cavalry general in the Civil War, organized the Denver & Rio Grande in 1870 to build southward from Denver to El Paso and then on to Mexico City. Palmer wanted to push his railroad into New Mexico as much as the Santa Fe wanted to reach Pueblo and Canyon City, which were already served by the D&RG.

By this time, Boston financiers Thomas and Joseph Nickerson had wrested control of the Santa Fe from Cyrus Holliday, although he continued as secretary of the board of directors. These two brothers recognized the need to expand the business of the railroad beyond carrying cattle and buffalo hides. They wanted to generate revenue from the rich mines in the Rocky Mountains of Colorado.

William Palmer did not want to build a railroad that would compete with the Santa Fe, so he traveled east to persuade the new owners of the Santa Fe to cooperate in building one line. The Santa Fe owners rejected his proposition, setting up a confrontation for control of two important mountain passes — the Raton Pass from Colorado into New Mexico and Royal Gorge in southern Colorado.

The first clash came in early 1873. Legal rights to the 8000-foot Raton Pass, located 15 miles south of Trinidad, Colorado, were ambiguous. Both railroads claimed title, although Thomas Nickerson did not see the urgency of crossing the pass to get to Santa Fe. Wagon traffic between Santa Fe and Colorado was not heavy, and Nickerson did not believe that the line would support a rail service. It was up to Cyrus Holliday to convince Nickerson and the board of directors of the need to expand into New Mexico.

Nickerson sent survey crews south to where Palmer had already ordered surveys and then leased the rights to construct a new line over the pass to a new railroad, the Canyon City & San Juan.

The Santa Fe and the D&RG were not the only railroads battling for the rights to the terri-

tory of New Mexico. (New Mexico became a state in 1912.) The Southern Pacific, under CP Huntington's shrewd leadership, was trying to stop the Santa Fe and the D&RG. Thomas Nickerson had ordered general manager William Barstow Strong to approach the New Mexico legislature to negotiate the required rights to build rail lines in the territory. When Strong reached Santa Fe, however, he discovered that Southern Pacific representatives had beat him there.

The SP men had persuaded the lawmakers to require that the boards of the railroad operating in New Mexico be dominated by residents of the territory. In addition, the law required the railroads to demonstrate that they possessed 10 percent of the building costs before starting work, which would make construction impossible for the Santa Fe.

Strong was not to be deterred, however. He stalked the halls of the legislature, seeking a way to get around the law. He found that the Southern Pacific agents had left one loophole. They had neglected to get New Mexico lawmakers to repeal the old law. Still in force therefore and superseding the new law, the old law allowed the Santa Fe to proceed without meeting the new requirements. Strong immediately created a new corporation—the New Mexico & Southern Pacific Railroad Company—to build from the Raton Pass to the border of the Arizona territory. He even convinced the law-

makers to exempt the new line from taxes for six years.

With business in Santa Fe completed, the stage was set for a construction battle with the D&RG for the Raton Pass. Strong returned to Kansas and instructed his crews to prepare to build a line across the Raton Pass—using force if necessary. He took a train to Trinidad, where he recruited a small army of men and armed them with rifles and shovels. Palmer, on the other side, had already recruited armed men to fight for control of the pass.

The opposing forces arrived at the mouth of the Raton Pass on the same day in 1873. Men from the two railroads growled at each other, but the expected fight did not erupt. The Santa Fe, having arrived just minutes ahead of the D&RG, took control of the Raton Pass, and its track crews went to work the next day.

On 7 December 1878, the first train traveled over Raton Pass by means of a switchback. The next year crews bored a 2000-foot tunnel through the summit, reducing the maximum grade from 316 feet per mile to 185. The Santa Fe had finally reached New Mexico.

The contest for Raton Pass was not the last time the two railroads would battle over Colorado land. Later, the Santa Fe and the D&RG fought for control of the Grand Canyon of the Arkansas—the Royal Gorge—a narrow rift 3000 feet deep through the granite Rockies west of Pueblo, leading to lucrative coal fields.

Once again, Strong ordered armed men into action and sent them to the Royal Gorge to prevent D&RG crews from advancing. He also ordered one of his engineers, William R Morley, to round up reinforcements from Canyon City. Since Morley could not travel on D&RG trains, he had to ride 63 miles on horseback to get help. The poor horse died from exhaustion, but Morley saved the day for the Santa Fe.

Meanwhile, Palmer and 200 armed men boarded a train and traveled to the mouth of the canyon to do battle. Morley led his own men back to the canyon to confront Palmer, telling the Denver & Rio Grande men that he would use all necessary force, including 'a bullet between the eyes' to stop them. The two

groups decided not to fight, yielding control of the pass to the Santa Fe.

Not willing to give up so easily, Palmer took his battle into the courtroom. Eventually, the Santa Fe gave up the rights to the Royal Gorge Canyon and was allowed to continue its transcontinental conquest, while the D&RG was allowed to expand locally in Colorado.

During this era of conflict, the Santa Fe decided to continue westward to California. There was little farming population in New Mexico from which the railroad could draw business and revenue, and it badly needed the business to be found in the Golden State.

After his success in the Colorado rail wars, William Strong became president and began

Left: Passengers relax on the 'veranda' of the Navajo *passenger liner.*

Below: Now at the Railroad Museum in Sacramento, California, engine No. 1010 is a remake of the Coyote Special.

Right: A passenger train passes through the arid West of the 1930s.

Below, right: A Santa Fe club car is the setting for this Roaring Twenties social gathering.

With new steel tracks and improved rolling stock came larger locomotives. Like other railroads, the Santa Fe had long favored the 4-4-0s, but in the 1880s, the Santa Fe began using larger locomotives, such as 2-6-0s and 4-6-0s from the Baldwin Locomotive Works and Brooks Locomotive Works, to pull trains of increasing length and load.

In the late 1880s, reduced rates and increased interest payments on company debts caused declines in revenues and earnings. Despite the fact that Strong was buying more locomotives and rolling stock each year, shortages continued to plague the system and the slide continued into the early 1890s, when the railroad, subject to the same economic pressures that were bankrupting competing lines, fell into receivership.

In 1896, Edward Ripley took over as president of the system and engineered the Santa Fe out of receivership. During his 24 years in control, Ripley expanded trackage to more than 11,000 miles and laid the foundations for the renaissance of the company. Ripley, who had worked for various railroads before coming to the Santa Fe, brought with him a reputation for honesty, integrity and leadership. He was responsible for making the Santa Fe one of the most successful railroads in the United States.

For those who traveled the Santa Fe's elite passenger trains, the name Fred Harvey conjured up great gastronomic memories. Harvey single-handedly transformed the business of serving food to rail travelers into an art—an art that has been lost with the advent of airline travel.

In the 1870s, some of the worst food in the United States was served at railroad depots. Fred Harvey changed all that. He believed that quality and service at the lunch counter were as important as speed and safety aboard trains. In 1876, he approached the Santa Fe with his idea. The superintendent of the railroad gave Harvey permission to set up a restaurant at the company's station in Topeka, Kansas.

Within a few months, passengers clamored to get off the trains for a taste of Fred Harvey's food, and the Santa Fe willingly financed Harvey at other stations. In no time at all, Fred Harvey restaurants were an institution, equally famous for their food as they were for the 'Harvey Girls,' the young women who worked as waitresses. After working for a short time, many a Harvey Girl became the bride of a Santa Fe employee or a local rancher, and it was said that the towns along the Santa Fe were soon filled with numerous babies named Fred or Harvey.

With the assistance of Fred Harvey, the railroad had built a reputation for fine food, and in 1905 'Death Valley Scotty' helped make the Santa Fe known for its speed, with the record-breaking run of the *Coyote Special*. On 1 July

expanding the Santa Fe system. The Santa Fe purchased a half interest in a charter owned by the St Louis & San Francisco Railway, permitting it to forge into California. Later, the railroad acquired the Chicago, Cincinnati & St Louis Railway, which owned track between Chicago and the Mississippi River. These two acquisitions gave the Santa Fe more than 7000 miles of track, with operations from the Great Lakes to the Gulf of Mexico and the West Coast.

Strong added rolling stock and spent money to improve trackage, increasing equipment from 5530 units in 1880 to 32,293 in 1895. He ordered new, heavier steel tracks on the main lines, and replaced old ties with treated ones.

1905, Walter Scott, aka Death Valley Scotty, wrote out a check to the Santa Fe for $4500 so that the he could reach Chicago in 46 hours. The Santa Fe put together a special train for the occasion, the *Coyote Special*, consisting of a Pullman observation car, a diner and a baggage car pulled by a 2-6-0 steam locomotive.

At one o'clock on the afternoon of 2 July, the *Coyote Special* left Los Angeles' La Grande Station. It pulled into Chicago at 11:54 am on July 12 — just under 44 hours after it left Los Angeles.

Though its many runs were never as dramatic as that of the *Coyote Special*, the *California Limited* contributed to Santa Fe's reputation for exemplary passenger service. Established during the tenure of President Ripley, the *California Limited* was one of the best known, most reliable and comfortable passenger trains from the Midwest to the West Coast.

The *California Limited* was extremely popular in the summer months when people headed to and from California. Each day as many as seven trains, each containing 11 sleeping cars filled with passengers, left Dearborn Station in Chicago or Union Station in Los Angeles within a half an hour of each other. At one point no fewer than 45 trains operated between the two cities — a record that still stands.

In 1937, Santa Fe introduced the *Super Chief*, the first all-diesel, all-Pullman streamliner in the United States. The *Super Chief* sped between Chicago and Los Angeles in 39.5 hours, which was more than 14 hours faster than its steam predecessor, the *Chief*. Known for its luxury and food, the *Super Chief* was *the* train of the rich and famous in the 1940s and 1950s.

A year after service on the *Super Chief* began, the Santa Fe launched *El Capitan*, an all-coach streamlined diesel that also operated between Chicago and Los Angeles.

When the diesel proved its value in passenger service, Santa Fe officials set about replacing its freight service fleet of steam locomotives. The Electro-Motive Division of General Motors delivered a 5400-horsepower engine to the railroad in 1938 nicknamed *The Jeep* and given the number 100. *The Jeep* hauled its first train of freight cars from Kansas City to

Below: The Chicago Exposition of 1938 exhibited the progress from diesel to state-of-the-art steam (second to left).

Right: The Santa Fe's Super Chief *streamliner featured daily service between Chicago and Los Angeles. Passengers were treated to all Pullman cars. Here, the* Super Chief *ascends the steep grades near Wooton, Colorado.*
Right, below: A map of the Santa Fe.

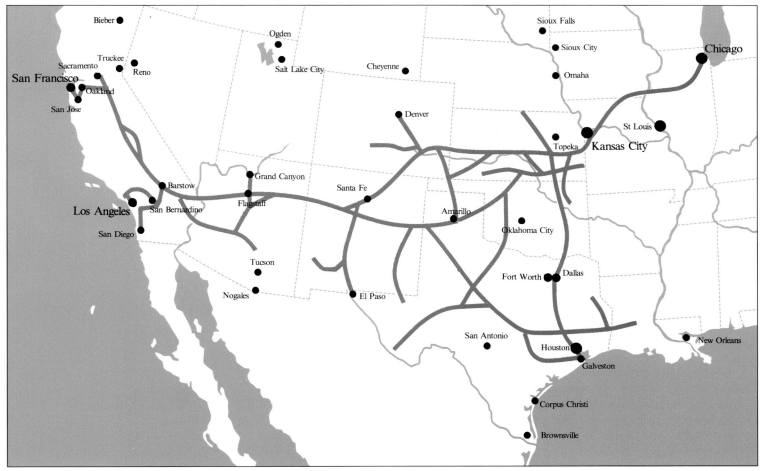

Los Angeles under regular operating conditions and proved that it could haul more freight cars up a grade at a higher speed than any steam locomotive in service at the time. No 100 trimmed the time it took a freight train to cover the distance from Chicago to Los Angeles from six days to four days, and then to three days. In 1938, hauling a freight train from the Great Lakes to the West Coast by steam locomotive required nine engines and a total of 35 stops for fuel and water. In contrast, *The Jeep* required just five stops.

Throughout the troubled times of the Great Depression and World War II, the Santa Fe stayed at the forefront of American railroads. However, the rail industry as a whole was entering a period of decline. Survival for many small lines was achieved only by merging with larger roads. During the 1950s and 1960s, the Santa Fe acquired numerous smaller roads and began diversifying so that the company was not dependent solely on its railroad profits.

Then, in 1983 the Santa Fe itself merged with another great American railroad—the Southern Pacific. Each railroad operated separately, each maintaining its own routes, pending the approval of the Interstate Commerce Commission (ICC). However, in June 1987, the ICC rejected the merger of the two railroad companies on the grounds that it would reduce competition in the West. Thus, the recently formed Santa Fe Southern Pacific Corporation, the parent corporation of the two historic railroads, would have to sell one (or both) of the lines and it elected to keep the Santa Fe. The Southern Pacific was sold to the Denver & Rio Grande.

Today, the Atchison, Topeka & Santa Fe Railroad continues the vision of Cyrus Holliday, operating over 11,000 miles, from Chicago to the Gulf of Mexico at Houston and Galveston, and throughout the Southwest to the West Coast ports of San Francisco, Los Angeles and San Diego.

Below: Two modern road switchers assist a Santa Fe freight train near Hesperia, California, by pushing from behind.

Right: The lead locomotives of this Santa Fe freight display the SFSP merger color scheme.

THE BALTIMORE & OHIO

Edited by Timothy Jacobs

*A*s the oldest railroad in the United States, the story of the Baltimore & Ohio Railroad is, in a sense, the story of railroading in America. The B&O was the first railroad to use a 'wagon,' a prototype of today's freight car (invented by Ross Winans); the first to build a railroad passenger and freight station at Mount Clare; the first to use iron box cars, the forerunner of the present all-steel cars; and the first to test an electrically-operated locomotive.

In 1827, the year that the Baltimore & Ohio was chartered, the population of the United States exceeded 12 million. The human tide had already overflowed the Atlantic seaboard and swept westward into the rich lands beyond. Suddenly, more people were living west of the Alleghenies than had lived in the entire original 13 states during George Washington's time. John Quincy Adams was the president of a nation that was rapidly forging ahead into the future. Toll roads and turnpikes took the places of Indian paths and wagon trails; the rivers and lakes were being linked with man-made canals. All attempts were being made to foster trade between the centers of population in the East and the forests and farmlands in the West.

In the days of the toll roads, Baltimore fared well in the competition for western trade, and her seaport flourished. But now, in the third decade of the nineteenth century, the city of 80,000 saw itself losing out. The Erie Canal carried many of the western products into New York. Other extensive canal works were under way in Pennsylvania, and these would draw still more of the trade away from Baltimore and into Philadelphia.

Baltimore had a great natural harbor, and her merchants hoped to make their city a great export-import center. But the only links Baltimore had with the West were the inefficient toll roads and turnpikes. At first, Baltimoreans

PETER COOPER'S "TOM THUMB" 1829-30 BALTIMORE & OHIO R. R.

thought that the newly chartered Chesapeake & Ohio Canal was the answer to their problem. But they were dismayed to find that the canal would end on the Potomac River near Washington, and that its trade would bypass Baltimore.

Among the more far-sighted Baltimoreans were Philip E Thomas, a Quaker merchant who in 1826 was president of the National Mechanics Bank of Baltimore, and George Brown, a director of the same bank. Evan Thomas, brother of Philip, returned from England in 1826 to give a glowing account of a new idea in transportation—a 'rail road.'

Philip E Thomas and George Brown became convinced that a railroad was the solution to Baltimore's transportation problem. They interested others in the idea of transportation by rail, and a committee was appointed to investigate the details.

The recommendation that a double-track railroad be constructed between Baltimore and the Ohio River was adopted unanimously, and the enthusiastic committee immediately asked the legislature of Maryland for permission to incorporate 'The Baltimore and Ohio Rail Road Company.' Mr Thomas was named president of the corporation; George Brown its treasurer. Thus began the first railroad to be chartered and built in America.

There were several possible routes to the Potomac River, but a route following the valley of the Patapsco River and then the depression carved out by Bush Creek to Point of Rocks on the banks of the Potomac, was deemed best. Proceeding further from Point of Rocks, the route lay within the narrow valley of the Potomac River to Cumberland. While construction of the road was proceeding this far, other

Below: The first locomotive to be built in America, the Tom Thumb, *was constructed by Peter Cooper in 1929 and this centennial recreation shows the engine hauling directors of the B&O in an open car.*

surveys would decide the location of the line west of Cumberland.

The first stone (stone blocks were often used in early railroad construction to support the rails, much the same way that the now-standard wooden ties are today) of the B&O was laid in Baltimore on the fourth of July, 1828, against the colorful background of a mammoth civic celebration.

The venerable Charles Carroll of Carrollton, the last surviving signer of the Declaration of Independence, spaded the first earth. When he finished his honorary task, Charles Carroll turned to a friend and said: 'I consider this among the most important acts of my life, second only to my signing of the Declaration of Independence, if even it be second to that.'

By 12 October 1829, 25 miles of the grading was complete. Within a few months, rails were laid all the way to Ellicott's Mills (now Ellicott City, Maryland), and on 24 May 1830, this 13 and one-half miles of road was put into service.

In the beginning, all of the Baltimore & Ohio trains were horse-powered. Usually rented from stagecoach companies, the horses were well cared for and carefully groomed, and were not required to pull a car for more than six or seven miles at one time. The horses were satisfactory for the first 13-mile route of the B&O between Baltimore and Ellicott's Mills, but the managers of the road foresaw difficulties if horse power had to be used all the way to the Ohio River.

Inspired by the English experiments with steam locomotives, the Baltimore & Ohio began testing a locomotive of American design. This was the *Tom Thumb*, constructed in 1829 by Peter Cooper, a New York merchant, inventor and philanthropist. After many difficulties, the little engine made a successful round trip between Baltimore and Ellicott's Mills in August, 1830, running at speeds of up to 18 miles an hour and pushing a car carrying 23 passengers.

For some time Cooper's engine was employed in pulling cars of distinguished visitors. On one occasion, the *Tom Thumb* engaged in an impromptu race with a horse-drawn car. Although the engine came in second—because the belt that operated the blower for the firedraft slipped off its pulley— still it proved itself, for the duration of its run, to be faster than the horse.

The *Tom Thumb* was, however, an experimental model, and was not practical for regular service. Two other methods of motive power were tested, with but little success. The B&O, in January of 1831, offered a purchase prize of $4000 for the best steam engine to be presented for a contest on 1 June of that same year. Only four engines were submitted: the *James*, built in New York; the *Costell*, from Philadelphia; the *Johnson*, a Baltimore product; and

Left: Peter Cooper, builder of the Tom Thumb.

Below: The 100th anniversary of the B&O was in 1927 and a special commemorative Fair of the Iron Horse was held. Original historic engines were displayed and run, such as this 1832 Atlantic shown pulling a pair of reproduction Imlay coach cars.

Right: Mount Clare station, built in 1829, is the first and oldest passenger station in America. The first train to enter Washington, DC on 25 August 1835, left from this station.

the *York*, built by a clever Pennsylvania watchmaker, Phineas Davis, at the town for which his engine was named. Davis had to dismantle his engine and trundle it in an ox-cart down the turnpike to Baltimore. The *York* was found to be best; it did much better than the specifications required.

The chief worry of the B&O directors had been that a locomotive large and powerful enough to be practical would not be able to negotiate the railroad's sharpest curves, built on a minimum radius of 400 feet. The *York* sped around the sharpest turns at 15 miles per hour, and on the straightaways it achieved the unheard-of speed of 30 miles per hour without mishap. A survey showed that locomotives such as the *York* could be operated for about $16.00 a day, whereas the same amount of work done by horse power would cost about $33.00.

In July, the Baltimore & Ohio introduced a regular passenger train powered by the *York*, and the capable Phineas Davis became for a short time chief mechanical engineer of the company. The *York* performed commendably, hauling at one time as many as five cars filled with passengers. It remained in daily service for many years, pulling trains on the 80-mile round trip between Baltimore and Frederick, Maryland.

By 1835, the Baltimore & Ohio was operating seven locomotives, not counting the already obsolete *Tom Thumb*, and it had 44 passenger cars and 1078 'burthen,' or 'burden' cars, as freight cars then were called. Improvements soon were being made in the passenger cars, which at first had been modeled after the horse-drawn stagecoaches. The versatile engineer Ross Winans, who had become associated

These pages: No 25, the William Mason, was built in the 1850s and is now on display in the B&O Railroad Museum in Baltimore, Maryland.

with the B&O shortly after its organization, produced in 1831 the first eight-wheel passenger coach. This had two 'trucks,' or a set of four wheels at each end of the car. It was named the *Columbus*. This truck arrangement permitted cars of greater length than was then customary to go around sharp curves without derailing, and passenger cars of a much roomier type could be built. Winans was also responsible for many other early developments in railroad car design, including the immensely important idea of axles that turned with their wheels, which is still a basic principle of railroad car design.

By April of 1832, the track of the B&O had snaked its way westward as far as Point of Rocks, Maryland, on the banks of the Potomac River, and by the end of 1834, the railroad had reached Harper's Ferry, where the Shenandoah joins the Potomac. The tracks reached Cumberland, Virginia on 5 November 1842. Some 25 days later, the B&O operated a special locomotive from Washington to Cumberland in five hours and 50 minutes—approximately *half* the time that had been expected for this 170-mile run. Miles of rugged mountain country lay between Cumberland and Wheeling, Virginia (now West Virginia). Eleven tunnels had to be drilled, 113 bridges had to be constructed, and hundreds of fills and cuts had to be made. When tunneling delays threatened to prolong the work, temporary bypass tracks were sometimes 'switchbacked' up the steep hills, or routed via lengthy and roundabout detours.

On 22 June 1852, the road reached the Monongahela River at Fairmont, Virginia (now West Virginia), 71 miles short of Wheeling. In addition, trackage had been laid eastward *from*

Wheeling, and on Christmas Eve of 1852, the last spike was driven at Roseby's Rock, 18 miles east of Wheeling. On 1 January 1853, the first train entered Wheeling. The B&O had reached the Ohio River at last. The time from Baltimore to Wheeling for passenger trains was set at 16 hours, a trip that had previously taken several days by horse or stagecoach.

Even before Wheeling had been reached, the B&O directors had turned to an even greater plan for westward expansion. Wheeling, it long had been realized, was not the most desirable western terminus. The city of Cincinnati, farther along the Ohio River, had grown and was still growing; it was a great midwestern trade center. Still farther west, St Louis was becoming an important Mississippi River terminal, and Wheeling was not on a direct line between Baltimore and these points.

By 1857 the United States had 'grown up,' and the B&O had grown with it. The nation's first railroad now consisted of 519 miles of line, including the Washington, Locust Point and Frederick branches, and the Northwestern Virginia Railroad. There were 226 miles of second track, additional sidings and other branch lines. The B&O also operated the Winchester &

Potomac Railway and other tributary lines with an additional 77 miles of track. Along the B&O there were 85 freight and passenger stations, and in 1857 the road hauled nearly 203 million ton-miles of freight. At that point in time, there were nearly 5000 B&O employees.

The growth of trade between the Northeast and the West enlarged and increased—by many fold—the cities and industries of New England and in the Middle Atlantic states. With the increased growth came wealth, primarily to the industrial North. The predominantly agricultural South was dropping behind, and the tension between South and North was increasing, as the drums of the American Civil War were beginning to beat in the background.

The Baltimore & Ohio was the main east-west route for Union troop transport for operations along the wide front from the Atlantic seaboard to the Mississippi River, and thus was a crucial military freight and troop transport for the Union war effort in general. The railroad was also the target of much destruction.

In June and July of 1861, Confederates ravaged Martinsburg and damaged the machine shops, the engine houses and other railroad buildings, in addition to confiscating 14 loco-

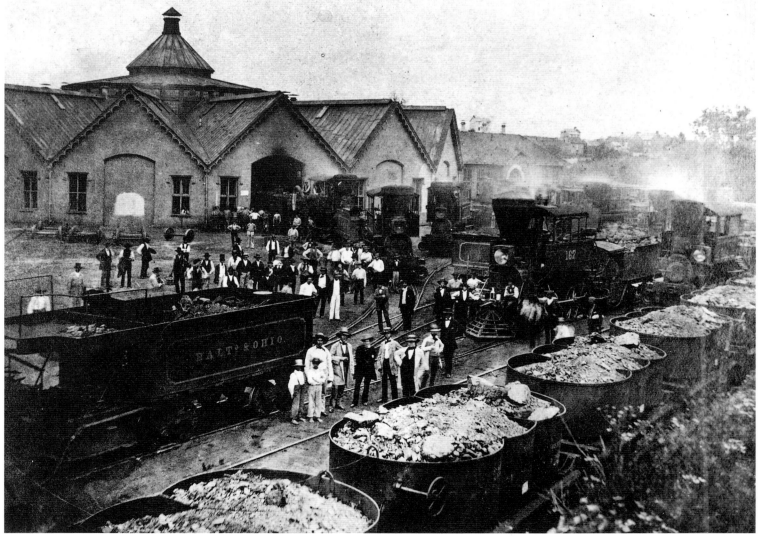

Left: This picture was taken at the B&O shops in Martinsburg, West Virginia during the War Between the States (1861-1865). In the foreground are iron pot railroad cars filled with coal and in the background are a group of Camelback locomotives.

Above: An old B&O iron boxcar used in 1863 as a powder car in the Civil War.

motives. These they hauled back down South, using teams of horses to pull the engines along the old dirt roads of the time, since sufficient fuel and trackage to the South was not quite yet available.

Other battles, sweeping over the right-of-way, resulted in the burning of 42 other locomotives and at least 386 cars between May and October of 1861. Twenty-three bridges were destroyed in that time; 36 and one-half miles of track and more than 100 miles of telegraph lines were torn down. Innumerable buildings were destroyed, and two additional locomotives were driven into the Potomac River. In the fall, General Stonewall Jackson's raiding forces added to the destruction, tearing up 40 more miles of track and wrecking more bridges, buildings and other equipment. Floods swept out trestles over creeks and rivers between the Monocacy River in Maryland and the Ohio River at Wheeling.

On 19 and 20 October 1862, the Confederate soldiers destroyed B&O tracks, made great bonfires of the ties, and upon this fire they laid the steel rails. The rails became hot and pliable, and the rails then were twisted around tree trunks so they could not be used again. This was a practice also used by the North, under the direction of the US War Department's General Herman Haupt, a railroad construction-engineering genius. In fact, the North may well have invented the practice—which made for many an uncanny landscape. Rails so wrapped around trees were known as 'Union bow ties.' Altogether, the destruction wrought by both

sides on the nation's railroads was phenomenal—due in large part to such inventiveness.

And so it continued. As the war dragged on, both armies had wreaked their full vengeance upon the B&O. The railroad's right-of-way was also battered by floods and weather of unusual violence. Raging waters thundered down the Potomac and Ohio and their tributaries again and again, repeatedly washing out many of the strongest bridges, sweeping away rolling stock, and wrecking telegraph lines and other installations.

The B&O's record of war- and weather-related disaster from 1861 to 1865 is one of monotonous destruction unequaled in the annals of private industry in America. Hundreds of thousands of dollars were spent to put the line into service after each calamity. That the railroad's engineers and workers—in conjunction with the US War Department's brilliant construction engineer General Herman Haupt and his men—rebuilt the road so quickly again and again, in the face of enemy gunfire and terribly destructive storms, is a tribute to their resiliency, skill and courage.

The aftereffects of the Civil War were to be reflected by the Baltimore & Ohio for many years. The war had actually helped to *strengthen* the road economically and administratively. Physically, of course, the B&O was in terrible shape, and a difficult job of reconstruction lay ahead. The B&O's trackage had to be rebuilt, improved and extended, and the rolling stock had to be upgraded and modernized.

Above, left: The interior of a 1915-era class A-18 B&O coach.

Left: Harper's Ferry in West Virginia, was on the B&O's main line, and was the scene of John Brown's rebellion in 1859. The piers to the left of the two modern bridges were the supports to a single covered bridge that spanned the Potomac during the Civil War.

Above: This late steam-era locomotive, No 2012, pauses for a switching operation.

It was a busy decade for the B&O. New projects were initiated by the score. The double tracking of the main stem went forward under the leadership of B&O president John W Garrett, whose plans for expansion exceeded the greatest dreams of the B&O's founders. His next task was to repair the weakest links in the B&O's main line, which meant that railroad bridges were necessary if efficient service was to be provided. The Wheeling bridge was begun in 1868, and was finished within 37 months. A gigantic structure, its length, including approaches, was 8566 feet. At Parkersburg, the second huge bridge was begun in 1869, and opened in January of 1871. By November 1874, Garrett had extended the B&O's northern main line to Chicago.

John Garrett's long tenure of more than 25 years as president of the B&O ended with his death in November 1884. The next four years would see three different men at the helm of the B&O. Finally, Charles F Mayer, a Baltimore merchant, took over the B&O presidency for the next seven years.

An administrator, rather than a railroad operating man, Mayer nevertheless contributed greatly to the expansion of the B&O. During his presidency, a second lake port with vast terminal facilities at Cleveland was tied into the B&O system. Mayer also added a third Atlantic Ocean terminal, in addition to those at Baltimore and Philadelphia, by completing a bridge over the Arthur Kill to Staten Island in

the New York harbor area. Partial ownership of the Staten Island properties had been purchased by the B&O some time before, but this bridge had to be built before they could be used to advantage. This third gateway to the Atlantic provided the capability of delivering huge volumes of freight directly to ocean-going vessels, and paved the way for a much-increased volume of foreign trade over B&O lines.

New rolling stock was purchased, and other improvements were added. President Mayer stretched new lines into the coal fields of West Virginia to capture increased soft coal haulage against very stiff competition from other railroads. He rebuilt the bridge at Harper's Ferry, to eliminate a bad curve, and increased control of the Staten Island lines. During his administration, President Mayer built 178 miles of new line, absorbed 743 miles of line from other roads, increased the B&O's locomotive fleet from 755 to 890, and increased the car fleet from 27,108 to 27,320 units.

Hard times were ahead, however, and on 29 February 1896 the B&O went into receivership for three years. Then, in 1901, Leonor F Loree was installed as president of the B&O by the Pennsylvania Railroad in 1901, following the purchase of 40 percent of the B&O's stock by the Pennsy.

At this time, the B&O consisted of 3221 miles of main line, one-fourth of this being double-tracked. It had a huge fleet of rolling stock, and the gross earnings, including those of the B&O Southwestern, had climbed to nearly $48 million for the fiscal year of 1901.

Mr Loree held the presidency until 1904. His achievements were varied and many, including a successful effort to expand and develop the system so that it could handle the B&O's now greatly increased freight traffic, and to facilitate the movement of Pennsy rolling stock on B&O lines. Leonor F Loree put into service the first Mallet compound locomotives ever to be used in the United States. These large engines were designed to haul the heavy freight trains of the B&O over the steep mountain grades of its main lines. With the invocation of the Sherman Anti-Trust Act by President Theodore Roosevelt in 1902, the Pennsylvania Railroad was forced to begin releasing its majority interest of the B&O, and the B&O began a slow progress down the road to independence. President Loree resigned in 1904, and was succeeded in the B&O presidency by Oscar G Murray, the railroad's former co-receiver.

On 1 January 1910, Daniel Willard began his 31-year term as president of the B&O. An 'operations' man, Willard was interested in increasing the efficiency of the system and improving its services. The new president first set about placing his road in shape to handle the increasing amount of freight that the second decade of this century offered. He borrowed $62 million so that he could regrade and double-track the right-of-ways, improve and add to the locomotive power and car fleet, and build new terminals and shops.

In his first 18 years as chief executive, Willard spent nearly $150 million to modernize the system. He increased the B&O locomotive fleet by 33 percent, the freight car fleet by 25 percent and the passenger car fleet by 50 percent. The majority of cars of all types were changed over from wood to steel.

Along with these material improvements, President Willard added greatly to the standing and the prestige of the road in the mind of the public—by encouraging an attitude, on the part of the railroad and its employees, of civic good will.

When the United States entered World War I in the spring of 1917, the B&O helped carry war materiel to the eastern seaports for shipment overseas. Other hundreds of thousands of tons of freight had to be moved within the country—raw material for manufacturing had to be moved to the factories that would use them, and completed products had to be moved from factories to civilian and military users. Millions of men, newly inducted into the army, had to be transported to training camps, three of the largest of these—Fort Meade, near

Right: The 4-6-2 Pacific locomotive typically headed B&O's passenger trains of the steam era. In this case, a streamlined P-7d pulls daylight flyer, the Cincinnatian, *between Washington, DC and Cincinnati, Ohio. The* Cincinnatian *later serviced the route between Cincinnati and Detroit.*

Below: Samuel Vauclain, president of the Baldwin Locomotive Works, and his family pose before one of the company's grand 2-6-6-2 articulated locomotives built for B&O.

Above, left: *Painted in B&O's* Royal Blue *color scheme, this diesel was bought in 1935 from GE's Erie Works and put into service on the Washington-New York passenger express route.*

Above: *An empty shell of B&O's No 51, an EMD EA 1800-hp diesel is preserved at the B&O Museum in Baltimore.*

Left: *The* President Washington, *a Baldwin 4-6-2 Pacific, one of 21 ordered by B&O president Daniel Willard to honor past US presidents Washington through Cleveland.*

Baltimore; Camp Sherman, at Chillicothe, Ohio; and Camp Taylor, at Louisville—being located on B&O lines. The B&O also played a big part in transporting troops to the seaports for shipment to France.

Late in 1917, President Wilson placed the railroads under government control, and on 28 December of that year, William G McAdoo, Wilson's Secretary of the Treasury, was named 'Director General of Railroads.' Under him, a large bureaucracy was set up to control railroad traffic and administer railroad business.

Government control of the railroads lasted through 1920, and had a damaging effect in many ways. Right-of-ways and rolling stock deteriorated, due to the government's low-maintenance policies, and expenses were allowed to mount until they exceeded income.

Despite the Great Depression and the fluctuations of the 1930s in general, the B&O continued to look to the future, and in some ways, led the nation in doing so. For instance, in 1930, the B&O introduced the first successfully air-conditioned car, a diner called the *Martha Washington*. Several months later, the first cars with individual reclining seats were placed in service by the B&O.

The first train in America to be completely air-conditioned was the B&O's streamlined, all-coach *Columbian*, which was put into service between Washington and New York in 1931. In 1932, the first air-conditioned sleeping car

train, the *National Limited*, was installed on the B&O between New York and St Louis.

The first nationwide radio broadcast from a moving train was made in March 1932, when the Columbia Broadcasting Company transmitted a feature from a B&O train traveling between Baltimore and Washington. Experimenting in lightweight equipment, the B&O in 1935 acquired two streamlined, high-speed passenger trains, one of aluminum alloy and the other of lightweight steel. The first self-contained diesel-electric road locomotive to be used on a long-distance passenger train in the US was placed in service on the B&O in August 1935. Additional diesel-electric locomotives were added to the B&O's passenger fleet in 1937. That year, the first 'stewardess-nurses' went to work on B&O trains, and the B&O's first road freight diesel operated in 1942.

When the Japanese attacked Pearl Harbor, the United States once again was plunged into war. The Baltimore and Ohio, along whose lines were hundreds of war plants and scores of camps and depots for the armed forces, and whose steel rails led to three of America's greatest seaports—Baltimore, New York and Philadelphia—bore a large part of the transportation burden. The man who headed the B&O during this period of turmoil and heavy duty was well qualified for the tremendous task. This man, Roy Barton White, who took over the presidency of the B&O in 1941, had spent many years of his career in railroading and knew the industry 'from the ground up.'

With the collapse of Germany and Japan in May and August of 1945, the decrease of wartime freight was offset by increased US exports of relief and rehabilitation supplies for the countries most damaged by the war. At the end of 1945, the railroads faced the problem of handling millions of returning servicemen. The wartime transport burden was not to be eased for some time after the armistice.

During the war, B&O designers had dreamed about the trains they would build for postwar passenger comfort. The first postwar fruit of their imagination was the *Cincinnatian*, a coach streamliner that went into fast daylight service between Baltimore, Washington and Cincinnati in January, 1947. Four mighty Pacific type 4-6-2 streamlined steam locomotives were built to power the twin *Cincinnatian*s on their daily runs. Each of the trains was made up of five 80-foot cars, including three luxurious coaches, a combination baggage-buffet lounge and a combination diner-observation lounge.

In 1949, the B&O added another new passenger special—the *New Columbian*. Built by the Pullman Standard Car Manufacturing Company at a cost of nearly $2 million, this train featured the first 'strata-dome,' or glass-topped, observation coaches to be used on any eastern railroad. The two eight-car sections of the *New* *Columbian* were placed in fast overnight service between Washington, DC and Chicago. Later, these 'strata-dome' sleeping cars were purchased for the B&O's *Capitol Limited* and its *Shenandoah*.

Wartime achievements in electronics enabled the B&O to install very high frequency ('VHF') two-way radios to control freight yard operations at New Castle, Pennsylvania, and at other points. The B&O, in conjunction with the American Telephone and Telegraph Company, also installed public telephone service on one of its trains. This service began on the B&O's *Royal Blue* between Washington and New York. Within a few years after the end of World War II, the B&O had adopted a program involving the expenditure of hundreds of millions of dollars for a large scale modernization and improvement program.

Millions of dollars went for new locomotives and new freight and passenger cars, as well as complete new trains. Millions more went for new coal and ore docks at Lorain, Toledo, Baltimore and Staten Island; for new railroad yards at Chicago, East St Louis and Cincinnati; for right-of-way realignment and new trackage; and for new bridges at Baltimore and at Point Pleasant, West Virginia. Money also went to such projects as the installation of new communications facilities throughout the B&O lines, and the building of new shops and diesel locomotive servicing facilities. The B&O's dieseliz-

Above: *An EMD E7 diesel leads the* Columbian *across the Thomas Viaduct. The* Columbian *was the first American train to be completely air-conditioned.*

Left: *These two post-war engines were ill-matched to compete in an increasingly competitive passenger and freight market. The advanced steam design on the left would never equal the efficiency of the diesels, like the EMD on the right, that would come to dominate the industry.*

Right: *A grimy B&O No 4814 rounds the bend on Salt Lick Curve.*

ation program moved ahead rapidly, as the diesel locomotive proved its efficiency. By the spring of 1951, the company owned more than 600 diesel locomotives. As the 1950s began, the B&O served 13 states and many of the largest US cities and industries in the highly industrial Northeast.

However, both passengers and freight revenues were steadily declining. In an effort to remain afloat, the nation's small railroads were engaged in a veritable merger fever that only increased as the decade drew to a close. The larger railroads—especially the eastern roads—took note of this.

In 1960, the Chesapeake & Ohio applied to the ICC for permission to purchase a majority share of the B&O common stock, and by the following year the C&O had gained control of 61 percent of the B&O common stock. Bucking the unions and most other eastern railroads, the ICC said 'Yes!' to the B&O/C&O merger on New Year's Eve, 1962. On 4 February 1963, the C&O formalized its control over the B&O. The ceremony took place at one minute after midnight, as that was the moment that the ICC approval became official. It was fitting that the knot be tied in Baltimore, in the old B&O boardroom, redolent with the history of the nation's oldest railroad.

The combined system was composed of 11,000 miles of trackage stretching from the Atlantic Ocean to the Mississippi River, and from the Great Lakes to the southern border of Kentucky.

The B&O obtained loans from C&O financiers to beef up its ailing fleet. Facilities were also refurbished, tunnels enlarged and freight yards upgraded. In March 1968, the ICC approved the taking of control over the Western Maryland Railway by the B&O/C&O, and this 800-mile line became part of what came to be known as the Chessie System. The C&O and B&O continued to operate separately, even though they had a common 'head' in the Chessie System offices in Cleveland.

As the 1970s drew to a close, plans were laid to make the Chessie System, and thus the B&O, part of what would become one of the largest railroad systems in the world. On 1 November 1980, the ICC approved a merger of the Chessie System with the Seaboard Coast Line (later, the Seaboard System), creating the CSX Corporation. The *C* stood for Chessie, the *S* for Seaboard and the *X* for the fact that the system was much larger than the simple addition of one system to another. Thus, the Baltimore & Ohio lives on as part of the CSX System, the largest railroad in the United States today.

Right: An ALCO GP-30 road switcher leads two diesels sporting the short-lived 'rising sun' paint scheme.

Right, below: An EMD road switcher, here equipped for B&O passenger service in 1962.

Below: An ALCO FA-2 freight diesel cab unit and boosters.

Overleaf: The fast 4-6-2 Pacific design saw service over five decades with B&O. This photo dates from the 1940s when steam was being superseded by diesel.

THE BRITISH COLUMBIA RAILWAY

By Bill Yenne

The British Columbia Railway had its origins in the Pacific Great Eastern Railway (PGE), a railroad which was born of the dream to unite the province of British Columbia. On 27 February 1912, the PGE was founded by a group of industrialists who reasoned that great wealth could be made in central and northern British Columbia.

Investment money for the project came from Great Britain—indeed the company's founders had named their project after Britain's Great Eastern Railway to attract English investors. A freight deal had even been worked out with the Grand Trunk Pacific Railroad, under which the PGE was to carry all of the Grand Trunk's freight between Vancouver and Prince George—then named Fort George.

The PGE's first locomotive, built by Manning Wardle of Leeds, England in 1874, was acquired when the company bought the Howe Sound & Northern Railway in 1912. Another famous locomotive of the early period was PGE Number 51, the first locomotive bought new by PGE and, despite its number, the third locomotive acquired by the railway. It was built in Canada by the Montreal Locomotive Works in 1913. This locomotive and its sister, Number 52, saw service until being retired and, sadly, scrapped in 1954.

Despite its promise, and the enthusiasm of its backers, the good times were not to last for PGE. Soon after it was founded, a severe and long-lasting recession hit British Columbia and the provincial government took control of a bankrupt PGE in 1918. The government thus acquired a political liability that would plague successive administrations for decades: keeping the railway was difficult to justify, but shutting it down would be political suicide.

Construction, however, continued on the railway until 1921, resulting in a popular, if unprofitable, passenger line running from the foot of Lonsdale Avenue in North Vancouver to Whytecliff in West Vancouver, and a main line that ran from Squamish to Quesnel.

For the next several decades the PGE was the object of great affection—from tourists, employees and the people who lived near its tracks—while being the object of ridicule by others. 'Neither Pacific, Great nor Eastern,' intoned the more witty of its detractors. The railway limped along with a very small operating budget and a lot of heart. Nails were straightened and reused, while machinists spent a lot of time rummaging around in the scrap heap. Even the popular North Shore passenger service closed in 1928.

However, by the late 1940s, the British Columbia economy was better. The province's interior had a new product that made the supporters of the railway gloat: lumber. The government wanted further construction to be done on the line. Soon the PGE had scores of modern diesel locomotives and the latest in microwave communications, and by 1952, the railway had reached Prince George. In 1956, the Howe Sound section was completed, and by 1958, the railway reached the Peace River district. In 1971, the line to Fort Nelson was completed. Despite this expansion, the British Columbia Railway continued to lose money—owing to an ambitious construction schedule and deficit financing. By 1976, the finances of the railway and its relationship with the provincial government became a matter of a Royal Commission of Inquiry. The Commission, among other things, recommended that the railway concentrate on operating as a business, rather than as a developmental agent of the government.

Another change for the railway was a new name. In the late 1960s and early 1970s, with nationalism sweeping the country, it was obvious that the name PGE had little to do with British Columbia. In addition, as the road and its business grew, PGE cars began showing up

Page 43: *A newly painted ALCO C-630 near Darcy.*

Above, left: *No 721, an ALCO road switcher dressed in the British Columbia Railway colors.*

Above: *Two BC Rail GF6-C electric locomotives head east on the Tumbler subdivision with an empty 98-car coal train.*

Left: *A British Columbia Railway diesel-electric locomotive, beside spectacular Howe Sound, pulls a southbound freight train on the last leg of its journey from British Columbia's interior.*

in various North American rail yards during this time and it was soon obvious that PGE's initials conflicted with those of the Pacific Gas & Electric utility company. PGE's name was changed to BC Rail in 1972—and was once more changed in 1984 to BC Rail Ltd.

Some of the locomotives of this more prosperous period were the Budd models RDC-3 (cab forward, with baggage compartment) and RDC-1 (cab rear, straight coach). These were built by the Budd Corporation of Philadelphia and delivered new in 1956. In the meantime, seven self-propelled Budd passenger cars were purchased by the railway to replace its aging coach fleet. (BC Rail now has nine Budd cars.)

Other newer locomotives include a 30-locomotive block of the MLW 700 Series, 3000-hp units featuring Alco 251 16-cylinder turbocharged engines which were purchased between 1969 and 1973.

The company also acquired 17 General

Motors diesel electrics from General Motors Canada under the designation SD-40-2. The first of these, Numbers 751 and 753, were both delivered in October 1980, while the last of the series, Number 767, was shipped in July 1985. Seven General Motors electric traction locomotives of the GF6-C class were built to haul coal on the 129 km Tumbler subdivision north of Prince George. Number 6001, delivered in December 1983, was the first built, while the last, 6007, was delivered in August 1984; these units generate 6000 hp and were also built by General Motors Canada.

Today, the British Columbia Railway is a corporation which is vital to the economy of the province, with assets in excess of 1.2 billion Canadian dollars. Its 50-kv electric coal line at Tumbler Ridge is recognized as one of the most advanced of its kind in the world. With about 1300 miles of track, BC Rail Ltd is the third largest railway in Canada.

THE BURLINGTON NORTHERN

By Bill Yenne

*T*he legacy of some of the nation's greatest railroads, the Burlington Northern can trace its roots as far back as 1850 to the predecessors' routes of the Chicago, Burlington & Quincy Railroad. The history of the Burlington Northern is also interwoven with the Northern Pacific and the Great Northern, which were founded in 1864 and 1889, respectively, and which between them literally defined the early industrial development of the entire northwest quadrant of the United States

Together, the Northern Pacific and the Great Northern acquired 97.2 percent of the Chicago, Burlington & Quincy in 1901, allowing it to operate as a separate entity for 69 years. Together again, the two 'Northerns' created the Spokane, Portland & Seattle Railway in 1905. It was these four principal entities which came together to form Burlington Northern on 2 March 1970.

The Burlington Northern Railroad came to life in 1970 as one of North America's largest railroads. It had 24,400 miles of main line, 35 percent of which came from the Chicago, Burlington & Quincy, and 34 percent of which came from the Great Northern. There were 1990 locomotives destined for the new 'Cascade Green' paint scheme, 33 percent of which came from the Chicago, Burlington & Quincy, with 31 percent coming from each of the two 'Northerns.' There were 110,741 freight cars, with 66 percent equally divided between the Great Northern and the Chicago, Burlington & Quincy, and 32 percent coming from the Northern Pacific. About half of the 1284 Burlington Northern passenger cars came from the urban commuter operations of the Chicago, Burlington & Quincy, as the other roads had retired most of their passenger cars during the 1960s.

In its first decade of service, Burlington Northern's revenues rose steadily from $1.2 billion to $5 billion, with operating income increasing from $96 million to $.5 billion. Of this, 83 percent of the revenue and 75 percent of the income was derived from the Burlington Northern Railroad. Air freight operations accounted for 11.5 percent of revenue and seven percent of income, while petroleum and minerals accounted for five percent of the revenue and 15 percent of the income.

On 21 November 1980 the St Louis-San Francisco Railway (the Frisco) was added to the Burlington Northern, with 431 locomotives and 17,392 freight cars operating over 4653 miles of track. The Colorado & Southern Railroad joined Burlington Northern on 31 December 1981, and the related Fort Worth & Denver was added on 31 December 1982. Together these two roads contributed 259 locomotives and 3772 freight cars operating over 1859 miles of track on a main line between Dallas-Fort Worth and Wendover, Wyoming.

By the end of its first decade, Burlington Northern operated 3200 locomotives and 109,000 freight cars—many of them acquired after 1970—over 27,000 miles of track. This compares to 24,400 miles inherited in 1970, and 30,240 miles operated in 1983.

Meanwhile, the Burlington Northern Corporation of the 1970s and 1980s owned in fee approximately 2,385,000 acres of land in the states of Wisconsin, Minnesota, North Dakota, Montana, Wyoming, Idaho, Washington, Colorado, Nebraska, Illinois and Oregon, and the Province of Alberta, Canada. It also owned mineral rights on an additional 6,044,000 acres of land, including 1,007,000 acres on which only coal and iron rights are owned, and 9000 acres on which only coal rights are owned. The greatest share of this acreage dated to the Northern Pacific land grant of 1874. The Northern Pacific brought into the Burlington Northern merger in 1970 approximately 2,180,000 acres in fee lands and mineral rights covering some 6,000,000 acres. Great Northern contrib-

Page 47: *Great Northern, a predecessor road of the Burlington Northern, purchased the SD45 as a reliable passenger locomotive for transcontinental service. The SD45 series was the top of the line at EMD and BN heads this train with two of the road switchers.*

Above, left: *A BN unit grain train carrying corn crosses Gassman Coulee bridge west of Minot, North Dakota, enroute to a Pacific Northwest port.*

Above: *A BN B30 GE road switcher, No 5509.*

Left: *Near Gillette, Wyoming, a BN unit train emerges from a silo at a mine carrying 11,000 tons of low-sulfur western coal.*

uted upwards of 160,000 acres of timberland, and the Chicago, Burlington & Quincy added coal holdings in Illinois and Missouri. Included in the total were land purchases by all of the predecessor companies for industrial development and property improvement.

The Burlington Northern Corporation also owned in fee approximately 1,344,000 acres of timber and timber-growing land, of which 196,000 are in the Douglas fir region of western Washington and Oregon; 260,000 in the western pine region of eastern Washington; 647,000 in the western pine region of northern Idaho and western Montana; 221,000 in the western pine region of eastern Montana; and 20,000 in northern Minnesota. Timber lands were managed on a sustained yield basis, with the orderly removal of mature timber permitting the production of new timber crops designed to reach maturity at regular intervals. The volume of marketable timber on these lands constantly changed due to increases from growth and decreases from harvesting and maturity, including losses from fire and disease and similar natural occurrences.

Reforestation of company lands was carried out on a consistent basis for many years by the Burlington Northern and its predecessor companies. Burlington Northern foresters also supervised the planting of some two million trees annually in the Cascade and Rocky Mountain areas.

When it was formed in 1970, Burlington Northern Corporation also held mineral rights on extensive acreage in Montana and North Dakota, which contained substantial reserves of sub-bituminous and lignite coal. The estimated reserves in North Dakota were 36 billion tons of lignite, and in Montana 26 billion tons of lignite and sub-bituminous coal. Another 833 million tons of lignite and sub-bituminous reserves occurred in Washington state.

Burlington Northern also leased 3335 acres of land to others on the Mesabi iron range of Minnesota. Millions of tons of iron ore and taconite were produced from this acreage annually. Industrial minerals, such as sand, gravel, clay, bentonite and travertine, were produced in limited quantities on other lands leased by the company.

Approximately 484,000 acres owned by Burlington Northern in fee (or on which it owns oil and gas rights) in North Dakota, Montana, Colorado, Nebraska, Illinois, Wyoming, Washington and Alberta were committed to leases or other agreements. Oil and gas were being produced on about 68,900 of these acres, and the company shared in the production of oil and gas from approximately 171,700 additional acres owned by others under utilization or pooling agreements.

Working interests were also owned by Burlington Northern in an additional 1540 productive acres leased from others, and net oil production averaged about 2,472,000 barrels per year (about 1,352,000 barrels working interest and some 1,119,000 barrels royalty interest during Burlington Northern's first decade). Burlington Northern's oil lands were managed under two programs: one of leasing for development, and another of company participation in development on its ownerships and on acquired leases. Both contributed heavily to Montana, North Dakota and Wyoming economies and provided large tax payments to state and local governments. All operations were, of course, conducted in a manner to maximize return to the company within the limiting factors of conservation.

A quarter century after the Cascade Green locomotives first ventured upon the tracks of the American Midwest and Northwest, the Burlington Northern Railroad serves more than 4000 American communities, including cities as large as Chicago (population three million) and hamlets as small as Bill, Wyoming (population three).

As of 1 January 1990, when it entered its first year as purely a railroad company, the Burlington Northern Railroad had a system of 25,474 miles, compared to 24,400 miles in 1970 and 30,240 in 1983. The longest railroad in the nation, it links Puget Sound to the Great Lakes, and reaches from Canada through vast grain, coal and timber belts in the heart of America to Gulf Coast ports in Texas, Alabama and Florida. Of the 25,474 miles of track operated at the start of 1990, 16,078 miles were main line, 6433 miles were branch lines owned by the company, while 2963 miles were operated under trackage rights. At the end of 1989, approximately 18,954 miles of the railroad's tracks consisted of 112-pound per yard (or heavier) rail, including approximately 9059 track miles of 132-pound per yard or heavier rail. At that same date, 8365 miles of track were equipped with centralized traffic control signaling systems and there were 14,002 track miles of continuous welded rail in place. In the 1980s and 1990s the transportation of coal was the railroad's largest source of revenues, contributing a 32.65 percent share in 1989. Approximately 91 percent of the railroad's 1989 coal traffic originated in the Powder River Basin of Montana and Wyoming, and was primarily destined for coal-fired electric generating stations in the North Central, South Central, Mountain and Pacific regions of the United States. The balance of the railroad's coal traffic came from mines in the Midwest and the South.

Nearly all coal tonnage transported by the railroad was carried in unit trains, typically

Above: Electro-Motive GP39Es were originally built as GP30s or GP35s, but EMD has rebuilt the locomotives to provide longer life to engines up to 27 years old. The GP39E comes with a 2300-hp, 16-cylinder turbocharged engine.

Above, right: Returning with grain empties from Stevens Pass, BN 2800 + 8 plays its part in shipping the nation's products.

Right: BN No 9924, the **Walter T Staunch,** *is an example of a major rebuilding project with Morrison Knudsen of Boise, Idaho. One of 21 E9As modified for passenger service, No 9924 serves the West Suburban Mass Transit District of Chicago.*

Above: A Burlington Northern unit grain train rolls through the Montana Rockies enroute to the Pacific Northwest.

Left: These BN unit coal trains pause for fuel at the Guernsey, Wyoming station.

consisting of 108 hopper or gondola cars, each with a capacity of 102 tons, powered by three to six locomotives.

Meanwhile, Burlington Northern continued to expand the use of double-stack cars in its intermodal service, offering better economies than standard flatcars. BN America, the company's domestic containerization program, began utilizing the double-stack technology in selected traffic lanes in 1989, and intermodal contributed 14.09 percent of revenues in 1989. Burlington Northern continued to serve the timber-rich regions of the Pacific Northwest, Midwest and the South, hauling significant volumes of lumber, panel products, wood chips, wood pulp and paper. Its Foods and Consumer Products Division provided logistical services to customers serving various food and finished products industries, and in 1989 contributed 8.97 percent of revenues. The geographic diversity of BN's physical plant, plus the creative use of transfer centers, was seen to offer many benefits to its customers.

The company's automotive traffic was evenly divided between domestic and import shipments. Domestic business is principally interchange traffic, as the railroad directly serves only the Chrysler facilities near St Louis. A growing portion of domestic traffic included foreign models produced in United States-based factories, while import traffic originated principally from Pacific Northwest ports. Automotive products contributed 3.34 percent of Burlington Northern's revenues in 1989.

During 1989, the railroad originated approximately 88 percent of the rail tonnage it handled. At the same time, approximately 96 percent of the total ton miles, both revenue and non-revenue generating, carried by the railroad was handled on its main lines. Revenue ton miles totaled 232.5 billion in 1989.

As of 1 January 1990, the Burlington Northern, now headquartered in Fort Worth, Texas, had 2309 locomotives (including 1227 that were leased), compared to 1990 in 1972; and 61,177 freight cars (including 14,036 that were leased), compared to 100,741 in 1972 at the time of the merger. Of the freight cars, 41 percent were covered hoppers (used primarily for Burlington Northern's coal operations), 26 percent were gondolas and open-top hoppers, and 17 percent were boxcars. There were 601 cabooses and 141 commuter passenger cars in service. The latter figure compares to the 1284 commuter cars with which Burlington Northern started in 1972. More than 32,000 forward-looking railroaders keep Burlington Northern working for America—moving its coal, grain, lumber, manufactured products and countless other goods.

THE CANADIAN NATIONAL

Edited by Keith MacKenzie

*I*n 1919, the Canadian National Railway Company, then known as the Crown Corporation, was created by the Dominion government to ensure that Canadians would always have the transportation necessary for their vast country. Just after World War I, several of Canada's largest railroads were financially weak and unable to continue operating independently. The government decided to incorporate them into a single railroad with stronger financial resources and access to government capital. Since then, the system has become one of Canada's most successful corporations and has branched out into other transportaton fields.

Although the CN is government held, many railroads comprising CN Rail were once private systems. The story of their individual origins and subsequent consolidation is the history of the Canadian National Railway.

One hundred and fifty years ago, Canada was a virgin landscape of impassable mountains, impenetrable swamps and bogs, and vast forests full of huge trees. Communities were isolated for many months of the year, separated by long, harsh winters of bitter cold and blizzards. The narrow dirt roads linking settlements were impassable for days after a rain or snow storm.

In the first half of the nineteenth century, Halifax, Quebec City and Montreal were Canada's most important cities, but all three depended upon waterways for supplies and goods. Ships and boats from Europe and the United States sailed as far up the St Lawrence River as Montreal, and passed cargo onto stage-coaches or carts. In the far west, large canoes capable of carrying 12 men were used. But every winter the ice blocked the ships and boats from navigating on rivers and lakes, and business slowed to a standstill. People had little choice but to wait for spring's thaw, which often brought rapids and flooding.

Businesses in Upper and Lower Canada, as well as the maritime provinces, desperately needed more reliable transportation to move people and supplies. Canadians followed with great interest the development of steam-powered railroads in the United States and England.

In 1832, a group of entrepreneurs known as 'The Company of Proprietors' built Canada's first railroad, the Champlain & St Lawrence, which made its maiden voyage in 1836. When the first trains started running, there was great celebration, with hundreds of people eager for rides. The Champlain & St Lawrence operated from the town of Saint Jean on the Richelieu River, and then headed just 23 kilometers north, to the St Lawrence near Montreal. The C&SL circumnavigated the rapids on the Richelieu River, and provided an alternative to the main roads and river links between Montreal and New York City.

The C&SL's first locomotive was imported from England, just like the *John Bull* in the United States. Called *The Dorchester*, it was a wood-burning steam engine with a tall smokestack. But it proved unreliable, managing on its first test run to pull only two of the six passenger cars. The other cars had to be pulled the old-fashioned way—by horses.

Despite problems with the locomotive, The C&SL Railroad was successful. The locomotive, about the size of a small automobile today, covered the distance from Saint Jean and the St Lawrence in about 30 minutes. The stagecoach, in the best of times, had required about three hours.

Motivated by the success of the C&SL, the government over the next 15 years granted permission to more than 40 companies to construct railroads. Yet, by 1850, only six were operating or laying track. It cost a great deal of money to survey the routes, clear and level the land and then build the tracks, not to mention purchase and import locomotives and freight

and passenger cars from the US or England. Lack of capital proved a major stumbling block to most small railroads, so money had to be borrowed from England or the United States.

Of the six railroads that managed to put down track, three were short lines built to avoid obstructions along river transportation routes. These were the C&SL, the Erie & Ontario Railway, built to avoid Niagara Falls, and the Montreal & Lachine Railroad which skirted the St Lawrence River rapids. The Scottish engineer of the M&L was so proud of his new Scottish-built locomotives that he took dignitaries and guests on a ride at speeds approaching 100 kilometers per hour, terrifying everyone. The force of the winds at those speeds crushed the men's hats and the women's hoop skirts.

The St Lawrence & Atlantic Railroad was the biggest project started before 1850. Two companies, one Canadian and one American, combined to build the railroad. The idea was to connect Lonueuil with the nearest ice-free port, in Portland, Maine, 480 kilometers away. However, the Canadians ran out of money and work had to be halted.

The government soon realized that if Canada were to build a viable railroad network, it would have to help purchase the equipment and finance the construction. In 1849, the governments of Upper and Lower Canada offered to pay for half the cost of railroads that were more than 120 kilometers long.

This legislation enabled private investors to complete the St Lawrence & Atlantic Railroad, while other investors started up other railroads. In the following 65 years, more than 56,000 kilometers of track were constructed between the Atlantic and Pacific oceans in a network which united Canada.

The Great Western Railway, struggling since 1834, started laying track only after the government offered financial aid. Within a few years, GW's 580 kilometers of track provided critical trade links between the United States and Toronto. The GW constructed Canada's first railroad suspension bridge, an engineering marvel stretching 250 meters over the Niagara River.

Canada's most important and successful railroad, the Grand Trunk Railway Company, was established in 1850. The name 'Grand Trunk' derived from the original plan to operate one main line railroad, with small lines branching out as from a tree trunk.

Construction proved to be expensive, but because of capital provided by English businesses the line was completed. Another rail line was constructed from a railhead east of Quebec City to Sarnia, connecting Montreal and Toronto. The job included construction of the world famous Victoria Bridge across the St

Previous page: CN Rail's No 5308 hauls grain across the Anderson Creek bridge in the Fraser River Canyon.

Right: This 1890 Brooks-built Grand Trunk locomotive takes water at Coopersville, Michigan.

Below, right: At the turn of the century, railroad companies were turning their energies to improving their passenger and freight service and expanding their routes. This included building repair shops and facilities such as this roundhouse in Durand, Michigan, still under construction in this 1912 photo.

Below: This Grand Trunk locomotive No 2109 was built by Baldwin Locomotive Works in 1873 and was in service 42 years.

Lawrence, which was completed in 1856. When the Grand Trunk made its initial run from Montreal to Toronto, 4000 people attended a banquet to celebrate the event.

The maritime provinces found railroad start-ups more difficult to finance and build. Many lines were attempted, but ran out of money after a few kilometers or into border disputes with the US. The Nova Scotia Railway, completed in 1854, used unusual rails for its system: they were shaped the same on the top and bottom so that when one side became worn the other could be used.

In the 1860s the maritime provinces constructed more than 3000 kilometers of track from Sarnia to Riviere du Loup. But the rails were only 5.5 meters long with wide gaps in between. First class passengers had cushioned seats to soften the jolts, but others had to endure hard wooden benches.

Dining cars did not exist, so trains had to stop at stations for meals, and again at night for hotels. The first sleeping car in the world was designed and constructed by Great Western. The accomodations were not luxurious: travellers were given rugs and pillows and directed to the nearest bench in a long wooden boxcar.

Train crews suffered as many hardships as the passengers. The firemen were required to climb outside on the engine to grease the bearings, and to load wood at each stop. If the train was running late, passengers were sometimes enlisted to bring some firewood aboard.

In smaller towns and villages, the arrival of the train was the big event of the day. When the train reached the station, people crowded around to see and perhaps chat with the travelers who got out to stroll. Young engineers were greeted by pretty girls at each stop, and the townspeople caught up on the latest news and gossip as reported by the crewmen.

When the time came to build a railroad connecting the eastern provinces with western Canada, the efforts of entrepreneurs became one of the most important chapters in the history of Canada. Some historians believe that had the line not been constructed, the western province of British Columbia would have joined the United States. Several times the necessary funds were raised just in time to keep the work progressing. Many men died in the effort. But in 1885 the last spike was driven in, creating the 4,666-kilometer Canadian Pacific line.

By the turn of the century, Canadian rails had grown from 130 kilometers of track to more than 27,350. Iron rails had been replaced with steel, and wooden bridges were replaced with iron. Then coal replaced wood in steam locomotives, allowing them to run farther without stopping to refuel.

In 1901 the Canadian government recognized that the nation needed more settlers to

Previous page: CN Rail's No 5308 hauls grain across the Anderson Creek bridge in the Fraser River Canyon.

Right: This 1890 Brooks-built Grand Trunk locomotive takes water at Coopersville, Michigan.

Below, right: The roundhouse in Durand, Michigan, still under construction in this 1912 photo.

Below: This Grand Trunk locomotive No 2109 was built by Baldwin Locomotive Works in 1873 and was in service 42 years.

bolster the economy, especially in the western prairies and mountains. Huge posters were slapped up all over England and in major European cities. Thousands of people poured into Canada, most heading for the wide, open lands of the west. New towns and settlements sprang up along the rail lines, along with farms and mining and lumber companies. The discovery of a new strain of wheat which ripened two weeks earlier than other varieties encouraged farmers to relocate farther north. Their migration doubled the amount of land that could be farmed in the prairies and created demands for new railroads.

In the early 1900s, two Ontario men, William MacKenzie and Donald Mann, built the Canadian Northern Railroad from Partage la Prairie in Manitoba north to Dauphin. When completed, they bought another line running west from Thunder Bay to Winnipeg. By 1905, their rails had crossed the Canadian prairie to Edmonton.

They were underfinanced, and construction was not always up to standard. In ensuing years, crews would have to go back and reconstruct much of the track; but completion of the project helped unite eastern and western Canada. In one of the stunning achievements of Canadian railroading, MacKenzie and Mann extended their Canadian Northern Railway all the way to Vancouver by 1915. The year 1915 was an historic one for Canada's railways. The National Transcontinental, the Canadian Northern and the Grand Trunk Pacific each inaugurated cross-country routes, giving Canada

more than 56,000 kilometers of lines, but there was not enough business to keep them profitable.

With the war in Europe under way, something had to be done to keep Canada's nationwide railway network operating; due to the war effort, the routes were needed more than ever. But with the exception of the Canadian Pacific, the railroads were deep in debt.

To save its investment, the government decided to take over the operations of troubled lines. In 1919, an act was passed creating a new company owned by the people of Canada, called the Canadian National Railway Company. The largest lines were the Intercolonial, the Grand Trunk, the Grand Trunk Pacific, the National Transcontinental and the Canadian Northern, and the combined lines made CN one of the largest railroads in the world. Canadian National then faced the task of eliminating parallel tracks, adjusting timetables, and making uniform the salaries and work rules of the coworkers who had so recently been competitors.

Henry Thornton, a progressive and visionary American, was hired to merge the disparate railroads into a cohesive network. Under Thornton's direction, the first diesel electric locomotives in North America were built by the CN. To attract new immigrants to regions served by the CN, Thornton instituted a special service to help them find jobs and adjust to their new lives. To entertain passengers during cross-country trips, Thornton created the first radio network in Canada. The system was later

Above: CN 4-8-4 No 6218 was the last steam locomotive in regular service on the Canadian National. It has been preserved for exhibition runs and is shown at rest on a siding in a CN yard.

Right, above: Locomotive 6400 is a 1943 4-8-4 Northern coal burner. Despite its streamline exterior and ride-smoothing 12-wheel tender, No 6400 would be rendered obsolete by diesel engines within the next decade.

Right, below: No 9000, one of CN's old electric double units, circa 1928.

Left, above: Grand Trunk Western is by far the largest and most important American railroad that came to be part of CN. GTW's vast rail network links some of the United States' great industrial cities—Detroit, Toledo, Chicago and Cincinnati. The company's principal customers are automobile manufacturers.

The gleaming spires of Detroit's Renaissance Center form the perfect backdrop for this modern Grand Trunk Western freight locomotive.

Above: VIA Rail provides passenger service on intercity trains across Canada and operated the luxurious passenger train, the Canadian *until 1991.*

Left, below: No 6500, a 1954 EMD FP9 with characteristic 'bulldog' nose, heads a Canadian National Railways passenger train.

taken over by the Canadian Broadcasting Company.

One of CN's more unusual assignments was the transportation of raw silk in the 1920s. Off-loaded in Vancouver from Japan, the silk was then sped to New York City, where it was transformed into expensive clothing. Raw silk rots if not processed within a few days, so the swiftest fleets carried the silk from Japan to Vancouver. From there, Canadian National trains sped across the country with special authority, ordering slower trains onto sidings as the silk trains moved eastward, stopping only 10 minutes at a time for fuel and water. The trip took less than 80 hours coast to coast.

The 1920s were a period of prosperity for the CN, due to the millions of tons of grain it moved from the prairies to Canada's large seaports. In 1929, new rail service was provided from The Pas, Manitoba to the port of Churchill on the Hudson Bay.

The construction of the Hudson Bay line had begun 20 years before, but the mushy terrain required the rebuilding of many sections of track. A supply train once slid off the track and was quickly sucked into the muck. All the crew members watched as their train, loaded with cargo, disappeared into the morass. Other crewmen faced derailments, collapsed bridges, epidemics, brushfires and floods, not to mention rampaging moose and ravaging wolves

drawn to the work camps by the smell of cooking food.

Ironically, Churchill never justified its labor pains; though it took less time for ships to reach Europe from Churchill, Thunder Bay remained the largest handler of grain shipments across the Atlantic.

Each fall during harvest season, the CN brought hundreds of young men from eastern Canada to the western farms to help harvest the wheat. At each stop on the prairie, farmers would come to the train, pick out the strongest, hardiest-looking workers, and offer them jobs. The CN often allowed hobos and other jobless men to travel for free to the prairie for temporary work with the harvest.

The Depression was a crucial time for the CN. The number of passengers dwindled because Canadians did not have the money to travel, while the number of hobos and other itinerants increased as men moved from city to city looking for jobs. When they had no luck, they slept in boxcars. Meanwhile, grain traffic, a major source of revenue for the CN, fell off dramatically.

The end of the Depression was signaled by the beginning of World War II. From 1939 to 1945, Canadian National carried wartime goods and soldiers. Traffic actually doubled, and demand was so great that the old cars and equipment had to be taken from retirement

and pressed into service. Women were employed to replace the 20,000 male workers who were called into uniform to fight the war.

During the six years of conflict, few locomotives and no new cars were constructed. Consequently, when the war ended, the CN began to fall apart. Many of its locomotives and cars were run down and worn out, and there was little money for replacement. The CN was put in the position of spending a great deal of money to make itself even barely competitive in the postwar era. Meanwhile, trucking had become a major means of transporting goods, and more Canadians were using those new-fangled machines, automobiles and airplanes.

To compete, Canadian National ordered specialized cars and rolling stock. Shippers liked these new cars because they were easier to load and unload and could carry more freight. New diesel locomotives were ordered and brought into service because they were cheaper to operate and maintain than steam engines. Even radar and computers were added in rail yards to speed the sorting and maintenance of cars; the CN also installed thousands of miles of electronically controlled switches so that trains could operate faster and closer together.

In 1949, when Newfoundland joined the Confederation, the CN took over its rail lines,

most of which were, and remain, narrow gauge. CN also began operating ferries between Nova Scotia and the new island province. It was during this period that the CN started to construct new lines in the west to link with the mining region along the Arctic Circle.

The most successful new line, the Great Slave Lake Railway, stretches from northern Alberta into the vast Northwest Territories. The 432 miles of this railway were built from 1962 to 1964 to tap the zinc- and lead-rich Pine Point, and to ship ore to smelters in British Columbia. Much of the construction was done during winter months, and the 50-man crew faced temperatures as low as 47 degrees below zero F. An automated track-laying machine laid and secured rails at the rate of 12 feet per minute, or a mile a day. Pulled along behind was a seven-car worktrain, including flatcars loaded with rail, ties and fastenings.

Today the CN operates a fleet of ferries and coastal vessels and provides a wide range of national and international consulting services. Railroad land was leased for the building of new industrial parks and shopping centers; old hotels owned by the CN system were renovated and new hotels were constructed. The CN rebuilt itself from the ground up, moving swiftly to fulfil its important function: serving and uniting Canada.

Above: CN 9452, a GP-40 diesel road switcher with three full-size radiator fans near London, Ontario.

Right, above: A 100-ton CN box car emblazoned with the 1980s-era CN logo.

Right, below: A CN unit coal train cuts through Alberta.

THE CANADIAN PACIFIC

By Jim Lotz

*T*he tracks of CP Rail, once known as Canadian Pacific Railway, could almost encircle the Earth. The railroad that helped to settle the Canadian west operates trains over more than 21,500 miles of track in Canada, and another 4600 miles in the United States. CP Rail's parent company, Canadian Pacific Limited, has assets in excess of $8 billion in land, sea and air transportation, as well as investments and holdings in telecommunications, natural resources, hotels, real estate and financial services. In the early 1980s, CP Rail deployed more than 1225 diesel locomotives and 62,000 freight cars and employed more than 29,000 workers.

The CP Rail system features one of the longest tunnels in North America—the Connaught Tunnel in British Columbia is five miles, 117 feet long—and operates over the longest and highest bridge in Canada: the Lethbridge Viaduct in Alberta is 5328 feet long and 314 feet high.

The history of CP Rail begins with trapper Alexander Mackenzie and other fur traders who ventured to rugged western Canada. By the 1830s, many Canadians were in favor of rails connecting eastern Canada and the trappers' settlements along the Pacific coast, but the British Dominion government needed almost 30 years' convincing. When a delegation from British Columbia discussed joining the confederation, they demanded that a rail connection be completed within 10 years. The government conceded, and committed itself to more than 2600 miles over mountains, thick forests and open prairies.

Stanford Fleming set out from Toronto to survey routes in July 1872. The task consumed six years, required hundreds of men and cost the Dominion more than $4 million. More than a half-dozen men died in fires and another dozen drowned.

Fleming himself covered 46,000 miles of possible routes before recommending a route running north of Lake Superior across the prairie to Edmonton and Yellowhead Pass. Once through the mountains, he recommended that the tracks parallel the Thompson River to Burrard Inlet, where the city of Vancouver is today.

After all of Fleming's travails, the government vetoed his recommendations and decided to build rails closer to the United States. Crews were ordered to begin at the coasts and meet in the middle. Work lagged while the government looked for private financers, but few investors in capital-poor Canada showed an interest.

Finally, private investors from England offered to complete the Canadian Pacific in exchange for a grant of $25 million and 25 million acres of land, plus rights to certain rail lines already constructed. The Dominion government, anxious to complete the work, accepted the proposal in 1881. The land for shops, buildings and yards would be given free by the government, while all construction material would be imported free of duties and taxes. Even the land grants would remain tax-free for 20 years.

Donald A Smith, a governor of Hudson's Bay Company in the Pacific Northwest, was named president of the new, privately-held CP system. Smith named his friend James J Hill—who would one day build his own railroad empire in the US Pacific Northwest—to the executive committee. Smith and Hill had originally met, according to legend, on a snow-covered prairie while driving dog sleds, 150 miles from the nearest house. It was a momentous meeting, destined to affect the future relations of the US and Canada.

The two were joined by Bank of Montreal president George Stephen. Earlier, Hill had persuaded the two men to invest in his St Paul &

Pacific line, which had been in decline for years. While on the board, Hill suggested possible routes and construction policies, but it soon became evident that his motivation was self-interest. When Stephen and Smith decided to keep the main line completely within Canada instead of using Hill's lines through St Paul and Minneapolis, he resigned from the company.

Although Hill had spent only a short time on the board, his influence was to last for years. He had brought William Cornelius Van Horne in as general manager of the railroad, the man who was to become the hero of the transcontinental project and of the Canadian Pacific Railway.

A telegraph operator on the Illinois Central at the age of 14, Van Horne at 27 had risen to superintendent of transportation for the Chicago & Alton Railroad. Later, he resurrected the bankrupt Wabash Railroad and, as president and general manager, did the same for the Southern Minnesota. It was there that Van Horne drew Hill's attention. When Van Horne joined Hill at the Canadian Pacific, he became a Canadian citizen and was eventually knighted by the British queen for his services to his adopted country.

Van Horne went to work immediately to get the project reorganized and under construction again. When crews lagged behind, he put them to work at night and doubled the number of employees.

The first engine used in Manitoba and on the Canadian prairies was the 38 ton *Countess of Dufferin*, a 4-4-0 woodburner. She had been brought in by way of the Great Lakes to Port Arthur, and then was barged to Duluth, where she traveled under her own steam to St Paul. She then was transferred to another barge for the trip up the Red River to St Boniface. Rails

Page 67: *No 5937 heads a CP Rail freight train outside Revelstoke, British Columbia.*

Left, top to bottom: Top: *Navvies of a CPR construction crew.* **Center:** *A freshly-excavated rock cut on the north shore of Lake Superior.* **Bottom:** *CPR's first locomotive, the* Countess of Dufferin. *A 4-4-0 American, No 1 was named for the wife of the Manitoba governor general.*

Above: *Probably Canada's most famous railway photograph, this photo was taken at Craigellachie, BC 9:22 am Pacific Time on 7 November 1885. Donald Smith is driving in the last spike of the first CPR transcontinental line carrying CPR directors, senior officers and other notables, to cross over the connection from Ross's rails to Onderdonk's. To Smith's right stands William C Van Horne, to his left is Stanford Fleming.*

Right: *Ties are carried forward from the supply train on the shoulders of the tracklayers in 1883.*

came from England, by way of the Mississippi River from New Orleans.

Van Horne's genius for organization paid off in time, as well. He completed his goal of 500 miles of track in one year, and continued to stay well ahead of schedule.

Moving westward into the Rockies, Van Horne decided to build well south of Fleming's proposed route to prevent US rail lines from monopolising border traffic. The decision was a risky one for Van Horne, because the route violated the government contract. Their agreement specified that the gradient over the Rockies be no more than two percent, and Kicking Horse Pass ran at 4.5, or 237 feet to the mile. Ultimately, Van Horne was vindicated: Hill had deviously wanted the traffic for his own railroad just across the border. The Canadian Pacific was able to move ahead, and later crews

returned to construct the Connaught Tunnel.

Despite generous terms granted by Parliament, the company was in serious financial difficulty. Van Horne kept crews working, even though they did not receive paychecks for months at a time. Before the line was completed, the directors pledged their private fortunes to keep the crews in the field. Then the government came through with a substantial loan. Canadian businessmen had invested so much money that, had the project gone under, the nation's economy would likely have plunged into a severe recession. But the risks proved lucrative for both the nation and the investors, and the directors soon recouped their investments handsomely.

On 1 November 1885, within the 10 year provision set by British Columbia, regular train service was instituted between Montreal and

Winnipeg. The same year, service began between Moose Jaw and Winnipeg, which was a region of granite broken with large tracts of muskeg, swampland that could not sustain the weight of track, much less fully loaded trains. In one section the track had to be relaid *seven* times before the ground could withstand the weight of a train, but Van Horne would not be thwarted.

The effort had taken 12,000 men with 5000 horse teams 10 years to complete. The last spike was driven at Craigellachie, British Columbia on 11 November 1885. The ceremony uniting the two coasts of Canada featured Donald A Smith, who delivered perhaps the shortest speech in railroading history: 'All I can say is that the work has been done well in every way.' Regular service began the next year between Montreal and Port Moody.

The CP proved its value even before its completion, when the railroad came to the aid of the Canadian government during the second Riel Rebellion. In the mid-1880s, Louis Riel, a brilliant but volatile French-Indian, roused a mob to capture the Canadian Fur Company's post at Fort Garry. Van Horne offered to move the government's troops to the scene, on one condition: he must have complete control of the train movements while moving the troops.

He had organized and helped move Union troops as a railroad employee during the US Civil War, and his experiences there undoubt-

edly helped make this mission a success. In 50 degree below zero weather, Van Horne transported men and artillery from incomplete sections of the track to sleighs, and back to the train again. The Canadian troops unloaded at Winnipeg just four days after boarding at Ottawa. Later, a train carrying reinforcements came to an untested trestle. The soldiers were evacuated, the equipment unloaded, and the brave crew took the train across. The soldiers followed, completed their journey and put down the rebellion.

The success of the effort enabled financier Sir John A McDonald to win more financial support for the transcontinental line from the House of Commons, and the Canadian Pacific now gave Canada one of the longest transcontinental lines in North America, running from Montreal in the east to Vancouver in the west. Comparable trains in the United States had to change in Chicago.

Within three decades of the completion of the Canadian Pacific Railway, the system was one of the biggest and best known in the word and operated a total of more than 22,000 miles of track.

Despite his refusal to give up US citizenship, Van Horne was made president of the Canadian Pacific. He designed a house flag that flew from steamship lines on both sides of the continent, as well as from company headquarters, reading: 'World's Greatest Travel System.' He said,

Right: A regal steam locomotive, No 2860, heads the Royal Hudson *H-1e streamliner in excursion service between North Vancouver and Squamish, British Columbia.*

Below: This photograph taken at 12 noon on 4 July 1886 recorded Port Moody's most significant event to date—the arrival of the first train from North Bend pulled by locomotive 371.

Above: CP No 5927 lets out a big head of steam as it hauls the trans-Canada passenger train, the Do-minion, *along the Bow River in Alberta. One of the Selkirk-type steam loco-motives, No 5927 was built by the Montreal Loco-motive Works in 1938 and scrapped in December 1957. The Selkirks were the largest and heaviest steam locos in the Common-wealth, boasting 10 63-inch drivers.*

Left: No 2203, a 4-6-2, was photographed on display in Ontario in June 1942.

however, that he would not remain for long; as soon as the stock of the company rose in par value and as soon as its mileage reached 10,000 miles, he would resign.

He achieved both goals in 1899. At Van Horne's resignation, Thomas Shaughnessy succeeded him as president, but Van Horne remained chairman of the board for another 12 years.

Later, he ventured to Cuba, where he constructed that country's first railroad. He agreed to undertake the project even though, in 1900, Cuba was not yet a nation. He completed the work in 1902. He then went to Guatemala City. Because of problems associated with insurrections and finances, work was not finished until 1908. Van Horne died in September of 1915.

Despite competition from other railroads, the CP prospered—so much so that the company became the subject of intense scrutiny, and complaints about high rates charged to freight customers by the railroad led the government to consider ending the CP's Canadian

rail monopoly. However, the rates remained high.

Dividends were paid from 1885 until the full impact of the Depression hit in 1932. Then no payments were made for 12 years, although the railroad profited from the sale of forest lands that had been granted by the government's original contract.

After the transcontinental line opened, Van Horne improved connections and branch lines, and acquired smaller lines. The CP set up head-quarters in Montreal—the home of its Union Station—and extended service to Quebec, Ontario and Chicago. The CP also extended lines to the maritime provinces, adding a con-nection to St John.

In the west, the CP constructed connections with the United States going south from Van-couver. It also bought control of two US lines that ran from Sault Ste Marie, Michigan, permit-ting an easy connection over the St Mary's River and ship locks. The St Paul & Sault Ste Marie Railway gave connections to St Paul, Min-nesota and from there northwest to Canada. This blocked the competing Grand Trunk Rail-way from moving into CP territory.

Meanwhile, in the west, problems erupted between the railroad and its neighbors, who resented the Canadian Pacific domination. The province of Manitoba granted charters to sev-eral provincial railways, disregarding CP's right to operate without competition for 20 years. Consequently, a battle arose at Fort Whyte between the Canadian Pacific and the Red River Valley Railway.

The first crossing was installed by the Red River Valley, but was immediately removed by CP crews and taken to a CP yard. Crewmen also deliberately derailed a provincial locomotive (there were no injuries). The standoff lasted for more than two weeks before CP crews relented, allowing the provincial railroad to cross the CP's tracks.

The Canadian Pacific continued to expand its empire. It bought other rail lines and built luxury hotels. By 1900, the CP was a major carrier of wheat, a world commodity. Shipping facilities developed on the Great Lakes, at Mon-treal and other ocean ports. The CP instituted a trans-Pacific steamship service soon after com-pletion of the transcontinental line. The British government granted CP the right to carry mail between Vancouver and Hong Kong in 1889. Two years later, the CP had three ocean liners—*The Empress of India*, *The Empress of China*, and *The Empress of Japan*—voyaging across the Pacific Ocean; later, the CP entered steamship service in the Atlantic.

In 1902, Canadian Pacific introduced a fast continental passenger train, *The Imperial Lim-ited*, to supplement the original service pro-vided by *The Pacific Express* and *The Atlantic Express*. In 1919, the first all-Pullman diner

train made the trip between Montreal, Toronto and Vancouver exclusively on CP tracks.

After 1900 the CP made major improvements to its main line through the Rocky Mountains, especially the steep descent known as 'the Big Hill' through Kicking Horse Pass. Eastbound trains were forced to climb it by dividing up their cars and using smaller locomotives to pull them up the hill in sections. But in 1909, workmen completed two spiral tunnels, now world famous. The first snakes more than 3000 feet under the Cathedral Mountains. It curves more than 234 degrees in its descent of 48 feet between entrance and exit. The second tunnel, almost 3000 feet long, drops 45 feet and makes a 232 degree turn through the mountains. Construction of the tunnels enabled the railway to reduce the grade up Kicking Horse Pass to 2.2 percent.

In 1916 the Connaught Tunnel, five miles long, enabled trains to avoid the dangerous curves through Rogers Pass. The original line along the west side of the Beaver River had been plagued by landslides.

The Canadian Pacific set the standards for intermountain locomotion. The company introduced engines of its own design that were perfect for working the grades over the Rocky Mountains between Calgary and Vancouver. These were a class of 2-10-4 that could be

favorably compared to any locomotive in use in the US.

The Montreal Locomotives Works constructed 36 of these machines, originally built to burn coal but later converted to burn oil. The popular 1200 class of 4-6-2s were used by the system until the advent of diesels in the 1940s. The CP also set the standard for rolling stock and locomotives and was especially known for its observation cars, first introduced in 1919 after World War I.

The Depression was an especially difficult time for the CP, because dividends had to be cut in the face of dwindling traffic. When government officials were obliged to examine the cost of maintaining competitive railroads in that time of great economic distress, some thought was given to eliminating competitive routes to save money, especially in the less-populated eastern sections of the country.

In the 1930s, following an investigation by a Royal Commission, the Canadian National Railway (CN) and the Canadian Pacific Railway agreed to pool passenger train service between Montreal and Toronto, and between Ottowa and Toronto.

Like the other railroads of North America, the CP and the CN were pushed to the limit to meet the demands of World War II. In 1944 the two railroads set a record, carrying 60 million

Above: An EMD F-series CP Rail diesel No 4075 was photographed in October 1969 in Glen Yard, Montreal.

Right: The Canadian, CPR's most renown passenger train, travels eastbound along the Bow River between Lake Louise and Banff, Alberta. The Canadian, taken over by VIA Rail in the 1980s, was discontinued in 1991.

passengers. Postwar adjustments were especially difficult for the CP when the demand to carry freight and passengers quickly dropped off as buses, trucks and commercial air traffic began to siphon off rail traffic. The management of the CP organized an airline subsidiary in 1942, taking over some bush airlines in northern Canada, and then expanding service outside Canada a few years later.

The decline in rail traffic was exacerbated following a lengthy strike in 1950. Although it lasted only nine days, it had a profound effect. Shippers turned to trucks to haul perishable goods during this period. They found that service was as good if not better than the train service—and they never went back.

Both the CP and the CN fought back in the 1950s, introducing faster transcontinental service on passenger trains. The CP introduced a train known as *The Canadian*, which featured all-diesel locomotives, streamlined stainless steel coaches and dome cars in every train. The CN then followed with *The Super-Continental*. Cross-country train times were reduced by as much as 16 hours because the new diesel locomotives did not have to stop as often as the steam for refueling and maintenance.

As traffic continued to decline through the 1950s and 1960s, CP officials asked for permission to drop operations such as its famed *Canadian* service. The last steam locomotive run took place in May 1960, although CP kept a few in working order for special occassions.

Today, passenger trains in Canada are operated much like passenger trains in the United States—under the control of a government corporation. In the United States, the corporation is known as Amtrak. In Canada, the crown corporation is VIA Rail Canada, Inc.

VIA, headquartered in Montreal, became independent of both the Canadian Pacific and the Canadian National on 1 April 1978, and since that time it has taken responsibility for managing all of Canada's rail passenger service, except subways and commuter lines.

CP sold VIA more than 300 passenger rail cars to get the government service rolling. Although VIA owns no track, it operates over the tracks of other railroads and employs more than 4000 workers. Meanwhile, locomotive engineers, brakemen and conductors remain on the payrolls of either the CP or the CN. VIA travels over more than 14,000 miles of track with regular passenger service.

In 1983, CP Rail began work on its $600 million Rogers Pass Project, the largest such undertaking since the completion of the transcontinental tracks in the 1880s. The project includes double tracking and the construction of a nine-mile tunnel through the Selkirk Mountains in British Columbia. The project will reduce the approach grade for westbound trains from the current 2.2 percent on the steepest parts of the line. When completed in the early 1990s, the tunnel will be the largest in North America.

Right: In 1983 CP Rail purchased 20 of these 2000-hp GP 38 diesel electric locomotives from GM's diesel division in London, Ontario, for use in grain service on Prairie branch lines. Another 30 3000-hp SD 40-2s were purchased for mainline service.

Right, below: CP Rail unit trains come empty and leave full of coking coal from their subsidiary Fording Coal.

Below: As many as six 3000-hp diesel electric locomotives are added to heavy freight trains for the nine-mile journey up particularly steep grades near Rogers Pass. These locomotives help pull a 108-car solid grain train up the 2.2 percent grade.

THE CENTRAL PACIFIC

By Bill Yenne

*T*he story of the Central Pacific is the story of five men whose foresight helped turn the dream of a steel track connecting the halves of a continent into an actuality. Four of these men turned the myth of California into a reality. It was the empire they created that bound together not only California, but the whole region that became known a century later as the Sun Belt.

Gold was discovered at Sutter's Mill on the western slopes of the Sierra Nevada in January 1848, and thousands of people flocked to California in the ensuing gold rush. California became a state of the Union in 1850 and in 1854 Sacramento was made its capital. Included in the hordes which swept across the wilderness and around Cape Horn were dozens who came to build vast fortunes in the new land and succeeded. Among them were the five men upon whose dreams the Central Pacific was built: Collis P Huntington, Leland Stanford, Charles Crocker, Mark Hopkins and Theodore Judah.

California was in a curious position. It was a state of the Union but it was not contiguous with any other territory that was also a state, and for all the difficulty of communication, it may as well have been a different continent. Transporting cargo between San Francisco and the East by sea meant a trip of several months around the tip of South America. Transporting goods overland required a difficult journey through the jungles of the Isthmus of Panama. The trip across the continent itself was also a grueling experience of several months' duration that involved encounters with a variety of natural obstacles and unpredictable Indians. Two ranges of high mountains, the Rockies and the Sierra Nevada, made crossing the continent with any significant wagonload perilous at best and impossible in winter. Four years before California became a state, 87 members of a group of pioneers en route west from Illinois,

known as the Donner party, either froze or starved to death in the Sierra, just a hundred miles short of Sacramento.

It was against this backdrop that Theodore Judah went to work on the Sacramento Valley Rail Road (SVRR), which was completed in 1856. On 22 February of that year, the locomotive *Sacramento*, a 4-4-0 transported around Cape Horn by ship, left the state capital with cars that carried the first paying customers to travel by train in California. It was less than five years since a locomotive of the Missouri Pacific Railroad had made its first run west of the Mississippi River, but still there was half a continent between them.

His first western railroad complete, Judah became one of the leading exponents of a transcontinental, or 'Pacific,' railroad, as it was known then. When Asa Whitney first suggested

Below: C P Huntington *was Central Pacific's No 3 locomotive, which began service in April 1864 at Sacramento, California. This photograph was taken during the building of the transcontinental line.*

such a railroad in 1845, his was a decidedly minority voice. However, by the time Theodore Judah arrived in Washington, DC, in late 1856, to lobby Congress for funding, the idea had grown in popularity. Senator Thomas Hart Benton of Missouri had placed the idea before Congress in 1849, and Pacific Railroad conventions had been held in Memphis, New Orleans and Boston that same year. It seemed as though the gold rush had won many converts to the dream of a railroad to the West. The only question, apparently, was that of what route the new road would take.

Judah was a delegate to the 1859 Pacific Railroad Convention in Washington, DC, where he presented the case for a central route. Though Congress was still not ready to subsidize the idea, Judah was not discouraged. Back in California the following year, he began to survey possible routes through the Sierra. At the urging of Dr Daniel Strong of Dutch Flat, Judah considered a possible course between that town and Truckee, north of Lake Tahoe. The Dutch Flat route was exactly what Judah had hoped for, and he publicly announced his findings—an indiscretion that cost him his job with the SVRR. Undeterred, he set off in November 1860 for San Francisco, the gleaming metropolis that the gold rush had turned into a major financial center in less than a decade. His objective was to find the financial backing necessary to build the railroad of his dreams but, one after another, the Market Street financiers turned him down. Judah returned to Sacramento, where he found a more auspicious reception for his ideas.

In Sacramento, Theodore Judah was introduced to four merchants who had come west in the wake of the gold rush to set up shop in California's capital. While Judah had been building the SVRR and pursuing his dream in the East, Charles Crocker had been presiding over a dry goods establishment and Mark Hopkins and Collis Huntington over a hardware store; grocer Leland Stanford had become a rising star in the state's new Republican party. Meeting with Judah above the Huntington-Hopkins store, the four merchants gradually developed an enthusiasm for Judah's idea and for the prospect of turning Sacramento into a major commercial hub. They were also interested in sharing the mineral wealth that lay on the eastern side of the Sierra, where a major discovery of silver had just been made near Virginia City, Nevada.

On 28 June 1861 they formed the Central Pacific Railroad, forerunner of the empire that was to be called the Southern Pacific. The Central Pacific was incorporated under the laws of California and dedicated to building a railroad across the Sierra via Dutch Flat. Leland Stanford became president of the new firm and Collis Huntington became its vice president. The fru-

Above: Central Pacific completed the first American transcontinental railroad by blasting over and through the rugged Sierra Nevada range. The 90-foot high Secrettown trestle, shown under construction in this 1867 picture, was built by crews of mostly imported Chinese labor with meager tools, and filled in with dirt carried by wheelbarrow and horse-drawn wagon.

Left: Chinese laborers with picks and shovels bank and cut a road for the Central Pacific at Sailor's Spur, 180 miles from Sacramento.

gal Mark Hopkins was named treasurer, and James Bailey, the jeweler who had introduced Judah to the Big Four, was made secretary. Judah became chief engineer and Crocker formed Charles Crocker and Company, a wholly owned subsidiary that was to undertake construction of the Central Pacific.

Across the continent, another Republican, President Abraham Lincoln, shared the vision. Presiding over a nation embroiled in a struggle for its survival, Lincoln could see that keeping California and the wealth of California and Nevada in the Union was essential. With the Union at war with the South, the southern transcontinental route was clearly not available, so the central route, long favored by Judah, was selected. Lincoln signed the Pacific Railroad Act on 1 July 1862, creating the Union Pacific Railroad Company to build a line westward from Omaha, Nebraska. The act authorized the Central Pacific to 'Start at or near San Francisco or some point on the navigable waters of the Sacramento River and build eastwardly to the western boundary of California, and continue construction until meeting the line of the Union Pacific.'

Below: An 1867 CP excursion train at Cape Horn, 57 miles from Sacramento.

It also provided for generous land grants to both railroads, allowed advance payments and eased security for loans. The Central Pacific received a land grant of 10 sections per mile, and the credit available from the use of government bonds to the amount of $16,000 per mile to the western base of the Sierra (as picked by California State Geologist JD Whitney), $48,000 for 150 miles over the mountains and $32,000 per mile across Nevada. The bonds constituted a first mortgage on the Central Pacific, with principal and interest payable in 30 years. (The government supplied bond credit rather than cash because it had used its cash to finance the war effort.) The Central Pacific accepted the terms of the act on 1 November 1862, but no investors could be found to undertake the building of the Union Pacific until the terms were liberally amended in 1864.

For quite some time there was controversy concerning the designation of the western base of the Sierra and hence the point at which the Central Pacific began receiving the government bond credit of $48,000 per mile as opposed to $16,000 per mile.

On 8 January 1863, Stanford, wielding a silver spade, broke ground at Front and K streets in Sacramento, and the railroad was on its way to becoming a reality. Theodore Judah completed his surveys, and as the railroad was gradually built westward, his role began to diminish. Though he still referred to the railroad as 'my little road,' it clearly belonged to the four 'associates' who were financing and building it. Animosity developed between Judah and Huntington, so Judah decided to go east to seek the financing necessary to buy out his partners. He arranged a series of meetings in New York and left San Francisco by steamer in October 1863. While crossing the jungles of Panama, he contracted yellow fever, and on 2 November he died in New York at the age of 38.

Although Judah died an exile from the enterprise that was his fondest dream, the dream lived on. As governor during the first year of Central Pacific construction, Stanford was able to aid the railroad with land grants and by approval of a $500,000 state subsidy that passed by a vote of 28 to 4 in the state legislature. The subsidy was popularly supported at the time, despite the appearance of conflict of interest when considered a century and a quarter later. An editorial in the *Sacramento Union* at the time commented that, 'The act shows the world that the State feels bound to advance some of her means, and lend the weight of all her moral and political influence, to promote this national enterprise.' The subsidy was never paid, and was superseded by an arrangement

Right: A CP construction camp in Utah in April 1869.

Above: CP track for the western link of the transcontinental railroad in 1868 was accompanied by telegraph poles and wires. Track was laid by rail layers (in the foreground) who were followed by Chinese gangs who spaced and spiked the rails to the ties.

Left: Water was scarce in the desert and had to be brought in by trainload as shown in this 1868 photo taken at Winnemucca, 325 miles east of Sacramento.

for the state to pay seven percent interest on $1,500,000 of company bonds.

On 7 October 1863, the Central Pacific's first locomotive arrived in Sacramento; on 9 November, having been dubbed *Governor Stanford*, it made its first run. On 25 April 1864, the first Central Pacific passenger service to Roseville began, and by 3 June the line had been extended to Newcastle. As the line stretched into the mountains, construction became more difficult. The situation was made worse when the city of San Francisco held up the issuance of $400,000 in bonds approved by its voters in May 1863 (it was April 1865 before they were released), and by a labor shortage created by desertions from the railroad camps to the more lucrative mines.

Charles Crocker, who had been impressed with the industriousness of Chinese workers and eager to address the labor shortage, urged his foreman, JH Strobridge, to hire a crew of Chinese workers. In later years, it was widely rumored that the Chinese workers were paid at a lower rate than white workers. In fact, company records show that everyone was paid at the same rate of a dollar a day. The discrepancy probably arose from the fact that white workers ate meals—consisting of generous portions of bacon and beans—provided free by the company, while the Chinese refused the company meals and opted to set up their own kitchens. Ironically, the Chinese diet of vegetables, fruits and fish was a good deal healthier than bacon and beans. Later, in the Nevada desert when bad water was a problem, the Chinese avoided dysentery by boiling their water for tea.

On 30 November 1866, the line reached Cisco, about five hours by rail from Sacramento. The line remained there for a year while the back-breaking work of punching tunnels through the Sierra summit was undertaken. Drills and black powder blasting were used for most of the job, which was painfully slow. Nitroglycerine was brought in for the main 1659-foot summit tunnel, and between February and April 1867 over 2000 blasts were made in the unrelenting granite.

Construction of the Union Pacific finally got under way on 5 November 1865, nearly three years after the Central Pacific, but the work was moving considerably faster. Laying tracks across the wonderfully flat expanses of the Nebraska prairie bore no similarity to the hardships encountered in the Sierra. While the Central Pacific had its sights set on completing its line east across Nevada and part of Utah to Salt Lake, Union Pacific surveyors had laid out a route westward all the way to the California border.

The Sierra summit tunnels, begun even before the tracks reached Cisco, took two painful years to complete. These years, 1866 to 1868, included the two worst winters on record, and men who weren't maimed in nitroglycerine mishaps ran the risk of freezing to death. Strobridge recalled that 'In many instances our camps were carried away by snowslides, and men were buried and many of them were not found until the snow melted the next summer. In the spring of each year the men were taken back from the Truckee River [at a lower elevation on the east side, where work continued year round] into the mountains, and an average depth of 10 or 12 feet of snow was cleared away before grading could be commenced.

'The total snowfall for the season was about 40 feet, and the depth of hard, settled snow was about 18 feet on a level in Summit Valley and Donner Pass, over which we hauled on sleds: track material for 40 miles of railroad, three locomotives and 40 cars from Cisco to Donner Lake, where all was reloaded on wagons and hauled over miry roads to Truckee, a total distance of 28 miles, at enormous cost.' The federal government bonds—$48,000 a mile—were being sold, but construction costs were running at least twice that.

The summit tunnel was completed at last in August 1867, but it took another 11 months before the railroad was completed over the Sierra. Meanwhile, the Union Pacific was easily traversing the plains.

In July 1868, the Central Pacific finally broke out of the mountains, and Charles Crocker gazed with relief and anticipation at the relative flatness of Nevada. The 150-mile crossing from Newcastle took the railroad 41 months; they crossed the 555 miles to Salt Lake in only 10.

Right: Goliath, *an 1867 wood-burning locomotive with a large, bonnet-type smokestack.*

Below, right: CP locomotive No 82 was built in 1868 and is pictured here in 1890 at Rocklin, California.

Below, left: Outside Tunnel No 8, 105 miles from Sacramento, a tea carrier pauses for this picture. By eating a well-balanced diet and drinking boiled liquids, Chinese laborers remained healthier than the Caucasian laborers.

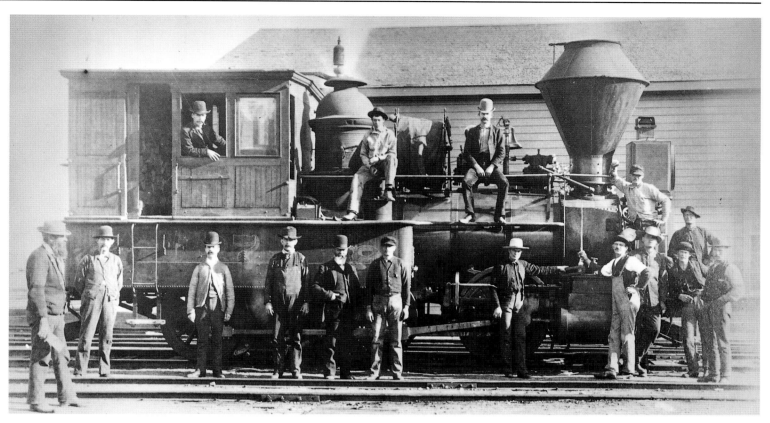

Left: CP No 166 is one of AJ Steven's valve-motion engines, commonly called 'CP Monkey Motions' or 'CP Monkeys.' They were so named because the return rod looked like a monkey hopping along when the engine was in motion.

Below: CP No 167 was built at this roundhouse in Sacramento in 1873 and was scrapped in 1927.

The final mad dash was on. Both railroads wanted to reach the lake first, and Leland Stanford personally made five trips to Salt Lake City to expedite the process. The Central Pacific crews, meanwhile, were laying more than a mile of track each day. The question of where they would meet was one of speed, until Congress stepped in on 10 April 1869 and dictated that 'The common terminal of the Union Pacific and Central Pacific railroads shall be at or near Ogden… and the Central Pacific Railroad Company shall pay for, and own, the railroad from the terminus aforesaid to Promontory Summit [north of Salt Lake], at which point the rails shall meet and connect and form one continuous line.'

In the meantime, the Union Pacific's chief engineer, General GM Dodge, was making a great deal out of his 'Irish terriers' having laid six miles of track in a single day. On 28 April 1869, Strobridge invited Dodge to have a look at what his Central Pacific crews could do. A train stood by before daybreak with two miles of rails, and the Central Pacific gangs went to work. Before dawn, the two miles were down.

In one instance, 240 feet were laid in one minute and 15 seconds. By the end of the day, two million pounds of rails were spiked, gauged and bolted. There were 10 miles and 56 feet of track laid that day, more than had ever been laid, or would ever be laid again, in so short a time. As General Dodge looked on, a Central Pacific locomotive rolled back and forth over the section.

As the sun set on those 10 miles of track and the hundreds that preceded it, the end was very near at hand. On 10 May 1869, the Central Pacific locomotive *Jupiter* moved toward Promontory pulling the private car of Leland Stanford. On the track ahead was the Union Pacific's No 119 and its vice president, TC Durant. Stanford had actually arrived on 8 May and waited in the rain for two days while Durant was delayed. (His train had been kidnapped by some unpaid contractors and was held until the account was settled.)

The rain stopped as the two locomotives paused within sight of one another, and the last rail was put into place. This was followed by speeches and the presentation of a golden rail-

Above: *A behind-the-scenes view of the historic meeting of CP and UP trains at Promontory, Utah.*

Left: *Atop UP No 119 at the ceremonial linking of the transcontinental railroad on 10 May 1869.*

Right: *Chief engineers Samuel Montague of the CP and Grenville Dodge of the UP shake hands after driving the last spike and connecting the two roads at the Golden Spike ceremony in Promontory, Utah on 10 May 1869. Behind them are the CP's Jupiter on the left and the UP's No 119 on the right.*

road spike to Governor Stanford. Nevada offered a silver spike and a speech, and Arizona presented a gold, silver and iron spike and another speech. Stanford responded with a speech. In place of the silver spade he had taken up in Sacramento six years before, he brandished a silver hammer. Telegraph lines that had been strung parallel to the two railroads were poised to carry the news east to Omaha and Chicago, and west to Sacramento and San Francisco. Both the spike and the hammer were wired into the telegraph so the moment of their contact could send a tiny spark of electricity exploding across the nation, waiting breathlessly for this monumental occasion.

A hush fell over the assembled crowd as Leland Stanford swung the silver hammer at the first gold spike. The hammer plunged down-

ward toward the final notch in the steel belt that would bind the nation... and missed. Stanford's second blow connected, but it was anti-climactic. Having seen the first blow fall short, a telegraph technician had tapped his key and the celebrations in Chicago and San Francisco had already begun.

Jupiter moved forward for the last few feet of the 690-mile distance from Sacramento, while No 199 inched ahead on the last of its 1086-mile trek from Omaha. As their cowcatchers clanged together, the champagne flowed and the Central Pacific and Union Pacific construction superintendents were photographed shaking hands. The gold and silver spikes were unceremoniously pulled, returned to Stanford and replaced with steel ones. Judah's vision had opened the way to the fruition of a whole nation's dreams.

THE CHESAPEAKE & OHIO

Edited by Timothy Jacobs

*T*he Chesapeake & Ohio had its beginnings in the Louisa Railroad, a central Virginia short line chartered in 1836. By 1850, the little road had stretched to Richmond and changed its name to 'The Virginia Central Railroad.' It soon grew into a line that reached from Richmond through Gordonsville, Charlottesville and Staunton to Jackson's River. Though the road was ravaged by the Civil War, Virginia and West Virginia lawmakers passed legislation to rebuild the line from 'the waters of the Chesapeake to the Ohio River' and changed its name to the Chesapeake & Ohio Railroad.

Collis P Huntington, one of Southern Pacific's Big Four, was assigned the task of building the road to the Ohio River. Despite Huntington's participation and financial support, however, the C&O went bankrupt in 1873. Five years later, Huntington organized a syndicate of investors and brought the line out of bankruptcy, renaming it the Chesapeake & Ohio Railway Co. Under Huntington's new ownership, the railroad prospered and expanded to the Virginia coast. During this period the C&O picked up the James River Company and merged it into its empire. By the turn of the century, the C&O consisted of 1445 miles from Newport News, Virginia to Cincinnati, Ohio and Louisville, Kentucky, and was seriously competing with the B&O for West Virginia coal.

Financial control of the C&O seemed to go from one set of hands to another in the 20th century—first the Pennsylvania Railroad and the New York Central, then the Van Swerigen brothers, followed by Robert Young and his Allegheny Corporation and, finally, in 1954, Cyrus Eaton. By this time, the C&O was a 5000-mile railroad with annual revenues of $350 million; an incredibly good coal traffic; diversified freight traffic (as a result of a 1947 buyout of the Pere Marquette Railroad); and

the virtuoso leadership of Walter J Tuohy, the C&O president since 1948.

C&O president Walter Tuohy was a dynamic, energetic and intelligent man, whose policies had made the C&O an efficient, high-grossing operation in an era when most American railroads were merging to save their lives. President Tuohy was in the position to call the shots, and he certainly did.

In 1960, the C&O, under Tuohy's guidance, had applied to the ICC for permission to purchase a majority share of the Baltimore & Ohio common stock. Baltimore & Ohio president Howard Simpson wanted to hold out for a direct, three-way merger between the C&O, the B&O and the New York Central, with control of the newly merged road shared by the leadership of the three pre-existing lines, but in 1961, President Tuohy of the C&O announced that the C&O had definitely gained control of 61 percent of the B&O common stock. This effectively told B&O president Simpson that the cards—all of them—were in the hands of the C&O. At the regular B&O board of directors meeting on 17 May 1961, Jervis Langdon, Jr was elected president, and former president Simpson was made chairman of the board and chief executive officer.

Before the merger could be made official, the approval of the Interestate Commerce Commission was needed. The US government had long been alert to the danger of common carrier monopolies, and the ICC was the chief watchdog for that sort of thing. Therefore, all mergers involving railroads, as well as other larger transport entities, had to submit to the approval of the ICC. Of couse, that meant having hearings, so that all parties involved could present their points of view.

By this time, the B&O was in terrible shape. Maintenance had been deferred for several years to defray costs, and freight service was starting to suffer. The C&O, on the other hand,

originated more coal traffic than any other US railroad, and as such, was snugly ensconced in a position of control as the hauler of the one commodity that no other means of transportation—save barges and ships—could haul in quantity with anything even approaching a reasonable economy.

Both B&O and C&O management pointed out that the B&O and C&O were complementary lines, rather than competitive, and that the stronger road could help pull the weaker one up. Unification was thus seen as a brake against the B&O's slide toward bankruptcy. Moreover, the C&O was willing to spend $250 million over five years to revamp the sagging B&O.

Bucking the unions and most other eastern railroads, the ICC said 'Yes!' to the B&O/C&O merger on New Year's Eve, 1962. It was felt in some quarters that the resulting road would be the strongest in the East. On 4 February 1963, the C&O formalized its control over the B&O. The ceremony took place at one minute after midnight, as that was the moment that the ICC approval became official. It was fitting that the knot be tied in Baltimore, in the old B&O boardroom, redolent with the history of the nation's oldest railroad.

The combined system was composed of 11,000 miles of trackage stretching from the Atlantic Ocean to the Mississippi River, and from the Great Lakes to the southern border of Kentucky. In March 1968, the ICC approved the taking of control over the Western Mary- land Railway by the B&O/C&O, and this 800-mile line became part of the system. Previously, in 1967, the C&O had aquired the Chicago, South Shore & South Bend Railroad, a commuter and freight service in the metropolitan Chicago area.

Over the years, C&O men slowly but surely replaced the B&O men on the B&O executive board. In 1964, Jervis Langdon left the B&O presidency for the presidency of the Rock Island Lines. Walter Tuohy was then elected president of the B&O, and upon his death in 1966, Gregory DeVine stepped into his twin presidencies on the B&O and C&O. By 1970, the B&O Board included six men that were also on the C&O board; 1970 also marked the 94th percentile in C&O holdings of B&O common stock.

In 1971, President DeVine retired, and was replaced by the energetic Hays Watkins, a C&O man since 1949. President Watkins had the appellation 'Chessie System' adopted as a marketing name for the C&O/B&O and Western Maryland conglomerate. The C&O and B&O continued to operate separately, even though they had a common 'head' in the Chessie System offices in Cleveland.

The name 'Chessie' obviously refers to the Chesapeake and Ohio Railroad, but in the sense in which the company uses and has used it, the name was first applied to a painting which portrayed a kitten asleep on a pillow, with a little blanket drawn up around its chin. In the

Previous page: No 8556 is a powerful 3500-hp Chessie System SD-50 diesel locomotive built by EMD-GM.

Right: T-1 No 3023, a 2-10-4 Texas, emerges from the Limeville bridge in 1943 with a full load of Kentucky coal. Built in 1917, the bridge is the strongest span ever constructed.

Right, below: Three massive C&O 2-6-6-6 Allegheny steam locomotives are ready for service at Russell, Kentucky in the 1940s.

Below: This 1947 photo shows Cincinnati and Northern Division traffic meeting at NJ Cabin, Limeville, Kentucky.

early 1930s, Lionel Probert, the C&O's assistant to the president, saw the artwork, and thought it would be an ideal advertising gimmick to emphasize the smoothness of passenger travel on the C&O. In 1933, the C&O sponsored an ad in *Fortune* magazine which included the picture and the tag line 'Sleep Like a Kitten.'

The kitten proved to be an immensely popular symbol, and 'Chessie' went on to an illustrious, extended career, selling war bonds during World War II, and, when the airplane and the automobile usurped the C&O's passenger traffic, Chessie sold freight haulage, with the slogan 'Purr-fect Transportation.'

For a while, management sought to give Chessie a playmate, by way of emphasizing the unification of C&O and B&O operations. This little kitty was to be known as 'Bessie' (for obvious reasons) but, after a survey of the shareholders brought forth almost no response to the idea, Bessie was erased from the promotional department's drawing boards. The Chessie System logo, 'Chessie' in silhouette within a 'C' shape, appeared on the equipment of the Chessie System's lines.

By 1979, total operating revenues for the Chessie System had risen by more than $800 million since the beginning of the 1970s. Net earnings had increased by over $85 million, with an inflationary skew. However, inflation or

no, there had been a two-for-one stock split back in 1974, and the price of the split shares rose on top of that, showing that the foundation of the system was going strong in a time of turmoil for many other railroads. The early predictions concerning the strength of the B&O/C&O merger were correct.

In 1980, the Chessie System merged with Seaboard Coast Line Industries to form the CSX Corporation, a holding company for the two large systems. Prime Osborn III, of Seaboard, became chairman, and Hays Watkins was elected president of the new entity. Following the merger, the Chessie System kept its headquarters in Cleveland and Seaboard remained based in Jacksonville, Florida. CSX set up its headquarters in Richmond, Virginia. In May 1982, Prime Osborn III retired and Hays Watkins, president and chairman of the Chessie System, succeeded him.

Today, CSX Transportation operates roughly 34,000 miles of track throughout 20 states in the East, Midwest and South; the District of Columbia; and the Canadian province of Ontario. Because of its strategic location in the southeast, the CSX is the United States' largest hauler of coal, carrying a record 179 million tons in 1990. In terms of operating revenue and track miles, CSX is the largest railroad in the United States.

Above: In 1947, C&O purchased the 500, a steam turbine electric diesel that was the longest (154 feet) passenger locomotive in the world. Pleased with this new model, C&O ordered two more just like it from Baldwin and Westinghouse Electric.

Right: An EMD GP road switcher in 1972 with the sleeping kitten logo on the nose. The Chessie kitten represented the railroad's passenger service motto 'Purr-fect Transportation.' After the 1980 Chessie System merger with Seaboard Coast Line, the paint scheme was changed.

THE CHICAGO, BURLINGTON & QUINCY

By Bill Yenne

*I*n 1849, a group of businessmen from Aurora, Illinois made plans to build a railroad from Batavia to Turner Junction (now west Chicago), Illinois, switching to the tracks of the Galena & Chicago Union Railroad, which had just been completed through to Chicago. The line was only 12 miles long, but it marked the beginning of a railroad that would one day span the entire state of Ilinois and provide a gateway to the West.

The Aurora Branch Railroad, as the new road was originally christened, was laid with secondhand scrap iron spiked to 12 miles of wooden rails, obtained from the Buffalo & Niagara Falls Railroad at a bargain price, after the New York legislature outlawed the use of wooden rails.

On 2 September 1850 the first train chugged its uncertain way over six miles of newly-built line. As neither the Aurora's secondhand cars nor its first locomotive had yet arrived from the East, the trip was made with equipment borrowed from the Galena line. The Aurora Branch thus became the second railroad to serve Chicago.

Progress over the next decade was rapid, aided largely by a group of Boston investors who bought the line in 1852. By 1864 the railroad had 400 miles of track—all in Illinois— and adopted the name Chicago, Burlington & Quincy Railroad Company, which properly described its trackage stretching from the Windy City to Burlington, Iowa and Quincy, Illinois on the Mississippi River. The name also had staying power, for it lasted 106 years, until the creation of the Burlington Northern in 1970.

The 'Burlington,' as the Chicago, Burlington & Quincy came to be known, had completed its own line between Aurora and Chicago in 1864, and the following year it had the distinction of operating the first train into Chicago's newly opened Union Stockyards.

Right: William Jennings Bryan, one of America's most influential Democrats and three-time nominee for president, poses with CB&Q No 288 and crew at a whistle stop.

Below: One of the CB&Q's earliest locomotives, No 27 Greyhound, a 4-4-0 American, was built by Amoskeag in 1855.

The Burlington's rapid expansion after the Civil War was based on financial management dominated by John Murray Forbes of Boston, who in turn was assisted by Charles E Perkins. Perkins, a powerful administrator, eventually forged a system out of previously loosely-held affiliates that virtually tripled the Burlington's size during his presidency, which lasted from 1881 to 1901.

From the basic Chicago to Burlington and Chicago to Quincy spokes of the road, Perkins began constructing a massive network that, by the turn of the century, would include a total of 204 originally independent railroads. Among the most noteworthy were the Hannibal & St Joseph Railroad Company and the Burlington & Missouri River Railroad Company.

Promoted by important citizens at each end of the route—including Mark Twain's father, John M Clemens—the construction of the Hannibal & St Joseph had begun in 1852 and was completed in 1859. The railroad brought mail across Missouri to connect with the Pony Express, and in 1862 it introduced the first railroad car equipped for sorting the US mail enroute. During the Civil War it was constantly

Left, above: No 380 was a Danforth-built 4-4-0 shown with its crew at one of the CB&Q shops.

Left, below: A CB&Q 4-4-0 American, No 205 was built in 1872 by Manchester. In that year, CB&Q established a connection with the Union Pacific Railroad at Kearney, Nebraska.

Above: CB&Q No 143 at 12th Street in Chicago, a 4-4-0 from the 1890s.

harassed by Confederate raiders, and afterward it became an occasional target of the notorious Jesse James, as well as other less colorful train robbers.

The Hannibal & St Joseph Railroad also sparked the beginning of Kansas City as a rail center and gateway to the Southwest. In 1869, under the direction of the great engineer Octave Chanute, the company completed the first railroad bridge over the Missouri River.

The Burlington & Missouri River Railroad was originally incorporated in 1852 to build across the state of Iowa, and operations began over the first few miles of track on New Year's Day in 1856. The road reached Ottumwa, Iowa by 1857, and was completed all the way to the Missouri River in November 1869. From the beginning, the line had financial help from John Murray Forbes and his Boston-New York group of investors, because it provided a natural westward extension of their rapidly-growing Chicago, Burlington & Quincy, which in turn was a feeder for the Michigan Central Railroad, which was also owned by Forbes.

In 1868 the Burlington itself completed its own bridges over the Mississippi, both at Burlington and Quincy, giving the railroad through connections with the Burlington & Missouri

River and the Hannibal & St Joseph railroads. Relations between the Burlington and the two smaller roads continued to be close and amicable until 1871, when they were severed by rail baron Jay Gould and his New York allies as they secured control of the Hannibal & St Joseph. For the next dozen years, Gould used the line as a pawn in bitter rate wars and shifting alliances. Traffic interchanges with the Burlington remained so important, however, that by 1883 Perkins finally bought the line, and it became an integral part of the Burlington system.

While the Burlington & Missouri River was still expanding westward in the 1860s, plans had been made for an extension into Nebraska. A separate company, the Burlington & Missouri River Railroad, was formed in Nebraska in 1869. During the summer of 1870 it reached Lincoln, the newly-designated capital of Nebraska, and a connection with the Union Pacific was achieved in 1872 at Kearney.

By the time its Missouri River bridge was opened at Plattsmouth in 1880, the Burlington & Missouri River had filled its territory in Nebraska with numerous branches and pushed into western Nebraska. The value to the Chicago, Burlington & Quincy of this westernmost feeder was now established and, in 1880, the

Nebraska line was purchased outright. In 1882 a line was completed to Denver, providing Colorado's capital with its first direct rail route to Chicago over a single railroad.

As Burlington and its subsidiaries were pushing westward, other segments of the Burlington system were built in the Midwest, notably links to St Louis, Missouri and Rock Island, Illinois.

The idea of building north to the Twin Cities also was gaining momentum. James J Hill's Northern Pacific had reached Puget Sound, connecting the forerunner of his Great Northern with the Canadian Pacific. Seeing this, it became apparent to Perkins that extension north-westward could put Burlington in a position to transport grain and lumber south, while moving coal and manufactured products to the north.

In 1885 Burlington lines were extended from Oregon, Illinois (on the Chicago & Iowa Railroad), and north from Fulton (on the route from St Louis) to Savanna, Illinois; and then northward along the Mississippi River, reaching St Paul in 1886.

While expanding its territory, the railroad also was improving technologically, with heavier rail, more powerful locomotives and larger cars. In 1886 and 1887 George Westinghouse conducted air brake tests on the grade at West Burlington, Iowa, during the course of his invention of the triple valve brake system. His device perfected the air brake and brought it into universal use.

More railroad building eventually gave the Burlington a main line from St Louis and Kansas City through St Joseph and Lincoln to Billings, Montana. During this same period, the Burlington either built or acquired a network of branch lines over the rich agricultural regions of northern Illinois, southern Iowa, northern Missouri and southeastern Nebraska. Throughout the years, products from farms and ranches were essential to the Chicago, Burlington & Quincy, and thus the company became known informally as a 'Granger Road.'

Congress granted the Burlington tracts of land in Missouri, Iowa and Nebraska to promote expansion and settlement. To attract settlers, the Burlington employed as many as 250 agents in the eastern United States, as well as opening offices in England, Scotland, Sweden and Germany. From 1870 to 1880 Burlington sold over two million acres of land to some 20,000 people.

Burlington's representatives continued to work closely with farmers and ranchers, and as early as 1854 the railroad advised prospective settlers on what crops could be successfully raised in Missouri. Alfalfa was introduced by the railroad as a commercial crop in Nebraska in 1875. Crop and stock improvement, and irrigation and soil conservation were aggressively promoted. Through seed and soil exhibits, poultry specials and livestock trains, the Burlington helped bring the most advanced agricultural methods directly to the farmer. Burlington would often employ farmers at shop work during winter months or until they were able to establish their farms and attend them on a full-time basis. Burlington built its first timber preservation plant at Edgemont,

South Dakota in 1899 and began a research laboratory at Aurora, Illinois in 1900.

The death of John Murray Forbes in 1898 symbolized the end of an era. For 47 years he had guided the company's finances, serving as a director for the last 41 years of his life. At the end of February 1901 Charles E Perkins resigned as president, although he continued as a director.

Although Burlington Northern as an entity did not exist until 2 March 1970, the three major elements of this conglomerate were actually joined in 1901 under the ownership of the flamboyant James Jerome 'Jim' Hill—'The Empire Builder.'

By 1901 Hill dominated the railroads of the northwest quadrant of the United States in a way that could not be imagined in any of the other three, yet he dreamed of a bridge to the eastern United States. His eastern terminus was at St Paul, Minnesota and he was eager to link his empire to the rest of the world through a connection with Chicago, the rail hub of North America and a Great Lakes port as well. As always, Jim Hill was seeking balanced traffic for his system and believed coal, minerals, livestock and agricultural produce from Texas and Colorado could be exchanged for imports from the Orient and timber and other products available from the Pacific Northwest.

Thus it was that in 1901 Hill, through the Great Northern and Northern Pacific, purchased 97.2 percent of the Chicago, Burlington & Quincy stock, paying $200 per share. Although Hill now controlled the three roads that would make up the lion's share of the ultimate Burlington Northern, they would exist as separate entities for the next 69 years.

Under the presidency of George B Harris, who would head the company from 1901-1910, and Davis Miller, who succeeded him until 1914, the Chicago, Burlington & Quincy continued to expand as it had in the preceding century—through acquisition.

First Hill and Harris noted that the Colorado & Southern and Fort Worth & Denver lines provided routes from Cheyenne, Wyoming and Denver south to Fort Worth, Dallas and the port cities of Houston and Galveston. With a link from Cheyenne to Billings, Montana, Hill reckoned that he could have a tidewater to tidewater line from the Puget Sound to the Gulf of Mexico—a diagonal transcontinental line through America! With this in mind, 70 percent of the Colorado & Southern and Fort Worth & Denver stock was purchased by the Burlington in 1908. A year later construction began, extending the Billings-Kirby branch southward through the Wind River Canyon to a connection with the Colorado & Southern east of Casper, Wyoming. By the time this major extension was completed in 1914, Great Northern had built into Billings, and both Northerns

had direct connections with Denver and the Gulf.

Hill was perhaps the first rail baron to seriously envision this land bridge route between the Pacific and the Gulf. Had it not been for the Panama Canal and the Panama Canal Act of 1914, which forbade the carrying of materials between the Gulf and the steamships of the Pacific Northwest (among which were some owned by Jim Hill), the line may have prospered more than it did.

Always anxious to employ the latest technology, the Burlington operated the first printing telegraph (a forerunner of the teletype) in 1910, and in 1915 was the first railroad to use train radio, utilizing a transmitter located at Riverside, Illinois. Communication with trains was achieved, but the need for a telegrapher on board the train made the device impractical.

Below: The Burlington Route's Pioneer Zephyr *opened the second year of the Chicago World Fair's Wings of a Century pageant on 9 April 1934. America's first diesel-powered streamline train, the* Zephyr *set a long-distance record with its dawn-to-dusk run from Denver, Colorado to Chicago, Illinois in only 14 hours.*

Train radio became a reality in 1943, when aircraft radios were successfully adapted to train operations.

In 1914 Hale Holden became president of the Burlington, serving until 1928, except for two years (1918-1920) at the end of World War I, when Charles E Perkins, Jr came in to serve in the interim role. Holden is best remembered for his later years in San Francisco, where he served as chairman of the Southern Pacific's Executive Committee from 1929 to 1932 and as chairman of the board from 1932 to 1939.

When Hale Holden left the Burlington presidency in 1928 to go west in the career move that would see him reach the apex of the Southern Pacific organization, he was succeeded by the great Ralph Budd. One of the preeminent figures in American railroading, Budd also served as president of the Burlington's parent, Great Northern Railway, from 1919 to 1931. At the time Budd took over the Burlington, it had 1575 locomotives, 62,225 freight cars and 1225 passenger cars operating over 9367 miles of main line track. Budd remained as president of the Burlington until 1949, after over 30 years in the president's chair of one of the roads which today form the Burlington Northern.

Budd led Burlington to establish a bus and trucking subsidiary in 1935. Known as the Burlington Trailways, it was sold in 1946. During this incredibly prosperous decade, Ralph Budd's trucking operation was expanded to over 10,000 route miles. Burlington Trailways also participated in piggyback traffic with its parent company as early as 1940.

Unlike the debacle faced by Hale Holden during World War I, Ralph Budd's experience during World War II saw the government adopt

a cooperative attitude toward American rail-roads. This translated into a hands-off approach, by which both the nation and the Burlington benefited.

Ralph Budd also saw the Burlington become the first railroad in America to introduce a diesel-powered, streamlined passenger train. The *Pioneer Zephyr*, with its high-speed, die-sel-electric propulsion system, was the fore-runner of thousands of diesels which, in the span of a few short years following World War II, replaced steam locomotives on virtually every railroad in the country.

On 26 May 1934, a three-car, articulated streamline train sped a thousand miles from Denver, Colorado to Chicago, Illinois in 14 hours in a dawn-to-dusk, nonstop run that was to officially open the second year of Chicago's great 'Century of Progress Exposition.' This famous trip culminated on the stage of the 'Wings of a Century' pageant on Chicago's lake-front, where at 8:09 pm the *Pioneer Zephyr* rolled onto the stage. Its run had set a world long-distance record and had firmly estab-lished the value of diesel-electric power. The applause of the World's Fair goers only added to the acclaim this unique train had received at every town along the Burlington's right-of-way. Thus, the *Pioneer Zephyr* ushered in a new era in rail transportation.

In the brief 14 hours of its spectacular run it had dramatized application of the internal combustion engine in main line railroad ser-vice; indicated practicability of the two-cycle

Above: *The* Zephyrs *continued to run on the Burlington Route into the 1970s. In 1945 the Burlington created the first Vista Dome observation car which made traveling aboard the* Twin Cities Zephyr *a visual treat.*

Left: *At the time of the Century of Progress Exposition in 1933, diesel engines were strictly experimental, but the* Pioneer Zephyr *drove home the point that diesel was the motive power of the future.*

diesel engine in rail service; and convinced railroad executives that the diesel engine had an important future in railroad power. Behind the story of that dawn-to-dusk run lies an account of inventive genius, teamwork and dedicated determination.

The successful trip of the *Pioneer Zephyr* resulted from three streams of action which occurred almost simultaneously. One was the successful development of a lightweight, two-cycle diesel engine by Charles F Kettering and his associates at the General Motors research laboratory. This development was of singular importance in the evolution of the diesel locomotive as we know it today, for it provided a new kind of diesel engine—one that was built, as Kettering said, 'the way it wanted to be built, not the way engineers thought it should be built.' Second was the desire of progressive railroad men to apply the inherent advantages of the internal combustion engine to main line railroad service. Ralph Budd was one of these men.

Last was the success of the Electro-Motive Company (founded in 1922 and a subsidiary of General Motors since 1930) in developing the gasoline-electric rail car for branch line service on United States railroads. Harold L Hamilton,

the founder of Electro-Motive, and Richard M Dilworth, his chief engineer, were key figures in Electro-Motive's development of the variable-voltage generator, and an electric transmission that could successfully harness the mechanical energy of a gasoline engine in rail service, using a control system operated by a single throttle.

In fact, Electro-Motive was the single most significant factor in the evolution of the diesel locomotive in North America. More than 80 percent of the locomotives which took to the rails over the next half century were built by Electro-Motive.

The prototype Electro-Motive diesel engines were used in 1933 to provide power for the Chevrolet assembly line at the Chicago 'Century of Progress.' Although at the time they were strictly experimental and difficult to keep running, the engines attracted the attention of Ralph Budd, who was then contracting with the Budd Company in Philadelphia to build the small, three-car *Zephyr* train. He needed a prime mover for the revolutionary new train and, through Hamilton, came into contact with Kettering.

Budd finally persuaded Kettering to make one of the new engines available for the

Zephyr. He later remarked that while Kettering expressed qualms about the feasibility of using such an experimental prime mover before it had been thoroughly tested in the laboratory, he and his Burlington associates had no fears because once Kettering had committed himself, he'd have to stand behind his decision. Subsequent events proved Budd right, and sowed the seeds for the tremendous locomotive power development which, over the next two decades, would see the end of steam power, which had dominated American railroad service for the preceding 100 years.

In reporting the maiden run of the *Pioneer Zephyr* to his directors on the Burlington board, Budd emphasized two facts: the fuel cost for the 1000-mile trip was $14.64, and the highest speed attained was 112.5 mph. In a nutshell, he was highlighting economy and speed, the basis for the coming revolution in railroading.

By the time that Ralph Budd relinquished the reins of the Burlington to Harry Murphy in 1949, Burlington was squarely in the forefront of what promised to be a new era in American railroading—but not one the railroads had expected. Faced with intense competition from airlines and private automobiles, rail pas-

senger volume plummeted, and in the 1940s and 1950s railroads came to depend more and more on freight.

Diesels as motive power, an innovation pioneered by Burlington in 1934, proved to be a key element in maintaining the efficiency of its operations. Burlington's first freight diesels were purchased in 1944, and by 1953, 95 percent of its operations were dieselized.

The yard at Galesburg, Illinois was equipped with electro-pneumatic retarders in 1931. In 1942, to meet sudden increases in traffic, a second hump yard was built. To match these facilities, the Lincoln, Nebraska yard was converted to hump operations in 1944. The car building shop was moved from Galesburg to Havelock, near Lincoln, Nebraska, in 1943, and the locomotive shops at West Burlington were expanded in 1946 to take care of heavy repairs to diesel locomotives.

In 1958 the railroad modernized its classification yard at Cicero, near Chicago, making it a modern, electronic facility. A new high-level bridge was constructed in 1960 at Quincy, Illinois to replace the original, 92-year-old span. Earlier, in 1954, Burlington completed 71 miles of new line in its Centennial cut-off between Brookfield and Maxwell, Missouri, which pro-

Above: CB&Q No 9966 passenger diesel, the California Zephyr II, *heads for North Kansas City, Missouri in July 1970.*

Right: Its twin, E-8 9934, also by EMD, pulls into Chicago. The first California Zephyr *route operated in cooperation with the Denver & Rio Grande Western Railroad and the Western Pacific Railroad between Chicago and San Francisco via Denver and Salt Lake City.*

vided a more direct route between the gateways of Chicago and Kansas City by shortening the route by over 20 miles.

It was apparent that Kansas City, the second most important traffic gateway on the Burlington, would become even more prominent after this merger. Consequently, in 1967, ground was broken for a new automatic classification yard at North Kansas City.

In 1958 Burlington revolutionized railroad refrigeration techniques by using foamed-in-place polyurethane to insulate rail cars. The new process produced the strongest, most efficiently insulated cars in America, and in many cases dramatically lowered transportation costs.

A large, three-track diesel maintenance facility was built at Lincoln in 1964. Soon after it opened, the facility was servicing over half of Burlington's motive power fleet.

As passenger service declined throughout the industry, Burlington continued to improve its service, particularly its Chicago area suburban commuter lines. In 1945 Burlington created America's first vista-dome car. In 1950 it ushered in the age of modern commuting, bringing to Chicago America's first double-deck, stainless-steel suburban equipment. In 1952 Burlington became the first railroad to completely dieselize a suburban service.

During this golden age of passenger travel that existed in the United States between 1920 and 1950, the Burlington's principal passenger routes were the *Denver Zephyr*, which oper-ated on the *Pioneer Zephyr* route between Chicago and Denver, the *Twin Cities Zephyr*, which operated between Chicago and Minneapolis, and the *California Zephyr*, which operated on the Chicago-Denver-Salt Lake-San Francisco route in cooperation with the Denver & Rio Grande Western Railroad and the Western Pacific Railroad. An all-new *Denver Zephyr*, which operated on the route between Chicago and Denver-Colorado Springs, entered service in 1956 and brought with it another railroading first: the Slumbercoach. These economy sleeping cars provided rooms for coach passengers for only a small occupancy charge.

With the advent of jet airliners in 1959-1960 and the global energy crisis of 1973-1974, this was the dark age of American railroads. During this period, many railroads succumbed entirely or banded together through mergers. Such was the case for the Burlington.

On 2 March 1970 the Chicago, Burlington & Quincy Railroad Company merged with the Northern Pacific, Great Northern and Spokane, Portland & Seattle railways to form the Burlington Northern Corporation. As the largest component of the new Burlington Northern, the Chicago, Burlington & Quincy Railroad contributed 665 locomotives, 36,264 freight cars, 624 passenger cars and a route structure totaling 8430 miles. Though the Chicago, Burlington & Quincy is no more, a part of its identity lives on in the name of the new corporation.

THE GREAT NORTHERN

By Bill Yenne

James Jerome Hill—'The Empire Builder'—was the visionary who founded the Great Northern Railroad, easily one of the half dozen greatest railroads in American history. When Hill retired in 1912, he remarked: 'Most men who have really lived have had, in some shape, their great adventure. This railway is mine.'

James Hill's 'great adventure' began in 1856. Then 18 years of age, he had left his birthplace, a farm carved from the forest by his parents near Rockwood, a settlement in eastern Ontario, Canada. Aspiring to be a sea captain in Oriental commerce, he headed for the Atlantic seaboard, but, not finding a seafaring job, he started west to sign on a ship sailing to the Orient. En route, he planned to visit a friend at Fort Garry—now Winnipeg, Manitoba.

Before he arrived in July 1856 at St Paul, head of navigation on the Mississippi River, the last ox cart caravan of the season had already left for the north. Hill had to find work for the winter, so he got a job as a shipping clerk in the office of a Mississippi River steamboat company. His lifelong career in transportation had begun.

Meanwhile, the Minnesota legislature, eager for rail lines in its territory, had granted charters as early as 1853 and had issued one in 1857 to the Minnesota & Pacific Railroad Company. The latter provided for construction of a line from Stillwater, Minnesota, on the St Croix River, to St Paul, St Anthony (now Minneapolis) and Breckenridge, and another by way of St Cloud to St Vincent on the Canadian border.

The federal government made a land grant at first of six sections to the mile and later of 10. Minnesota, as soon as it became a state, also undertook to help with a bond issue, using the land grant as security. The sum of $100,000 was allowed for every 10 miles of grading, and the same amount for every 10 miles of completed road. The loan was exhausted in 1859 and the

road went bankrupt, later to emerge as the St Paul & Pacific.

Under the terms of the Federal Act, the line had to be completed in 10 years or the land would revert to the United States. The time limit was extended and the St Paul & Pacific figured in Hill's plan for using the railroad mainly as a basis for credit and for drawing in immigration, which would make business for the line.

After many delays and difficulties, the St Paul & Pacific Railroad Company completed the first 10 miles of construction in Minnesota—from St Paul to St Anthony—and began regular operations on 2 July 1862. At that time locomotives and rolling stock had to be brought up the Mississippi on barges. Among them was the pioneer wood-burning locomotive of the St Paul & Pacific, which was named *William*

Crooks after the railway's chief engineer. In 1939 the *William Crooks* went to, and returned from, the New York World's Fair under its own power.

Hill's early judgment of the prospective earnings of the railroad, if rehabilitated and properly managed, was thoroughly vindicated by the time he became president in 1882. That year, notwithstanding large expenditures for improvements, a seven percent dividend was paid to stockholders. For half a century thereafter, until the depression year of 1933, the company maintained an uninterrupted record of dividend payments.

The expansion of the railroad in Minnesota and into Dakota Territory continued at a steady pace, and by the close of 1885 the system of main and branch lines had grown to 1470 miles. It has been said of other sections of the

Below: This perky St Paul & Pacific 4-4-0 American wood-burning locomotive was the first locomotive to come to the Northwest. Known as the William Crooks *it arrived by barge in St Paul, Minnesota, in 1861, prepared to run on the 11 miles of track between St Paul and St Anthony (now Minneapolis).*

West that they were settled from the ox cart, while 'Hill country' was settled from the boxcar. Hill laid his rails first, then labored tirelessly to create traffic for his trains. The success of his plans for rapid expansion depended upon quick and sound colonization. Having sold his country, it was up to him to make it 'make good' after the settlers moved in, so he started showing the farmers how to improve their methods, and in the process became an authority on agriculture and livestock. He was an early ecologist, an advocate of diversification and conservation of natural resources. He imported purebred stock, introduced improved strains of seed, established experimental farms and credit facilities for producers and he held rates at a level which would enable settlers to sell their products competitively in distant markets. This formula enabled Hill and his associates to expand their mileage rapidly without land grants or government subsidies of any kind, other than the limited original grant of the Minnesota & Pacific.

Meanwhile, in 1881, Hill had acquired the Minneapolis & St Cloud Railway for $30,000. Chartered in 1856, the Minneapolis & St Cloud existed only on paper. In a quarter of a century it had built no track, yet it held very broad charter rights, an asset which James J Hill would bring into play eight years later.

In 1886 the main line of the St Paul, Minneapolis & Manitoba was extended westward from Devil's Lake to Minot in Dakota Territory, to set the scene for one of the great epochs of railroad construction. Between April and mid-October 1887, 545 continuous miles of line, reaching across largely unsettled wilderness all the way from Minot to Great Falls in Montana Territory, was graded, bridged and laid with track.

The logistics of an operation so distant from sources of supply were staggering, with 8000 men and 3300 draft horse teams pushing the construction. In one all-time record day, 11 August, 44,100 feet of track were laid.

By 18 November another 97 miles were completed between Great Falls and Helena by the subsidiary Montana Central Railway Company, which Hill had created in 1886, bringing the season's total to 642 miles. At Helena the new line connected with the Northern Pacific, which had been completed to the Pacific Northwest four years earlier.

It was now time for Hill to utilize the assets of the Minneapolis & St Cloud Railway, the obscure paper company that existed neither in Minneapolis nor St Cloud, but on a very important document in Jim Hill's desk drawer.

On 18 September 1889 the name of the Minneapolis & St Cloud was changed to Great

Left: The StP&P Minneapolis Terminal in 1874 bustled with traffic. In this photo are three balloon-stack 4-4-0 locomotives, freight cars and passenger cars.

Above: Built in New Jersey in 1861, the William Crooks *4-4-0 made its trial run to St Anthony in 1862 and thus opened a predecessor road to the Great Northern.*

Northern Railway Company. On 1 February 1890 the new Great Northern took over the properties of the St Paul, Minneapolis & Manitoba Railway, which actually had a smaller land grant than the anonymous Minneapolis & St Cloud.

The Rocky Mountains loomed ahead, and beyond, the Pacific. John F Stevens, a locating engineer later responsible for the Panama Canal, was hired to determine an easy, low-altitude route over the Rocky Mountains. He found Marias Pass, at the headwaters of the Marias River in Montana. A bronze statue of the engineer as he appeared that wintry day in 1889 was later built at Summit, Montana, 12 miles west of Glacier Park Station, within a stone's throw of Great Northern's passing transcontinental trains. Summit, only 5213 feet above sea level, is one of the easiest crossings possible through the Rockies, and is the highest point on the railway's transcontinental line.

Marias Pass had been known as an Indian legend for a half century or more. Lewis and Clark nearly found it, but were misled by the Blackfoot Indians. The Great Northern's Stevens went ahead after his Indian guide left him and a little while later 'walked right into the pass.' The snow was too deep for him to build a fire, and to keep from freezing to death that night he had to tramp back and forth until morning.

Due to the lower elevation, however, the climate is actually milder than at many points further south. The region is rich in natural resources and possesses numerous rivers—the Missouri, the Flathead, the Kootenai, the Spokane, the Pend d'Oreille, the Columbia and countless smaller streams—which have an abundance of water power capable of producing hydroelectric energy.

Construction of Great Northern's Pacific Coast extension began early in April 1890 at Pacific Junction, four miles west of Havre in what now was the fledgling state of Montana. Between here and Puget Sound lay 815 miles of mostly wild and rugged mountain land. Except for the town of Spokane, it was virtually uninhabited. Construction proceeded through 1891 and was virtually completed in 1892 while other railroads were going into bankruptcy or at best marking time. For 430 miles, the route ran through heavy timber, and for more than 200 miles there was no sign of a trail. The heights of the Cascades had to be scaled by a switchback, until such time as the projected tunnel could be undertaken.

At the close of 1892, however, less than three years since Havre, only a seven-mile gap remained in what once was referred to as 'Hill's Folly.' On 6 January 1893, in the towering Cascades near Scenic, Washington, the final spike was driven by 'The Empire Builder' himself.

Above: During 1887, pioneer rail laying gangs built 636 miles of track on the StPM&M Railway from Minot, North Dakota to Helena, Montana.

Left: Construction began 2 April 1887 and was completed on 19 November 1887. Four world's records were established in the process.

Right: James Jerome Hill, 'The Empire Builder' (1838-1916).

The Panic of 1893 swept a quarter of the nation's railroad mileage into receivership. Hill's first effort was to unify the operations of the Great Northern and the Northern Pacific. At the same time, a plan in which the Great Northern would agree to guarantee both the principal and interest on bonds of the reorganized Northern Pacific was found by the Supreme Court to be in conflict with a Minnesota statute prohibiting consolidation of parallel and competing lines.

James Jerome Hill had set about the task in his usual way. Fifty engineers and hundreds of assistants had been kept busy for three years locating and surveying the route. In an order to the chief engineer in 1890, Hill had said: 'We do not care enough for Rocky Mountain scenery to spend a large sum of money in developing it either on the Spokane or elsewhere. What we want is the best possible line, shortest distance, lowest grades and least curvature that we can build between the points to be covered. It would be unfortunate to find out afterward, as so many companies have, that we have left the best places unoccupied on some part of our line.'

The issue had been clear-cut, but as often happens, the ramifications of argument possible on both sides were anything but simple. Other Northern Pacific stockholders had alleged that the agreement with the Northern Pacific was illegal. They based this on two state of Minnesota statutes. An act of 1874 provided that 'No railroad corporation or the lessees, purchasers, or managers of any railroad corporation, shall consolidate the stock, property or franchises of such corporation with or lease or purchase the works or franchises of, or in any way control, any other railroad corporation owning or having under its control a parallel or competing line.' Furthermore, a law passed in 1881 stated that 'No railroad corporation shall consolidate with, or lease, or purchase, or in any way become owner of, or control, any other railroad corporation or any stock, franchise rights, or property thereof, which owns or controls a parallel or competing line.' A question of fact was presented as to whether the Great Northern was a 'parallel or competing line' with respect to the Northern Pacific and a question of law as to whether these statutes applied to the Great Northern.

The contest centered chiefly on the question of law. When the Great Northern was organized in 1889, it took the charter of the old Minneapolis & St Cloud Railway Company under which the link from St Cloud to Hinckley had been built, and simply changed the name. This charter was granted by the territorial legislature in 1856 and had authority to construct a railroad on an indicated route, to connect its road by branches with any other road in the territory, or to become part owner or lessee of

any railroad in the territory or to 'connect with any railroad running in the same direction with this road, and where there may be any portion of another road which may be used by this company.'

The incorporating act also provided that it might be 'amended by any subsequent legislative assembly in any manner not destroying or impairing the vested rights of said corporation.' In 1865 an amendatory act authorized the railroad 'to connect with or adopt as its own, any other railroad running in the same general direction with either of its main lines or any branch roads which said corporation is authorized to construct,' also 'to consolidate the whole or any portion of its capital stock with the capital stock or any portion thereof of any other road having the same general direction or location, or to become merged therein by way of substitution, to consolidate any portion of its road and property with the franchise of any other railroad company or any portion thereof; and to consolidate the whole or any portion of its main line or branches with the rights, powers, franchises, grants and effects of any other railroad.'

The Great Northern contended that the laws forbidding consolidation could not apply to it because it had been given these sweeping powers by earlier legislation; and under the doctrine that a charter was a contract, the state was prevented by the United States Constitution from taking away the rights that had been granted since to do so would impair the obligation of a contract.

With regard to the reservation of the right to amend in the act of 1856, it contended that the rights granted therein vested as soon as they were accepted by the corporation. The case was submitted on 16 December 1895, and the decision was handed down 30 March 1896. It was a keen disappointment for the Great Northern. The Supreme Court reversed the circuit court and found against the legality of the agreement. Not only did it do this, but in its language, the court made it clear that it considered the plan contrary to public policy.

The power to make such an arrangement of consolidation, although granted by the charter was, it held, an unexecuted power and not a

The decision did not mean the end of the effort to bring about a harmonious operation of the two railroad systems. Meanwhile, an alternative plan of reorganization had been worked out by the companies, to accomplish the same result without encountering the same legal obstacles. As soon as the court's decision was announced, steps were taken to put into effect the other plan.

Legislatures could, and did, prescribe just where the rights of property of a corporation could begin and end, but they could not for a person. That which had been forbidden to the Great Northern as a corporation — owning a controlling interest in the Northern Pacific —

Right: Construction of the St Paul, Minneapolis & Manitoba Railway took place in what is today western North Dakota, but what until 1889 was hostile Dakota Territory. This 1887 photo shows the crews accompanied by soldiers for protection.

vested right. It was a mere license revocable at the will of the legislature.

'We think it was competent for the legislature, out of due regard for the public welfare,' the court said, 'to declare that its charter should not be used for the purpose of stifling competition and building up monopolies. In short, we cannot recognize a vested right to do a manifest wrong.'

The court's opinion clearly reflected the popular philosophy of the day that railroads must be required to compete.

'While in particular cases, two railways by consolidating their interests under a single management may have been able to so far reduce the expenses of administration as to give their customers the benefit of a lower tariff, the logical effect of all monopolies is an increase of price of the thing produced, whether it be merchandise or transportation. There are, moreover, thought to be other dangers to that moral sense of the community incident to such great aggregations of wealth, which, though indirect, are even more insidious in their influence, and such as have awakened feelings of hostility which have not failed to find expression in legislative acts.'

could, in fact, be done legally and properly by stockholders as individuals.

The plan as adopted provided for a foreclosure and organization of a new company with common and preferred stock. The JP Morgan interests, as well as Jim Hill's interests, bought a very considerable part of this stock.

Meanwhile, in 1896 the Great Northern became the first American railroad to serve Japan as Hill negotiated an agreement with Nippon Yusen Kaisha (NYK), then the largest steamship line in the Pacific, resulting in the establishment of service between Seattle and Oriental ports. It was a bold challenge to the established commerce between Europe and the Orient, and marked the beginning of Seattle's ascendancy as a world port. NYK and Great Northern established rates that soon enabled them to gather up steel rails from as far east as Pittsburgh, flour from Minneapolis and cotton from the South for shipment to the Orient.

It was against this backdrop that James J Hill decided upon the necessity of a direct route to Chicago to give his Seattle to St Paul operation a connection with the grand rail hub of North America. Hill abhorred an empty boxcar, and the normal movement of freight over his

Above: No 38 is a Rogers 4-4-0 American, built in 1878 for the St Paul & Pacific.

Right: Great Northern crews lay track in Whitefish, Montana, circa 1903.

Laying Steel into Whitefish.

newly-completed Pacific Coast extension was certain to be predominantly westbound. To avoid the waste of hauling empty cars eastbound and to develop the lumber industry in his territory, he drastically reduced lumber rates, opening new markets in the Mississippi and Ohio valleys to Pacific Northwest mills.

Thus it was, that in 1901 he finally was able to arrange for the purchase by the Great Northern and the Northern Pacific of nearly all of the outstanding stock of the Chicago, Burlington & Quincy Railroad, giving the parent lines access not only to Chicago but to the markets of the Midwest and South as well. (Please refer also to the chapter which discusses the Chicago, Burlington & Quincy in detail.)

The year was 1901, for the United States a time of mergers and rumors of mergers. It was as though the advantages of mergers had suddenly been realized and every power in the economic world was hastening to avail itself of the new discovery. The industrial field was especially marked by this trend, but the transportation field was also feeling the effects. An outstanding example was the United States Steel Corporation, the so-called 'billion dollar steel trust.'

There were a great many rumors circulating over the questions of whether Jim Hill was in the market for the Burlington or some other Chicago line. Every trip that he made to the East was accompanied by newspaper speculation that a deal pended at least for securing a road to Chicago, and frequently for enlargement of much vaster scope. Edward H Harriman, the head of Union Pacific, was active in strengthening and extending his system, and if the Great Northern sat idly by, it might soon

Left: No 515 was one of the immensely popular Consolidation locomotives built by Brooks.

Above: No 98, an 0-6-0, was built in 1887 by Rogers for the St Paul, Minneapolis & Manitoba.

find itself hemmed in, cut off from desirable markets and threatened with discriminatory rates.

In January 1901, Jim Hill was in New York conferring with Pierpont Morgan. Something big, something unprecedented in size, comparable only to the steel corporation, was in the wind. Hill and Morgan had an option on the Chicago, St Paul, Milwaukee & Pacific (aka the 'Milwaukee Road'). They had an option on the Burlington, they had purchased the Erie and they were buying stock in the Baltimore & Ohio. The tabloids suggested that they were going to construct a colossal system extending from one end of the country to the other.

The Great Northern and Northern Pacific had to be assured of an outlet to Chicago. They could not depend on past alliances, for at any time, hostile interests might buy control of a connecting road. On the other hand, there was no legal bar to their buying a Chicago road. The prohibition was against buying a *parallel or competing* line, *not* one which was a continuation.

'What are the things that limit the development of railway systems?' Hill had said. 'Markets, geography and commerce, aside from the law. What good would a system be that reached from coast to coast and was operated as one road? The man west of the Mississippi would still ship his grain, his livestock, to Chicago or St Louis, and there it would change owners. Compared with such consignments to Chicago or St Louis, the amount of through shipments would be inconsiderable.'

Contrary to the rumors, Hill believed in the process of arranging the railroads in groups on the basis of territorial control. His interest in Erie was only, as he declared, to get that property fairly established so that it would no longer be a 'financial derelict and a discredit to American management.' His connection with the Baltimore & Ohio had the same purpose. The story that he held a one-fifth interest in the Milwaukee Road and was blocking it from building to the Pacific coast was completely unfounded. The truth turned out to be that he had been acting on his principle of regional

Left: *Celebrating the completion of the Oregon Trunk Railway, James J Hill drives the gold spike in Bend, Oregon on 5 October 1911.*

Right: *Rogers Locomotive and Machine Works in Paterson, New Jersey, built a number of locomotives for the St Paul, Minneapolis & Manitoba. No 324 2-6-0 was built in 1887.*

Below: *A Great Northern train crosses Two Medicine Bridge in Montana in 1891. This was one of many engineering feats created to enable trains to cross the Rockies.*

competition and in conjunction with Morgan had bought the Burlington on behalf of the Great Northern and the Northern Pacific jointly to round out the northern transcontinental system and 'protect' the Northwest. It was the same thing that had been done by Southern Railway, the Pennsylvania, the New York Central and the Union Pacific, each in its respective sphere.

'I do not regard a transcontinental system, one extending from ocean to ocean, under one management or ownership, practicable,' said Hill. 'Conditions differ so radically East and West that a system under one ownership couldn't be managed to advantage. Under one ownership, there would be a demand for uniformity in rates over the entire system.'

The actual negotiations for the purchase of the Burlington began in March 1901, and in April the deal was admitted as an accomplished fact.

'Well, the "Q" is ours,' Hill said, using the popular name for the Chicago, Burlington & Quincy. 'We've headed off the Union Pacific. At the same time we've made sure we can take care of the Oriental trade. We have to look not only to cotton but to anything that will furnish us business going to the West. We had to have access to the main centers. Out here it is a case of getting fuel or freezing.'

Hill and Morgan had gone about acquiring the road in a different way from the Union Pacific interests. They had dealt directly with the executive committee of the Burlington. They had made an offer of $200 a share and this had been accepted. The market price had ranged lately from $175 to $180. The shares were in the hands of 15,000 stockholders, hence it was obvious that the method followed was the only one by which a successful transaction could be made. The Burlington shareholders received a good bargain, measured by the 20 to 25 point profit they were given, and the two purchasing companies received something of immense value to themselves and capable at the same time of returning a profit, even on the new capitalization. The stock of the reorganized company was to be $100,000,000, divided equally between the Great Northern and the Northern Pacific.

The statement of the purchase laid before the directors described the acquisition as follows: 'The Burlington system includes 7,992.6 miles of standard gauge track and 178.7 miles of narrow gauge railroad. The territory served by the Burlington produces most of the machinery and implements used in the farms, in the forest, mines and mills of the tier of states reached by the Great Northern and the Northern Pacific. It also produces a large part of the iron and steel products exported to Asia via the Pacific Ocean. Chicago, Kansas City, St Joseph and Omaha are the largest provision centers in the country. At St Louis it connects with the chief cotton-carrying lines of the South and Southwest. On the other hand, the Burlington territory takes payment for fattening the livestock raised on the northern and western farms and ranches. It consumes lumber in all shapes on a large scale.'

It seemed indeed to be the ideal completion of the system formed by the two Northerns. It was the capstone of a railroad empire. It assured the Northwest of independence, of freedom to proceed in its development unthreatened and unhampered.

Meanwhile, however, there was trouble brewing. On 6 May 1901, Northern Pacific common stock opened at 114, climbed to 133 and receded to 127.5 at closing. The number of shares changing hands reached the vast total of 350,000. There was general bewilderment as to the cause, but the following day, indications pointed to Edward H Harriman, the owner of the Union Pacific and the Illinois Central, as the headlines on the first page screamed 'Hill Loses NP Control,' and 'Harriman Syndicate Defeats GN Magnate.' The price of NP common had gone up to 149.75, and the transactions involved 179,300 shares. In St Paul, President Mellen of the Northern Pacific scouted the idea that the Hill-Morgan group had been overthrown. The Harriman syndicate had a majority of the total stock, while the Hill-Morgan group was sitting tight with a majority of the common stock and knowledge of what they could do with it.

Nothwithstanding the denials of both sides that they were still dealing in the stock market, newspapers persisted in picturing the Wall Street frenzy as a combat between giants. The part that Northern Pacific had played in the ruin of Jay Cooke and Henry Villard in 1893 was recalled, and the thought expressed whether it would not also prove of evil omen to James J Hill.

The climax came on Thursday, 9 May, when the cry of the headlines was, 'Money Kings in Death Struggle,' 'Fight for Northern Pacific Sends Common Stock to 1000,' and 'Morgan-Hill Forces Supposed to Have Defeated Harriman Syndicate.' It was the worst panic to hit Wall Street until the crashes of 1929 and 1987.

These pages: One of the great name trains of all time, GN Empire Builder No 2517, a Class P Mountain, is seen here at the St Paul Union Depot on the day of its inaugural run, 11 June 1929. This luxurious passenger train was fast too, cutting five hours from previous schedules between Chicago and Seattle.

There was no bottom to stock market prices. Under an immense mass of forced liquidation sales, the market crumbled in every direction. At the same time, people were offering any price to get Northern Pacific stock, and the price rushed up quickly from $170 to $1000. Three hundred shares had actually changed hands for $300,000 *cash*! In other stocks, utter demoralization set in and there was a frantic rush to get out of the market at any price. Northern Pacific broke to 600 and closed at 325.

The real cause of the panic came out in the announcement of the after-hours agreement by Harriman's Kuhn Loeb & Company and Hill's JP Morgan & Company to settle at 150. It was evident that many speculators had sold stock that they did not have in their possession and were now making efforts to cover their bargain.

'I have no statement to make,' Hill declared. 'I have been too busy today buying locomotives.'

'Who in your personal opinion now controls the Northern Pacific?' he was asked.

'My personal opinion is that the control of Northern Pacific rests with the same interests that have held it for the last five years, and I think it will continue there for the next five, and that without qualification is my opinion.'

The Harriman syndicate was certain of $41,000,000 of preferred and $37,000,000 of common stock in Northern Pacific. This made a total of $78,000,000, an indisputable majority of the $155,000,000 capital stock. The annual meeting was fixed for October, and at that time Harriman's Union Pacific interest could, as matters stood, name a new board of directors. But the preferred stock could be retired on any 1 January, so the present board had the right to postpone the annual meeting. It could take such action and retire the preferred stock before the time for the postponed annual meeting. Control would then be in the hands of those who had a majority of the common stock. At the beginning of the fateful week Hill could count on only from $18,000,000 to $20,000,000 of common stock, and Morgan & Company $7,000,000 to $8,000,000. The Morgan and interests had bought about $15,00,000 on the open market, and the result was that the Hill-Morgan group now controlled about $42,500,000 of the common stock.

The danger was past. The Great Northern was safe, and the Northwest could not be exploited.

On 13 November the holding company was incorporated in New Jersey under the name 'The Northern Securities Company.' It had finally been decided to make it big enough to take in all Great Northern and Northern Pacific stockholders who wished to be admitted, and therefore the capital stock was fixed at

$400,000,000. This development grew out of Hill's disinclination to set up anything which could be said to benefit himself and a part of his stockholders and not all of them. The Harriman Union Pacific interests agreed to participate and exchanged their Northern Pacific holdings for about $82,500,000 of the new stock, thereby making a lasting peace doubly sure. In all, about 96 percent of Northern Pacific came in, on a basis of $115 for $100, and about 76 percent of Great Northern on a basis of $180 for each $100. The board of directors consisted of 15, six from Northern Pacific, four from the Great Northern, three from the Harriman Group and two at large. For president there was no thought of anyone but James J Hill. There had been so many combinations of one kind or another the past few years, that the public was suspicious. As Oscar M Sullivan so eloquently pointed out, every 'trust-buster' was a David going out to battle with a Goliath, and every politician could picture himself enacting such a role to the utmost satisfaction. The new railroad holding company was too promising an opportunity to be missed. By a little distortion, just a little pulling out of perspective, just a slight overlooking of evident facts, it could be made to appear as a gigantic merger.

However, as Hill pointed out in December, the new company was 'purely an investment company, and the object of its creation was simply to enable those who hold stock to continue their respective interests in association together, and to prevent such interests from being scattered by death or otherwise; to provide against such attacks as had been made upon the Northern Pacific by a rival and competing interest, whose main investment was hundreds of miles from the Northwest, and whose only object in buying control of the Northern Pacific was to benefit their southern properties by restraining the growth of the country between Lake Superior and Puget Sound, and by turning away from the Northern lines the enormous Oriental traffic which must follow the placing on the Pacific of the largest ships in the world.'

The case went to the United States Supreme Court, and on 14 March 1904 the court held against the Securities Company and sustained the action of the lower court, which had enjoined the company from voting stock, acquiring additional stock, paying dividends or exercising corporate control. The great financial plan of 'The Empire Builder' for insuring railroad harmony in the Northwest was shattered.

'I have not yet read the complete decision,' Hill was quoted as saying, 'but I wish to say that the three roads are still there, and there they will remain, despite the learned jurists of the Supreme Court of the United States. The properties are as good as ever, and they will con-

Right: The Empire Builder *flies along the Middle Fork of the Flathead River between Belton and Marias Pass.*

Left: A trio of Great Northern Railway giants, shown at Appleyard, near Wenatchee, Washington in 1958. From left to right: a 5000-hp single-cab electric, a 5400-hp four-unit diesel-electric and a 2-8-8-2 Chesapeake oil-burning steam locomotive.

Below: Baldwin built the GN Mallet-articulated locomotive in 1910. Here is an M class No 1959 2-6-8-0 compound with 23/35 x 32-inch cylinders.

tinue to make money for their stockholders.'

And so they did. In the meantime, new construction of Great Northern lines and acquisition of smaller operations continued, so that by the end of 1901, the Great Northern had more than 5000 miles in service. The building of a railroad never ends, and Great Northern lines constantly were upgraded and frequently relocated for more economical operation and better service.

In 1901, notwithstanding a decrease of 218 cents per ton mile in freight charges, Hill reported an increase in revenue per freight train mile of 12 cents per mile. The revenue per freight train mile for the Great Northern in 1900 had been $3.38, which was larger than that of any other important railway system in the country. The average rate charged per ton mile had been steadily reduced. The average for the entire West was about 20 percent above the Great Northern rate in 1900.

One of the features of the 'Hill methods' which resulted in a high revenue per freight train mile was his success in consolidating freight into big trains, and to bringing about a low cost of operation by avoiding 'empties.'

After paying seven percent dividends on $98,682,520 stock, there remained a surplus of $1,689,064 to appropriate to the fund for improvements. Such a record in a year of crop failure astounded Wall Street financiers.

Major changes in the first two decades following the Pacific Coast extension included the original 2.6-mile Cascade Tunnel built in 1900, which eliminated a series of hazardous switchbacks over Stevens Pass; a 69-mile relocation of the main line between Columbia Falls and Rexford, Montana in 1904; and completion in 1912 of the Surrey cutoff between Fargo and Surrey, North Dakota, reducing Great Northern's transcontinental route by 52 miles, or about an hour of through-train time.

In 1905, under Hill's aegis, the Great Northern and Northern Pacific formed the Spokane, Portland & Seattle Railway Company, which built a line from Spokane, Washington to Portland, Oregon, and subsequently acquired other lines in Oregon by purchase, lease and building. Important new markets and sources of freight resulted. (Please also refer to the chapter which discusses the Spokane, Portland & Seattle Railway in detail.)

On 11 May 1910, thanks in part to the lobbying efforts of James Jerome Hill and the great environmentalist George Bird Grinnell, President William Howard Taft signed the bill creating Glacier National Park. The new park, located on the Canadian border in northwest Montana on the main line of the Great Northern, encompassed an area larger than the state of Rhode Island. Hill viewed Glacier as potentially the 'playground of the Northwest,' and the Great Northern set out to attract tourists to visit the newly christened park—and, of course to ride the rails of the Great Northern to get there.

Hill's son Louis, who would later succeed his father as president of the Great Northern, was assigned to the company's tourist facilities in Glacier. Under his direction, the railroad embarked on an ambitious building project of hotels and chalets to service travelers in Glacier.

Although in 1911 the younger Hill planned only to involve the railroad in the hotel business for two or three years, it was to be an involvement spanning half a century. Historian Michael Ober wrote that during this 50-year period, 'The Great Northern gave to Glacier the housing it needed, the advertisement and notoriety that it demanded.'

The first of the great hotels constructed by Great Northern in the park was the sprawling complex known as the Glacier Park Hotel, which was located near Midvale (now East Glacier), Montana at the point where the Great Northern main line first reaches the park from the East. Fifty railroad carloads of Douglas fir logs were brought in from Oregon and Washington for the hotel. The largest, which formed pillars for the grand, six-story lobby, weighed 50 tons each and were almost six feet in diameter and 52 feet long. The hotel cost over $500,000 and took 18 months to construct. The main section opened in 1913, with an annex added the following winter.

Two years later another opulent hotel was completed at Many Glacier, near the northeast corner of the park, about one day's coach trip north of the Glacier Park Hotel. Unlike the Glacier Park Hotel, the hotel was built almost entirely with cedar and other materials from the area. More than two million board feet of lumber was cut from the forest east of the hotel, with a sawmill built on the site to turn out finished lumber. In fact, the only prefinished woodwork brought to the hotel site were window sashes and door frames. Almost all of the hotel's woodwork, including furniture, utilized native timber. The stone foundation for Many Glacier also was built with native materials. The Many Glacier Hotel opened in August 1915, outfitted not only with a rustic appearance but comforts such as telephones, hot and cold running water and steam heat.

Below: A 1947 view of the famed Empire Builder, *drawn by an early EMD streamline diesel.*

Great Northern also built Swiss-style chalets at Two Medicine Lake, Cut Bank Creek, Gunsight Lake, Sperry Glacier, St Mary Lake and Sun Point on St Mary Lake. Construction had to surmount Glacier's obstacles. In the case of the Going-to-the-Sun Chalets at Sun Point, logs were cut at the upper end of St Mary Lake, floated in rafts down the lake, and then hauled up a cliff to the construction site.

The last of the Great Northern's projects, Granite Park Chalet, also presented a challenge. Since the chalet was above the timberline near Swift-current Pass, a stone, rather than log, structure was required. Quarrying crews worked on site to put up the completely native stone facility. Other materials—ranging from cement to furniture to food—came up from Many Glacier in 60-horse pack strings. Granite Park's 17-room chalet and six-room dormitory were completed in 1915 and capped Great Northern's building program in Glacier Park. The Chalet still exists and is still reachable only by trail. In 1927, the company put up its third Swiss-style hotel, the Prince of Wales, in Canada's Waterton Lakes National Park. Three years later Great Northern acquired the Lake McDonald Hotel from John E Lewis, who had expanded the previous Snyder Hotel into the large, three-story Glacier Hotel.

Through its subsidiary Glacier Park Company, the Great Northern continued as the primary park concessionaire until 1961, when Don Hummel bought the company. He ran it for two decades before Greyhound, Incorporated took over the concession.

In 1907 James Jerome Hill left the railway's presidency to become chairman of the board. He retired in 1912 from the chairmanship and active direction of the railroad system his genius had created. On 29 May 1916 he died in St Paul, the headquarters city for the railway he had founded and nurtured.

Fame as a transportation genius and 'Empire Builder' has largely eclipsed Hill's other noteworthy accomplishments. He was also instrumental in the building of the Canadian Pacific, the St Paul, Minnesota & Manitoba and the Spokane, Portland & Seattle, as well as the Great Northern. His addresses on economic topics are still read in the light of later history. He became an authority on agriculture and livestock and established experimental farms and credit facilities for producers. He was a staunch advocate of conservation of natural resources, and many educational institutions still carry on now with the aid of his endowments.

Subsidies of large grants of land and cash had helped build earlier lines to the Pacific Coast, but Hill's venture was unique in that land grants or other government aids were neither sought nor given. The only government lands ever received by Hill's company were those attached to the 600 miles of railway in Minnesota constructed by predecessor companies and acquired by purchase.

Throughout his years of creating, encouraging and directing, Hill's creed was to develop the resources of the region the railway served. He knew the railway could not prosper unless its territory prospered. That concept, that

Right: No 5012, an electric locomotive, emerges from the Cascade Tunnel at Skykomish, Washington.

Below: No 5018 is one of the world's two largest single-cab electric locomotives, both of which were operated by GN on the electrified segment of the Cascade Mountains of Washington State. The two identical General Electric locomotives were designed primarily for heavy mountain duty. Each was 101 feet long, weighed 360 tons and developed 5000 hp.

objective, guided Great Northern throughout its entire history. There is probably no other single human being who did more to affect American railroad development than James Jerome Hill. At the time of his retirement, the region that depended upon his rails as its lifeline to the world was larger than Britain, France and Germany combined. 'The Empire Builder' had created a domain that exceeded—in both scope and riches—those of all but a handful of the world's potentates.

The influence of James Jerome Hill on the history of American railroads is truly awesome; his stamp on the history of the American Northwest is indelible.

The years immediately following James Jerome Hill's death found the United States involved in World War I, a global calamity which resulted in the de facto United States government nationalization of America's railroads between 1918 and 1920. This exercise was in itself a disaster of immense proportions and is discussed in full detail in the chapter devoted to the Chicago, Burlington & Quincy. Hale Holden, then the president of the Chicago, Burlington & Quincy, was a member of the Executive Board that attempted to keep the

Left: Over 3400 of EMD GP9 road switchers, including No 910, were built between 1954 and 1959. Upgrading the GP7s from 1500 hp to 1750 hp made the GP9 a formidable engine.

Below: The Empire Builder in 1947 near Glacier National Park in Montana shortly after the fleet of streamliners was introduced on the Chicago to Pacific Northwest line.

governmentally contrived monstrosity of railroad nationalization under control during the wartime emergency.

Federal control of the Great Northern, along with that of all American railroads, ended on 12 March 1920, and at that point there began a decade of brilliant achievement by Great Northern under the presidency of Ralph Budd. Improvements to the railroad in that period totaled $160 million, including two historic engineering projects.

The weakest link in the Great Northern's route to the West Coast was its tortuously circuitous line across the Cascade Mountains of western Washington. This line was costly to operate and difficult to maintain, and was conspicuously out of place in a system that constituted the shortest rail link between the Great Lakes and the Pacific, with the least curvature and lowest grades. The original line built in the Cascades in 1892 was carried over the summit on a series of switchbacks, with maximum elevation of 4059 feet above sea level. In 1900 a tunnel 2.63 miles in length was completed, reducing the summit elevation to 3383 feet. This bore, electrified in 1909, was destined to

be supplanted by another, greater tunnel. On Thanksgiving Day 1925 the railway's directors authorized construction of the 7.79-mile Cascade Tunnel, and the relocation of all but seven miles of the 50-mile line between Peshastin and Scenic, Washington, in addition to the elimination of 12 miles of tunnels and snowsheds and the electrification of 75 miles of track between Wenatchee and Skykomish.

The total cost of this historic Cascade Tunnel project was approximately $25 million, and its completion on 12 January 1929 was signalized by a nationwide radio broadcast in which President Herbert Hoover participated. The Cascade Tunnel is as straight as a rifle bore and is still the longest tunnel in the Western Hemisphere. (The second longest is the seven-mile Flathead Tunnel in northwestern Montana, begun by Great Northern in 1966 and completed by Burlington Northern in 1970.)

By 1929 the Great Northern had 8368 miles of main line track and a fleet of 1164 locomotives drawing 55,777 freight cars and 946 passenger cars.

From 1929 through 1956, the Great Northern utilized a fleet of huge, 5000-hp electric

locomotives to pull its trains through the Cascade Tunnel, but in 1956 a ventilating system was installed, which permitted the operation of diesels through the tunnel. This shaved as much as an hour of switching time off the duration of the St Paul to Seattle run.

The second major project undertaken by the Great Northern in the 1920s was the California extension through central Oregon, which began in 1927 with 68 miles of construction from Bend to Chemult. Traffic rights over Southern Pacific lines provided a link to Klamath Falls, Oregon, and the Great Northern itself then built from there 92 miles into California, while the Western Pacific was building 112 miles north from Keddie. The two lines met at Bieber, California on 10 November 1931, giving the Great Northern a direct connection to San Francisco.

With the addition of California, the Great Northern now served 10 states: Minnesota, Wisconsin, North and South Dakota, Iowa, Montana, Idaho, Washington, Oregon and Cali-

fornia, as well as the Canadian provinces of Manitoba and British Columbia.

During this period, the Great Northern also inaugurated increased maintenance and improvement programs. When traffic soared from the low levels of the 1930s to ever higher levels in the prewar and war periods, the Great Northern was ready for this momentous task. During World War II, the railway flourished as a military supply line, and set yearly all-time records for freight traffic in 1942, 1943 and 1944. Record highs for passenger volume were recorded in 1944 and 1945.

This heavy wartime traffic was handled by a growing number of diesel locomotives, as well as oil- and coal-burning steam locomotives, and by electric motive power in the Cascades area. Improvement of other railway facilities also continued, subject to wartime shortages, but with the war's end, this program was accelerated.

In the all-time record freight year of 1944, ton miles (a ton mile equaling the movement of a ton

Right: An impressive GN 5400-hp diesel locomotive built by EMD hauls a plywood freight train.

Below: Traveling along Puget Sound between Seattle and Everett, Washington, Great Northern Railway's revered passenger train, the Empire Builder, heads west.

of freight one mile) totaled 19,586,780,000. In the all-time record passenger year of 1945, passenger miles (each representing transportation of one passenger one mile) amounted to 1,305,138,000.

The Great Northern system was traditionally known as 'The route of the Empire Builder.' The basis of this title is dual, for it pays tribute to the memory and achievements of James Jerome Hill and also distinguishes the line's principal passenger train, which traversed the immense territory to which Hill had devoted his life. The *Empire Builder*, the premier transcontinental passenger train of the Great Northern Railway, began daily service between Chicago and the Pacific Coast in 1929, soon after the completion of the Cascade project.

Great Northern's galaxy of streamlined trains began to take form in 1944 with the wartime announcement that five completely new *Empire Builder*s would go into service between Chicago and the Pacific Northwest 'as soon as they could be assembled.' On 23 Febru-

ary 1947 these streamliners, each having 12 cars and a 4000-hp, two-unit diesel-electric locomotive, began daily service. With the *Empire Builder*'s 45-hour schedule between Chicago on the east and Seattle and Portland on the west, the Great Northern became the first northern transcontinental system to inaugurate streamliner service. These 1947 cars were the first completely new sleeper and coach transcontinental trains built in the nation after World War II ended, and the first since 1941, before the United States entered the conflict.

Another completely new fleet of five *Empire Builder* streamliners—the third generation under this name—entered service on 3 June 1951. Each had 15 cars and a 4500-hp, three-unit diesel-electric locomotive. These trains, again representing the most modern equipment and accommodations, took over the run and schedule of their predecessors. In the summer and early fall of 1955, four dome cars—three dome coaches and a full length dome lounge, all equipped with the ultimate in mod-

ern conveniences—were added to each of the five streamliners. During the summertime months of peak travel, the *Empire Builder* included 15 passenger cars, but that number was reduced during the winter months.

Also on 3 June 1951 the five *Empire Builder* streamliners that had begun operating in 1947 were joined by a sixth completely new train, the *Western Star*, which became the companion train of the *Empire Builder* on the Chicago to Seattle/Portland run. Thus, travelers on Great Northern's transcontinental line had their choice of two daily passenger trains, both westward and eastward.

Between Chicago and St Paul the routes of the *Empire Builder* and the *Western Star* were on Burlington route lines, and between St Paul and Seattle they were on Great Northern lines. Between Spokane and Portland, cars from both trains were part of connecting routes of the Spokane, Portland & Seattle Railway.

When the initial transcontinental streamliner fleet took over the *Empire Builder* name in 1947, another famous Great Northern train name was revived. The *Oriental Limited* had first become a Great Northern name in 1905, when the train began operating as a vital link with trade of the Orient in the empire-building era of James Hill. New equipment was added in 1924 and in 1931, two years after the first fleet bearing the *Empire Builder* title went into operation. The *Oriental Limited* was 'honora-

bly discharged' as a name train, and remained unused until 1947, when it was reassigned to the six non-streamliner trains, which since 1929 had operated as the first-generation *Empire Builder*s. When the fleet of *Empire Builder*s that was new in 1947—the second-generation of that train name—was renamed the *Western Star* in 1951, the latter took over the run and schedule of the *Oriental Limited*, and that name was dropped.

In June 1960 three additional and completely new streamliners, each with five cars and diesel power, all began operating on faster schedules than previously in effect. These new trains were the twin *International*s, which made round trips between Seattle and Vancouver, British Columbia, and the *Red River*, which operated between St Paul and Grand Forks, North Dakota.

The *Empire Builder* passenger service was abandoned by Burlington Northern after the 1970 merger, but when the United States government-owned National Railroad Passenger Corporation (Amtrak) resumed passenger service on American railroad lines in 1971, the name *Empire Builder* was assigned to the Amtrak route that used the same tracks as those of the original Great Northern *Empire Builder*.

The steam era on the Great Northern officially ended in the spring of 1958, and *all* regularly scheduled freight and passenger trains

Above: This F45 diesel bears the short-lived 'Big Sky Blue' corporate color and the new 'Rocky' silhouette logo.

Right: No 3036 is an EMD light road-switcher built for GN and used for local and branch line freight and passenger duties.

were then powered by diesel-electric locomotives, which had supplemented steam locomotives on the Great Northern for two decades.

Meanwhile, Great Northern began to use electronics in an ever-increasing way. At the railway's data processing center in St Paul, the Univac electronic computer was used for such diverse duties as payroll, accounting, labor distribution and inventory control. The original installation, finished in 1957, was the second among United States railroads to go on-line and the first among Western railroads. In 1963 Great Northern installed an updated Univac II computer that could handle an expanded workload. This installation was augmented in 1967 with new hardware in Great Northern's extensive data processing center — the Univac 418, the railway's first 'real time' electronic

computer that could instantaneously make information available for all facets of the railroad's operations. Two of these computers were connected with a network of 38 on-line reporting stations, which were equipped with IBM 1050 data control facilities, thus enabling the railway to pinpoint immediately any one of some 40,000 freight cars on its line.

Extensive use of radio in freight train operations and in switching and yard areas began in 1953, and early 1956 saw the completion of Great Northern's very high frequency (VHF) radio network between the Twin Cities and the Pacific coast. Radio was thereafter to be routinely installed on passenger, freight and yard engines, on cabooses, snow-fighting and other maintenance equipment, and on supervisors' rail cars and automobiles.

Construction of Great Northern's largest freight classification yard at Minot, North Dakota was begun in 1955 and concluded in the early fall of 1956. This ultramodern, electronic 'push-button' yard, built at a cost of $6.5 million, was dedicated on 12 October 1956 and named in honor of Frank J Gavin, Great Northern's seventh president.

Great Northern opened its $6 million taconite pellet-handling facility at Superior, Wisconsin in early 1961, inaugurating a new era in the railway's association with the Iron Range of Minnesota. Pellets from the National Steel Pellet plant near Keewatin, Minnesota and the Butler Taconite plant near Nashwauk, Minnesota were moved by unit train to the facility, where they were unloaded onto an intricate conveyer system and then into holds of ore boats alongside the dock at Superior, or stockpiled for later shipment.

Freight piggybacking, or trailer-on-flatcar service, was initiated on Great Northern in 1954, and was substantially expanded over the next 16 years. Great Northern acquired its first bi-level and tri-level cars in late 1960, and in 1968 moved 8987 carloads of new automobiles on this type of equipment. Still in use, tri-level racks carry as many as 12 standard-sized automobiles or 15 compacts. To further meet its expanded requirements for specialized piggyback and auto rack flatcars, Great Northern in 1960 joined the Trailer Train Company, a railway-owned agency operating the largest fleet of such equipment in the country.

In 1964 Great Northern, in cooperation with three other railroads, began faster freight service from New Westminister, British Columbia, Canada, to Whittier, Alaska. The Alaska Trainship Corporation's SS *Alaska*, a 520-foot streamlined vessel, transported 56 fully-loaded rail cars in enclosed decks to the nation's 49th state at a cruising speed of 18 knots.

In the spring of 1966 the first phase of construction on the giant $352 million Libby Dam project in northwest Montana was begun. Damming the Kootenai River a short distance above Libby created a 90-mile long reservoir that extended into Canada. The Great Northern's main line was inundated for 48 miles, and its relocation required 59 miles of new line and the construction of the seven-mile Flathead Tunnel, which became operational in 1970.

The new line was the largest railroad construction project of its decade in the United States, and the most extensive single undertaking on Great Northern in 36 years.

In October 1965 Great Northern reached a financial milestone when it became a billion dollar enterprise. The principal commodities in its diversified traffic 'mix' at that time included (in order of importance): grain and grain products; lumber and products; iron ore and taconite pellets; wood, pulp and paper and products; smelter products; automobiles and trucks; petroleum products; iron and steel manufactured articles; coal and coke; aluminum; logs and pulpwood; canned goods; and apples.

Above, left: GN No 3007 in 1965 before it became part of the BN in 1970. Dominating the scene to the right is 5639-foot Mount Index.

Above: Three U33C diesels totaling 9900 hp, pull an eastbound freight train on the 1.1 percent grade of the Index line, as it crosses the Skykomish River.

At the time of the 2 March 1970 merger that created the Burlington Northern, the Great Northern Railway was, by a narrow margin, the second largest component of the new conglomerate. It had served a vast, diversified and productive region comprised of the upper Midwest and the Northwest. On a system 8277 miles in length (compared to 8430 for the Chicago, Burlington & Quincy), its trains carried passengers, freight, mail and express in the vast area between the Great Lakes and the Pacific Ocean. At the time of the merger, the Great Northern possessed a fleet of 609 locomotives, 415 passenger cars and 36,300 freight cars. Its principal main lines extended from the Twin Ports of Duluth, Minnesota and Superior, Wisconsin, and the Twin Cities of St Paul and Minneapolis, Minnesota, to the Puget Sound on the Pacific coast. It had more than 15,000 employees who earned over $130 million annually, and 42,000 stockholders who owned over six million individual shares.

Spanning more than half a century of history and half the American continent, the Great Northern Railway had been the greatest adventure, not only for 'The Empire Builder,' James Jerome Hill, but for the thousands who followed him in the gleaming, black steam locomotives and the bright orange streamliners that bore the name *Empire Builder*.

THE GULF, MOBILE & OHIO

By Bill Yenne

Between 1880 and 1890, 70,301 miles of railroad main line were built in the United States. This amounted to nearly half of the railroad that had been built in the country since the first rails were laid more than 60 years before. In that one single decade, 30 percent of all the main line *ever* laid in the United States was built!

This incredible achievement was unequaled in the economic history of any other country of the world. Within 10 years, the people of the United States built as many miles of railroad as the people of the three leading countries of Europe had constructed in 50 years. The building operations were carried on in all sections of the country, but the largest increases were made in the central and western states, where settlers were rapidly taking possession of the unoccupied agricultural and grazing sections of the vast public domain, and where vast mineral wealth was causing cities and states to be established on the great Rocky Mountain plateau.

Capitalists, confident of the growth of the country, and assisted by generous aid from federal and local governments—and individuals of the sections to be served—constructed railroads to create the traffic upon which the earnings of the roads must depend. In many cases, the railroads built during the 20 years following the Civil War were to serve pioneers entering unsettled regions beyond the Mississippi and Missouri rivers and opening the highways by which immigration was rapidly able to occupy the prairies and mountain valleys of the West.

After 1890, railroad construction was not as swift. Less than 30,000 miles were completed for the decade ending in 1900. By 1890, the most urgent need for railways had been met and the country had been so well covered with the railroad net, only minor extensions were necessary.

Thus it was that 1890 was the high water mark in American railroad development. It was also the birthdate of the Mobile, Jackson & Kansas City Railroad.

The Mobile, Jackson & Kansas City was born in the soft wood logging country of the deep South, in the same area that saw the genesis of such other roads as the New Orleans, Jackson & Great Northern, and the New Orleans, St Louis & Chicago, both of which had already been joined to the Illinois Central by 1890.

The idea behind the Mobile, Jackson & Kansas City was obvious: to connect the Gulf of Mexico with the Midwest heartland. However, the Depression that began in 1893 and lasted for nearly five years compelled the railway companies to practice rigid economy and to extend their systems slowly. During the five years between 1894 through 1898, the annual construction averaged less than 200 miles for the entire country, a yearly increase of only a little more than one percent. For the Mobile, Jackson & Kansas City, this meant only 50 miles were constructed between Mobile, Alabama and Merrill, Mississippi by 1898.

By 1902, the line had been completed to Hattiesburg, Mississippi. When the road was sold, and in turn merged with the Gulf & Chicago Railroad, this optimistically named road extended from Pontotoc, Mississippi, not to Chicago, but just 62 miles to Middleton, Tennessee. By 1906, however, 240 miles of new track had been laid, connecting the two systems into a respectable deep South rail network.

At this point, however, the Mobile, Jackson & Kansas City went into receivership. It seems that most of the money used to construct the new rail lines, like that of most railroad construction nationally, was obtained by borrowing money. The bondholders had furnished most of the capital used in railroad construction. When times were good and business

active, railroad companies had no difficulty paying the interest on their debts; but when times were bad and business slow, many corporations had found their income insufficient to meet their obligations. When a corporation such as the Mobile, Jackson & Kansas City was unable to make its payments, the bondholders, or those from whom equipment had been purchased, requested a court to take over the management of the company from the officers of the railroad until the road again became solvent. When the court took control of a road in the interests of the creditors, it took the place of the corporation for the time being. If the court found that the road could be put upon a paying basis, the court kept the road running until the financial troubles passed. If, however, the court found the railroad to be hopelessly insolvent, it would sell the property to pay the creditors.

The Mobile, Jackson & Kansas City finally re-emerged from receivership in 1909 as the New Orleans, Mobile & Chicago Railroad, a new entity which was, in 1911, placed under the joint stewardship of the Louisville & Nashville and the St Louis & San Francisco (the 'Frisco'), two major regional railroads with considerable influence in their respective areas east and west of the Mississippi River Valley. Neither of the larger roads had access to New Orleans and found that the New Orleans, Mobile & Chicago could provide this. The new arrangement was short-lived, and the New Orleans, Mobile & Chicago was again forced into receivership in 1913.

It was not until 1917 that Isaac B Tigrett, a banker from Jackson, Tennessee, got the rail-road back on track, so to speak. Tigrett christened the revived railroad the Gulf, Mobile & Northern, a name which more clearly defined its actual region of activity than any of the preposterous earlier appellations. The Gulf, Mobile & Northern initiated operations on New Year's Day in 1917, but within five days of the United States' declaration of war against Germany on 2 April 1917, the Railroads War Board was organized under a resolution signed by the chief executive of practically every railroad in the country. The resolution bound the railroads individually, for the duration of the war, to voluntarily coordinate their operations within the continental railroad system, 'merging during such period all their merely individual and competitive activities in the effort to produce a maximum of transportation efficiency.'

While the controlling motive behind the War Board was one of patriotic endeavor to make the railroads the greatest possible aid to the government in winning the war, there undoubtedly was a desire on the part of many railroad executives to demonstrate to the public that American railroad men, under *private ownership and control* of railroads, could do their part in the emergency without formal government action, such as that taken in England. The demonstration, if successful, would curb the activities of the growing number of people who then looked with favor upon government ownership of the railroads.

Each railroad was individually operated by its chief executive under instructions from the Executive Committee of the War Board. Outside of freight car utilization and troop move-

Page 139: No 710, a 1500-hp diesel electric locomotive, ran in the late 1940s and early 1950s for the Gulf, Mobile & Ohio Railroad.

Left: This 4-6-0 ten-wheeler was built by Rogers Locomotive Works for the Mobile & Ohio Railroad, a predecessor road of the GM&O.

Below: A woodburner of the 1854 era, uncoupled from its cars, pauses for fuel while a few friends stop to chat with its crew.

ments, an excess of centralized control of detail was avoided. While at first the energy of the Railroads War Board was devoted to satisfying the demands of the army and navy, efforts were made to also take care of the needs of other branches of the government, while imposing only a minimum of hardship upon the civilian population. Considerable progress was made in bringing about the joint use of terminals and running racks, in reducing the volume of traffic moving via what the Board deemed to be circuitous routes and in curtailing superfluous passenger trains routed by the various railroads for competitive reasons. The statistical records of April to December 1917 show considerable improvement in the efficient utilization of locomotives and freight cars, and the inconvenience to the civilian travelers was much less than that experienced during the same period in England.

Yet, as a whole, the positive results began to wane toward the end of 1917, and freight congestion began to occur on the lines serving the Atlantic seaboard. Yards, sidings and even running tracks became clogged with cars. Overall freight service on the lines between Chicago, Pittsburgh and the Atlantic ports was badly demoralized. One reason for this congestion was the failure of the railroads to keep up their prewar programs of enlargement and improve-

ment, and to maintain their usual acquisition of equipment, locomotives and freight cars. This was seen as the natural result of government over-regulation in the early part of the century.

The failure to control the flow of export traffic was another cause of congestion on the lines. Freight for export was accepted without regard to the capacity of the available ships. Part of the war materials for the Allies was ordered from American manufacturers under contracts which provided that a large percentage of the invoice would be paid as soon as the materials were loaded on cars. There was, therefore, every inducement to load the materials into the cars at the earliest possible moment. The result was that the export tonnage on the rails very much exceeded the capacity of the ships, and the cars containing the excess were held for months at a time. If something like the permit system, which was later adopted by the United States Railroad Administration, had been put into effect, or if the Railroads War Board had been able to curb the spirit of competition, the flow of this traffic might have been controlled at the source and the crisis might have been avoided.

The original 1887 Act to Regulate Commerce provided that 'The railroads, in time of war, should give preference and precedence over all other traffic to the movement of troops

and materials of war, and should adopt every means within their control to facilitate and expedite military traffic.' Under this authority, each branch of the government insisted upon priority in the movement of *its* freight, but there was no effective agency for coordinating these demands.

By December 1917 the railroad situation had become acute. The Interstate Commerce Commission, in a special message to Congress, recommended that complete unification of the railroads should be effected, either by the carriers themselves, with the assistance of the government, or by the operation of the nation's railroads by the President as a single government-owned agency for the duration of the war. Commissioner McChord, in a dissenting opinion, disagreed with the majority recommendation that the carriers be permitted to bring about complete unification themselves with aid from the government. Instead, he argued that 'The supreme arm of governmental authority is essential,' either by the exercise of the President's authority to operate the roads or by the creation of a single government administration control. In his opinion, unification of diversified governmental control was as vital as unification of the properties.

On 26 December 1917 President Woodrow Wilson took possession of the railroads of the country as a war measure. He placed them under the control of the newly-created United States Railroad Administration (USRA) and appointed William McAdoo, Secretary of the Treasury, as Director General of Railroads, to act for the President under the authority granted to the President by the Army Appropriations Act of 29 August 1916.

During the period of federal control, a great deal of publicity was given to the administration's policy of standardizing the design of locomotives and freight cars. McAdoo's statement in July 1918 that there were '2023 different styles

of freight cars and almost as many different descriptions of locomotives,' appealed to the public imagination, as did the announcement that a committee of experts of the Railroad Administration had agreed upon 12 standard types of freight cars and six standard types of freight locomotives of two weights each. Obviously, the process of standardization would make the problems of new construction much easier and eventually would reduce the cost of maintenance. In 1918 USRA's McAdoo ordered 1430 locomotives and 100,000 freight cars of standard design.

Under the terms of the contract between USRA and the railroad companies, he was required to secure the approval of the corporation before he could permanently assign any of the new standard equipment to that corporation. There was much opposition to the universal adoption of these standards, and long, drawn out controversies over the assignment of the new equipment to individual companies.

Under the Transportation Act of 1920, federal control of America's railroads terminated at 12:01 am on the first of March, and Isaac B Tigrett again took control of the Gulf, Mobile & Northern.

Tigrett's railroad was far from being the model of efficiency. In the 14 years since its ancestor had first gone into receivership in 1906, it had actually operated as a railroad for *less than five years*. Tigrett was undaunted, however. He completed a 40 mile connection to link the Gulf, Mobile & Northern at Middleton, Tennessee to the Illinois Central trunk line at Jackson, and in 1926 he commenced operations north to Paducah, Kentucky over track leased from the Nashville, Chattanooga & St Louis. Compared to the first two decades of the century, which had found the Gulf, Mobile & Northern in miserable condition, the 1920s were an era of robust expansion. In 1924, Tigrett took over control of the Birmingham &

ROGERS LOCOMOTIVE COMPANY,
PATERSON, NEW JERSEY - UNITED STATES OF AMERICA.

Below: Dating from the 1880s, No 36 of the Mobile & Ohio is a Rogers 2-8-0 Consolidation type locomotive with an extended smokebox.

Above: No 151, a 4-6-0, is also manufactured by Rogers Locomotive Company.

Northwestern, a railroad whose *only* claim to fame was that it ran the 49 miles from Jackson to Dyersburg, Tennessee, but this was only the beginning of Tigrett's empire building. In 1928, much to the chagrin of Illinois Central, which sensed a rising competitive spirit, he merged the Birmingham & Northwestern into the Gulf, Mobile & Northern.

The following year Tigrett and the Gulf, Mobile & Northern acquired two more small regional roads: the Meridian & Memphis that ran from Meridian to Union, Mississippi, and the Jackson & Eastern, which connected Union, Mississippi with the state capital at Jackson, a city served by the Illinois Central but not yet by any of Tigrett's roads. This move gave the Gulf, Mobile & Northern interchange points with the Illinois Central at *both* Jackson, Tennessee and Jackson, Mississippi, each a vital rail hub in its respective state.

At the end of December 1929, two months after the stock market crash that launched the Great Depression, Tigrett added the New Orleans Great Northern to his empire.

The New Orleans Great Northern Railroad had been founded in 1905, and like the majority of the region's roads, it was a logging railroad. It was originally part of the empire of Charles and Frank Goodyear of Buffalo, New York, who are best remembered for their great Buffalo & Susquehanna Railroad. Having started the New Orleans Great Northern, the Goodyears immediately bought the East Louisiana Railroad, which had a small network imme-

diately north of New Orleans but no direct access over its own tracks *to* New Orleans. By merging the East Louisiana into the New Orleans Great Northern, this problem was solved, and the latter prospered for the next decade.

After the cessation of federal control of American railroads in March 1920, the New Orleans Great Northern found itself with vastly diminished passenger traffic, and the crash of October 1929 forced it under the control of the Gulf, Mobile & Northern. On 7 November 1932, the troubled New Orleans Great Northern went into receivership and the receiver was none other than Isaac B Tigrett!

By July 1933, Tigrett had reorganized the New Orleans Great Northern *Railroad* as the New Orleans Great Northern *Railway* and had leased it to his Gulf, Mobile & Ohio. At this time, the road had 14 locomotives and 14 passenger cars operating over 263 miles of track, compared to 28 locomotives, 29 passenger cars and 1354 freight cars operated over 277 miles of track in 1929 when it was last independent.

Isaac Tigrett's Gulf, Mobile & Northern entered the Great Depression in 1929 with 77 locomotives, 39 passenger cars and 1573 freight cars operating over 734 miles of track. He faced down this crisis by severe cost cutting measures and belt tightening, and by 1935 the Gulf, Mobile & Northern was ready to improve passenger service by the institution of the famous *Rebel* passenger liners, which offered through service on the extensive network that Tigrett had built in the 1920s. To the success of the *Rebel*s of Gulf, Mobile & Northern was added Gulf Transport in 1936, a bus and trucking subsidiary that was intended to do on the highways of Mississippi, Alabama and Louisiana what the Gulf, Mobile & Northern rolling stock was doing on Tigrett's empire of steel.

As early as 1934, Gulf, Mobile & Northern had begun to consider buying the moribund Mobile & Ohio Railroad, but it was a 1936 disagreement with Illinois Central that served as the catalyst for their eventual merger. It seems that in 1933 the Gulf, Mobile & Northern had begun leasing trackage between Paducah, Kentucky and Jackson, Tennessee from the Illinois Central after seven years of using the tracks of the Nashville, Chattanooga & St Louis to connect the two cities.

In 1936, Illinois Central started insisting that Gulf, Mobile & Northern begin using Illinois Central *crews* on this segment. There ensued two years of squabbling that ended with a 30 June 1938 ultimatum being issued by Illinois Central that gave Gulf, Mobile & Northern three weeks to make the change or stop getting its trains into Paducah. Gulf, Mobile & Northern pulled out of Paducah and signed a traffic agreement with the Mobile & Ohio Railroad to take up the slack, and by the end of 1938, the Gulf, Mobile & Northern had been turned into a holding company to preside over the merger of the two roads.

The name says it all. One of the oldest railroads in what is today the Illinois Central Gulf,

the Mobile & Ohio Railroad was formed in 1850 to build north from Mobile toward the Ohio River Valley. The Mobile & Ohio was, in fact, part of the original Federal Land Grant that made the Illinois Central possible.

The first segment of the Mobile & Ohio to be completed covered the 30 miles from Mobile to Citronelle, Alabama, which was opened in 1852. The line was then extended to Columbus, Kentucky on the Mississippi River immediately south of Cairo, Illinois. This line had the misfortune of opening for business in April 1861, ten days after the first shots were fired in the Civil War, so it was to be many years before the Mobile & Ohio would be able to operate as first conceived.

During the Civil War, the infrastructure of the Mobile & Ohio was severely mauled, and the rebuilding effort that began in 1865 was so costly that the railroad fell into receivership in 1875. By 1882, the Mobile & Ohio finally finished the last 20 miles to the Ohio River at Cairo, 32 years after it was chartered.

Four years later, the Mobile & Ohio acquired the narrow gauge St Louis & Cairo Railroad and converted it to standard gauge. As time went on, the importance of Columbus, Kentucky declined and the Mobile & Ohio finally abandoned its line to the town in favor of the main line to Cairo.

By the turn of the century, the Mobile & Ohio was facing stiff competition from major roads in the region, such as the Illinois Central and the Louisville & Nashville, and was seeking an alliance with a more powerful benefactor. A

Below: Pulling the funeral train of President Abraham Lincoln is Chicago & Alton No 57, a 4-4-0 American built by Schenectady. It is draped in black bunting and carrying a picture of the president on the front.

Right: This artist's cutaway illustrates the comfort of the dining car on Chicago & Alton passenger service between Chicago and Kansas City in the late 1870s.

'white knight' was found in the Southern Railway, which was perhaps the most durable railroad in the South. An exchange of securities brought about the alliance in 1901, and there would have been an outright merger had it not been for the governor of Mississippi, who vetoed the essential permit legislation.

The Southern Railway continued to control the Mobile & Ohio profitably until the onset of the Great Depression in 1929. In June 1932, the Mobile & Ohio went into receivership and the Southern Railway, strapped for money itself, could not bail it out. Six years later, the Southern Railway sold its share of the Mobile & Ohio to the Gulf, Mobile & Northern, and in 1940 the two merged as the Gulf, Mobile & Ohio.

north into the region that was the 'home turf' of the Illinois Central.

Between 1944 and 1947, the Gulf, Mobile & Ohio conducted negotiations toward the eventual takeover of the bankrupt Alton Railroad (formerly Chicago & Alton), a system which served the Kansas City/Chicago/St Louis triangle with 959 miles of main and feeder lines.

The oldest current member of the Illinois Central Gulf family tree, the Alton, was originally chartered as the Alton & Sangamon in 1847 to connect the central Illinois farm country with the Mississippi River port of Alton, Illinois. This initial line was completed in 1851, and eventually the name was changed to St Louis, Alton & Chicago, although the railroad

At the time of this transaction, the Mobile & Ohio operated 119 locomotives and 31 passenger cars over 1180 miles of track. This compared to 231 locomotives, 112 passenger cars and 8368 freight cars on 1159 miles of track eleven years earlier, at the time that the Mobile & Ohio started sliding into debt in 1929.

The Gulf, Mobile & Ohio was born on 10 November 1938 as a holding company for the assets of the Gulf, Mobile & Northern and the Mobile & Ohio. This was accomplished by foreclosing on the Mobile & Ohio on 1 August 1940 and merging with the Gulf, Mobile & Ohio six weeks later, on 13 September 1940. On this date the holding company became a real railroad, a major road with 180 locomotives operating over 1808 miles of track that extended from New Orleans to Mobile, Birmingham and Montgomery, Alabama to St Louis via Jackson, Tennessee.

This three-forked trunk gave the new company a system which fully served the New Orleans/Montgomery/St Louis triangle, an area immediately to the east of the Illinois Central's Chicago to New Orleans corridor. It was during the frantic yet profitable years of World War II that the Gulf, Mobile & Ohio began looking

served neither St Louis nor Chicago. By 1861, however, lines had been extended north via Bloomington to Joliet, which was in proximity to Chicago. Also in 1861, the St Louis, Alton & Chicago was sold and renamed Chicago & Alton.

In 1864, the road merged with the Joliet & Chicago Railroad, which did in fact provide service to Chicago. This joint entity retained the Chicago & Alton name because, after all, Joliet was now just another station along the road, but Joliet & Chicago president Timothy B Blackstone retained the presidency of the new company.

With the end of the Civil War, the eyes of the nation turned once again to exploration of the West. For Timothy Blackstone, one of the men behind not only the Chicago & Alton Railroad but the Chicago Union Stockyard as well, this meant creating through service between Chicago and Kansas City. The first piece of the puzzle was the leasing in 1870 of the Louisiana & Missouri River Railroad, which controlled service through the Mississippi River port of Louisiana, Missouri, upstream from Alton and hence closer to the straight line axis between Chicago and Kansas City.

In 1878, the Chicago & Alton leased the Kansas City, St Louis & Chicago Railroad. This completed the link that the Chicago & Alton had sought, and for ten years the road controlled the shortest route between Chicago and Kansas City.

By 1899, the profitable Chicago & Alton, with its network in the Chicago/Kansas City/St Louis triangle, became a much sought after prize by the great empire builders. Edward H Harriman, who directed the Illinois Central, carried the day with a bid of $1.75 on the dollar for Timothy Blackstone's majority interest.

Harriman set up this deal by incorporating a Chicago & Alton *Railway* on 2 April 1900 to take over a piece of Peoria to Springfield track that he owned, and then leased it to the vastly larger Chicago & Alton *Railroad* on 3 April. This intricate 970 mile labyrinth was in turn consolidated as the Chicago & Alton Railroad in 1906.

By 1912, three years after Harriman's death, the cattle transport business, which was the Chicago & Alton's mainstay, began to decline

Above: No 254 is a 4-6-0 Baldwin locomotive built for the Chicago & Alton.

Right: This Baldwin 4-6-2 Pacific, No 623, was part of the Chicago & Alton motive power in 1910.

due to the proliferation of other cattle railroads and stockyards outside of Chicago. As as result, the Chicago & Alton began to lose money hand over fist and plummeted downward toward eventual bankruptcy in 1929, the year of the stock market crash. The once-desirable railroad was picked up at a foreclosure sale by the Baltimore & Ohio Railroad. At this time, the Chicago & Alton had 292 locomotives, 232 passenger cars and 13,066 freight cars running over 1028 miles of track.

The Baltimore & Ohio incorporated its new purchase in 1931 as the Alton Railroad and operated it as part of the Baltimore & Ohio system until March 1943, when it was made an autonomous unit. During World War II, the Alton Railroad became a sought after road once again because of its access to the Great Lakes at Chicago and the Baltimore & Ohio began taking calls from would-be buyers.

In 1945, the Gulf, Mobile & Ohio got serious and paid $1.2 million for the Alton, which had been stripped to half its 1929 proportions. In 1945, the Alton had 193 locomotives, 212 passenger cars and 5362 freight cars operating on 959 miles of track.

When the acquisition of the Alton Railroad became final on 31 May 1947, the Gulf, Mobile & Ohio had a network that involved over 375 locomotives, 300 passenger cars and 12,000 freight cars operating on over 2700 miles of track. The pre-merger Gulf, Mobile & Ohio had doubled the track mileage of the pre-merger Alton, but the Alton actually came into the merger with more locomotives and rolling stock than its new parent.

Although passenger service in general declined in the postwar years, the Gulf, Mobile & Ohio was in an expansive mood with the 1947 introduction of the first streamliners in the South—the *Rebel*, between St Louis and New Orleans and the notable *Gulf Coast Rebel*, which ran from St Louis down to Mobile, until it was finally discontinued in 1958. On the Alton lines, the Gulf, Mobile & Ohio operated the *Abraham Lincoln*, *Ann Rutledge* and *Alton Limited* passenger trains between Chicago and St Louis, commuter trains between Chicago and Joliet and a joint St Louis to Kansas City passenger service in cooperation with the Burlington route.

Between 1949 and 1950, the Gulf, Mobile & Chicago acquired three roads that had long been leased by the Alton Railroad. These were the Kansas City, St Louis and Chicago Railroad, the Louisiana & Missouri River Railroad and the Joliet & Chicago Railroad, a name that was a spin-off of the road which had merged with the railroad responsible for helping the old Chicago & Alton reach the Windy City in 1864.

By the end of the 1960s, railroads in general and passenger railroads in particular were in decline. Nevertheless, although it abandoned its *Rebels* in the 1950s, the Gulf, Mobile & Chicago maintained its Chicago to St Louis passenger service until 1971, when the National Rail Passenger Corporation (Amtrak) put nearly all of the nation's rail passenger services under federal control. At this same time, the Gulf, Mobile & Chicago began looking for a merger partner. The obvious choice was the Illinois Central, its occasional opposition road, whose route network was a virtual shadow of the Gulf, Mobile & Chicago. The merger became final on 10 August 1972, and the Illinois Central Gulf was born.

THE ILLINOIS CENTRAL

By Bill Yenne

*I*t all started in 1851. As so much of American railroad history traces its roots to that decade before the Civil War, so it is with the Illinois Central. And just as it was with so many other railroads, its name defined exactly what its creators intended it to be!

The starting point of the Illinois Central was Cairo (pronounced Kay-Roe, mind you) at the southernmost tip of the state where the waters of the Ohio River flow into the great Mississippi River. At that time, Cairo was one of the key transportation hubs of the Midwest. Goods were transferred here from Ohio River traffic to ships and barges on the Mississippi (and vice versa) for the trip down to New Orleans and beyond, and goods traveling north on the Mississippi were changed onto smaller vessels that could negotiate the shallower waters north toward St Louis.

The basic idea followed by the founders of the Illinois Central was simply to create a railroad which superimposed a 'T' shape over the entire center of Illinois. The base of the 'T' would be at Cairo and the cross bar would run from Galena on the Iowa border east to Chicago.

The Illinois Central Railway was chartered on 10 February 1851 with a federal land grant—the first ever—signed by President Millard Fillmore himself the year before, and the benefit of a few miles of graded road bed that existed from an earlier, failed venture. The Illinois Central Land Grant Bill, which was passed by Congress to facilitate the road's construction, was a true milestone in American history.

The federal government began assisting railroad construction later than the states, but it ultimately contributed even more than they have given. Most of the aid given by Congress to the railroads consisted of grants of land from the public domain, although a few companies received large loans from the Federal Treasury. The Illinois Central Grant was part of the first

extensive grant of land to further railroad building. Under this grant, Congress gave about 4,000,000 acres of land to Illinois, Alabama and Mississippi, to be used by those states in aiding the construction of the Illinois Central, as well as the Mobile & Ohio lines, by which Chicago was to be connected with New Orleans and Mobile, Alabama. During the next 20 years, about 80 such grants were made to states in the Mississippi Valley.

In aiding the construction of roads built within the boundaries of the states, Congress did not at first donate land directly to corporations, but gave the land to the states as trustees, which were to turn the land over to the railway companies. This was because the tendency in the 1850s was to interpret the Constitution more narrowly than it has been interpreted since the Civil War, and many people ques-

tioned whether Congress had the power to donate land located within a state to a railroad corporation.

In making these grants to railroads, the United States sought, among other purposes, to increase the accessibility and value of the public lands not given away. The grant to Illinois for the Illinois Central Railroad—the first large one—was the model followed in all its subsequent donations. Some companies received more land per miles of road than others did, but all the grants had the same general terms.

According to the Illinois grant, the railroad company was given a right of way 200 feet wide through the public lands, and was also given alternate (the even-numbered) sections of land on each side of the line for a distance of six miles from the road. The company thus secured half the land within a strip 12 miles

Below: Built by Rogers Locomotive Works for the Illinois Central Railroad in the 1880s, this 2-4-2T locomotive No 1401 was photographed at the 1934 Chicago World's Fair, with the handsome General Motors building in the background.

wide, or six square miles of land, for each mile of track built. If any of the land within this 12-miles strip had previously been disposed of by the government, the railroad was able to select an equal area within 15 miles of the railroad. The alternate (odd-numbered) sections retained by the government within the 12-mile strip were not to be sold for less than $2.50 per acre. In the grants made at a later date, a wider strip of land was donated, and in some cases the government did not agree to charge $2.50 or more an acre for the sections it retained within the land-grant strip.

Construction on the Illinois Central line began at each end, but the first section opened for service was the 14 miles from Chicago to Kensington, serving Hyde Park and Grand Crossing, which was inaugurated in May 1852 after 15 months of work. By January 1855, a total of 706 miles between LaSalle and Chicago had been completed, and in 1856 the entire 'T'-shaped trunk had been completed, along with a branch line from Centralia directly into the Illinois Central Station in Chicago. At the time of its completion to this status in 1856, the Illinois Central was the longest railroad in the world!

The Illinois Central station in Chicago was located on the northwest corner of the juncture of Randolph Street and Central Avenue, and the tracks ran due south between Lake Park and Lake Michigan itself. The first stop on the

line was at Thirty-ninth Street on the South side.

The Illinois Central's Chicago yard was located adjacent to Indiana Avenue between Twelfth and Sixteenth streets, and the Illinois Central shared a depot at Twelfth and Indiana with three other railroads: the Chicago & West Michigan, the Michigan Central and the Kankakee line of the Cleveland, Cincinnati, Chicago & St Louis.

Having constructed what stood as the world's largest railroad in 1856, the Illinois Central established a Mississippi steamboat service to connect its Cairo terminus with New Orleans. The Civil War period was an era of retrenchment for the Illinois Central, but soon afterward, the road spanned the distance between Galena, Illinois and Dubuque, Iowa.

In 1857, the railroad entered into a leasing arrangement with the Dubuque & Sioux City Railroad that gave it access to central Iowa as far as Iowa Falls, which is midway between Fort Dodge and Waterloo. The line to Sioux City via Cherokee was not, however, completed until three years later, in 1870.

By 1872, it became obvious to the Illinois Central that a railroad link south of Cairo was preferable to a steamboat line in order to save valuable travel time. Although the company approached this project piecemeal, hoping to accelerate the process by leasing existing

Below: No 114, a 4-4-0 American locomotive built by NJL&M, is pictured at the Illinois Central roundhouse in Centralia, Illinois in 1861.

Right: This archival photo of the interior of an early Pullman sleeper car shows a few of the upper and lower berths made up and the elegant curtains which afford privacy to the rail traveler.

Below, right: It is no surprise that this Amboy sleeper car looks much less luxurious from the outside, compared to the early Pullman. However, the introduction of a sleeping car on the Illinois Central in 1856 marked a great forward step in passenger travel.

track—as it had done successfully in Iowa—rather than by building new lines, timing proved to be advantageous. At this time, most of the railroad infrastructure in the South that was basically sound had recovered operationally from the ill effects of the Civil War, yet the railroad companies there were so financially strapped, lease deals were easy and inexpensive to negotiate. It was indeed a buyer's—or, in this case, a lessor's—market.

The first segment the Illinois Central acquired under its new program was that of the New Orleans, Jackson & Great Northern. Founded in 1858 and running from New Orleans to Canton, Mississippi via Jackson, Mississippi, the New Orleans, Jackson & Great Northern had been built to serve a then-active logging industry in the deep South. Another road leased by the Illinois Central was the Mis-

sissippi Central Railway, which had been completed in 1860 and connected Canton with Jackson, Tennessee. These two deals gave the Illinois Central about 80 percent of the rail mileage that it needed to connect Chicago with New Orleans, but it still left a gap of more than one hundred miles between Jackson, Tennessee and Cairo. The Illinois Central could use the tracks of the Mobile & Ohio between Jackson and Columbus, Kentucky, but this was not desirable because it still meant off-loading cargo onto barges at Columbus for the last few miles into Cairo.

The choice was obvious, and a year-long track laying effort extended the Illinois Central south from East Cairo, Kentucky to interchange with the Mississippi Central at Jackson, Tennessee. The entire network south of East Cairo was, however, built to the five-foot gauge

Left: This Illinois Central 4-8-0 Twelve Wheeler was manufactured by Brooks and photographed in 1899.

Right: No 1224 is a Brooks 4-4-0 American with the coal in its tender visible.

Left: Illinois Central had a number of Brooks locomotives. No 905 is a 4-4-0 American.

Below: No 213 was the first suburban engine on the Illinois Central Railroad. It is a Rogers 2-4-4T, and its configuration is known as a 10 wheel double-ender.

favored in the South and was not converted to standard gauge until July 1881.

Meanwhile, in 1874 the Illinois Central took over both the Mississippi Central and the New Orleans, Jackson & Great Northern, merging them into a single entity as the ambitious-sounding New Orleans, St Louis & Chicago. This subsidiary was in turn merged with the Mississippi Central in 1877 as the Chicago, St Louis & New Orleans, a name which underscored the railroad's reordered focus from the South to the North, and thus reflecting how the corporate powers then viewed their empire.

A principal area of interest in the South at this time was the fertile Yazoo River Delta that stretched between the Mississippi River and the main line of the Illinois Central's New Orleans, Jackson & Great Northern line. To exploit the potential business in the Yazoo

River area, Illinois Central decided in 1882 to build a new railroad westward out of Jackson, Mississippi. This line, the Yazoo & Mississippi Valley Railroad, immediately ran afoul of the rival Louisville, New Orleans & Texas Railway that was then constructing a line between Memphis and New Orleans via Vicksburg on the Mississippi.

However, the Louisville, New Orleans & Texas was no ordinary line, but a pet project of Collis P Huntington of San Francisco. One of the original 'Big Four,' Huntington, who had built the Southern Pacific—which then connected New Orleans with California—was one of the world's foremost rail barons. He scrambled to finish the Louisville, New Orleans & Texas, which he yearned to have as a link between the great Southern Pacific with his Chesapeake, Ohio & Southwestern. This road

Left, above: This Baldwin woodburner 4-6-0 belonged to the Central Railroad of Georgia in 1884. It was E H Harriman who, in 1909, sold the C of G to the Illinois Central and completed a coveted rail network linking the upper Midwest and the southeastern corner of the Southeast.

Left: Locomotive No 101 belonged to the Mississippi Central and ran at the turn of the century.

Left, below: No 76 of the Yazoo & Mississippi Valley is a Schenectady 4-4-0 American.

Above: Engine No 1003 is a Rogers 4-4-2 Atlantic of the Illinois Central Railroad.

was completed in 1884, and Huntington went one step further by acquiring the Mississippi & Tennessee Railroad, a short line that served to link Memphis with Grenada, Mississippi. It was also an important Illinois Central feeder line, and so the battle lines were drawn. It was Collis Huntington versus the Illinois Central. A classic showdown, it had all the drama any modern day screen writer could want.

However, the Mississippi & Tennessee could not stand without Illinois Central's business, and this started a domino effect that ended in defeat for Huntington. In the end, the Illinois Central not only won this test of wills, but it wound up owning both the Mississippi & Tennessee *and* the Louisville, New Orleans & Texas! These lines were then consolidated with Illinois Central's little Yazoo & Mississippi Valley Railroad, and tracks were then extended all the way west to Shreveport, Louisiana.

Edward Henry Harriman was arguably the single most important person to visit his influence upon the Illinois Central since its inception in 1851. This mousy looking man in the spectacles and shaving brush mustache is best remembered for his control of the Union Pacific and, briefly, of the Southern Pacific, but he also controlled the Illinois Central for 26 of the most important years in American railroad history.

Born on Long Island, in the village of Hempstead, New York in 1848, young Edward aspired to high finance, becoming a partner in a Wall Street brokerage firm when he was just 18. Only three years later, this enterprising Long

Islander bought his own seat on the New York Stock Exchange. In 1872, he founded Harriman & Company, and was soon a name to be feared in the wheeling and dealing world of railroad stock manipulation. He took an interest in the Illinois Central, and by 1883 he was on its board of directors, becoming its president in 1887. One decade later he performed his masterstroke, seizing control of the great—albeit bankrupt—Union Pacific for $62 million, a stunning sum for its day.

In the meantime, Harriman diligently worked to enhance the infrastructure of this acquisition. In 1889, a bridge was constructed across the Ohio River to link the Illinois lines terminating at Cairo to the southern port of the Illinois system.

The creation of the Chicago, Madison & Northern in 1886 provided a link between Illinois Central's Freeport, Illinois terminal and the Wisconsin state capital at Madison via Podgeville, Wisconsin. In 1893, Harriman, through the Illinois Central, bought the Chesapeake, Ohio & Southwestern, which ran from Louisville, Kentucky to Memphis. Two years later, he built a line out from St Louis to connect this acquisition to the northwestern corner of the Illinois Central network.

Also during this period Harriman extended the Illinois Central lines west from Fort Dodge, Iowa to Omaha, Nebraska and Sioux Falls, South Dakota. These would be the westernmost points in the Illinois Central map.

Any doubt about Harriman being the king of American railroading was eradicated in 1900

Above: This photo was taken 22 November 1934 at the Chicago World's Fair. No 2411 is an ALCO-Schenectady 4-8-2 Mountain locomotive that was built in 1923.

Left: A Brooks 4-6-2 Pacific, No 1142, is pulling the Panama Limited *passenger train on Illinois Central track between Chicago and New Orleans.*

upon the death of Collis Porter Huntington, the last of the Big Four, and a long-standing adversary of the Illinois Central. (See the first chapter.) When Huntington died, Harriman bought his estate, and along with it, a 46 percent interest in the Southern Pacific.

A year later, Harriman got into a struggle with James Jerome 'Jim' Hill, the legendary Empire Builder, who headed the Great Northern and the Northern Pacific, which in turn owned the Chicago, Burlington & Quincy. The latter, like the Illinois Central, was headquartered in Chicago, America's foremost rail hub. Harriman's ambition was to control both railroads, and Chicago in the bargain. His acquisition of the Chicago, Burlington & Quincy, along with the Union Pacific and Southern Pacific, would have given him command of rail transportation which covered over 60 percent of the total land area of the United States.

However, the Empire Builder outmaneuvered Harriman in this scheme, but Harriman retaliated with a flanking maneuver in which he started buying Northern Pacific stock. The ensuing battle between the two titans so severely disrupted the national economy that it resulted in the Wall Street Panic of May 1901. In the end, Hill kept his railroads and Harriman survived, but a large segment of the American economy never recovered. It was the end of the Golden Age of the American rail baron. An

Interstate Commerce Commission investigation later cleared Harriman of willful wrongdoing in this affair and in his takeover of the Union Pacific.

In 1907, Harriman bought the Central of Georgia Railroad (which had been controlled by the Illinois Central in the 1890s) with a plan in mind to connect it to the Illinois Central and subsequently assemble a huge network that would link the upper Midwest with the southeast corner of the Southeast. The link between the Central of Georgia and the Illinois Central came by means of lines leased from the Mobile & Ohio, the St Louis & San Francisco (the Frisco) and the Southern Railway system, combined with 80 miles of new track.

By the time he died at his sprawling Arden, New York estate on 9 September 1909, Harriman had become the master of 25,000 miles of railroad and had a controlling voice in the management of another 50,000 miles. Among these were the 4459 miles of the Illinois Central.

The Central of Georgia Railway dates back to the Central Rail Road & Canal Company, which was incorporated in 1833 to build a rail line from Savannah to Macon to compete with the South Carolina Railroad, which connected Charleston with Augusta, Georgia in 1830 and had diverted business away from the port of Savannah. It took two years for work to begin, and it was not until October 1843 that the now-named Central Rail Road & Banking Company of Georgia completed the 191 miles of track to Macon. A connection with the city of Augusta was finally accomplished a decade later through the use of leased lines.

After the Civil War, the Central of Georgia recovered from being heavily damaged, and in 1869 expanded westward to Columbus, Georgia, on the Alabama boarder, and in turn on to Eufala, Alabama. In 1875, the Central of Georgia acquired the Georgia Railroad and the Western Rail Road of Alabama, giving it a network in Georgia and Alabama that was as comprehensive as any, although an attempt to expand eastward was thwarted by the state government in South Carolina. Nevertheless, a line was built to Chattanooga, just across the Tennessee border, giving the Central of Georgia a relatively ample system of track totaling 2600 miles.

Hard times for the Central of Georgia began in 1888, when it was taken over by the Richmond Terminal Railroad and in turn leased to the Georgia Pacific Railway, which was owned by the Richmond & Danville, that later evolved into the sprawling Southern Railway system. Outright bankruptcy of the Central of Georgia occurred in 1892 on the eve of the Panic of 1893, and the road was then actually run for several years by the Illinois Central.

In 1901, reconstruction of the road got under way and the badly dismembered road began to resemble its former self. That year, the Chattanooga line was restored, and in 1905 the line between Columbus and Greenville, North Carolina was widened from narrow to standard gauge, providing Central of Georgia a standard gauge main line from Atlanta to Columbus, over which it shared operations with the Atlanta & West Point.

In 1907, Edward Harriman purchased the Central of Georgia in order to link it to the Illinois Central. Just before his death two years later, after having completed the necessary leasing and track construction required to join the two systems, Harriman sold the Central of Georgia to the Illinois Central, under whose direct control it would remain until 1948, when it once again became an independent line. It continued largely under its own control until 1963, when it was made a subsidiary of the Southern Railway System.

In 1906, there were 222,000 miles of track in the United States, nearly 40 percent of the railway mileage of the world. The mileage in the United States exceeded that in all of Europe by more than 15 percent. The American railroad system carried 798 million passengers over 25,167 passenger miles in 1906, compared to 501 million over 13,380 passenger miles only eight years earlier. By 1929, the total mileage had increased to only 229,530. By 1939, it had decreased to 220,915, and by 1980 to just 164,822. Thus the turn of the century truly marked the point at which America's railroads turned from expansion to management of existing lines.

The Illinois Central had, by this time, 4459 miles in its trunk line, more than the Union Pacific or the New York Central! The Illinois Central ranked twelfth in track mileage among the nation's railroads as it entered the 20th century, and, indeed, it had a greater passenger density than many of the longer roads such as the Atchison, Topeka & Santa Fe or Jim Hill's Great Northern, which spanned vast, but sparsely populated, regions.

The prominent railroad expert George R Blanchard was quoted as saying that the Illinois Central illustrated an excellent distribution of ownership among the stockholders. In 1905, for example, it had 9123 shareholders, two-thirds owning less than $10,000 each of stock. Fully half of the shares were owned in lots of $50,000 and less, the average of all holdings being $10,310. In May 1908, the Pennsylvania Railroad Company, one of the most powerful American roads, had 59,406 shareholders owning 6,291,893 $50 shares, the average holding being 106 shares, with a par value of $5300.

Although the railroad corporations were becoming larger every year, and the amount of railroad securities was increasing, there was a remarkably wide distribution of ownership. The control of railway properties was coming

more and more into the hands of a small number of groups of capitalists, such as Jim Hill and Edward Harriman, but each *group* of capitalists comprised a multitude of individual owners, and the concentration of control was really the result of the delegation of authority to a limited number of financial leaders in whom investors had special confidence. It was not necessary for an individual to own a majority of the stock in a corporation to obtain the practical control. As the corporations became larger and the stockholders became more widely distributed, control by the individuals or groups of individuals holding a minority of the shares became easier.

In 1906, Illinois Central's Indianapolis southern subsidiary added a link between Indianapolis and Effingham, Illinois. In the south, the Illinois Central's empire was pushed eastward by a connection between Fulton, Kentucky and Birmingham, Alabama in 1908, and in the following year by the acquisition of the Central of Georgia Railway, which is discussed at length in the preceding section.

The Illinois Central prospered during the 1920s, and by 1929, on the eve of the Great

Above: An advertisement for the new diesel-powered locomotives made by GM-EMD. It features the observation-lounge car of the luxurious Panama Limited.

Right, top: The IC's diesel-powered streamliner, the Green Diamond. *Its distinctive turret-cab was part of an articulated five-car train operating between St Louis and Chicago.*

Right, bottom: Two ALCO C636-models, 1101 and 1102, head a train of 100-ton coal-laden hoppers. The C636 was the last model produced by ALCO before ending locomotive manufacture.

Depression, it operated 1762 locomotives, 2034 passenger cars and 65,035 freight cars over 6712 miles of track, up from the 4459 of 1906 and supplemented by the 1944 miles of the Central of Georgia. All told, this gave the Illinois Central a system of 8565 miles, still more than the New York Central/Boston & Albany/Ohio Central system.

The Illinois Central served states embracing a third of the nation's population, and a region of widely varied agricultural, mineral, lumbering and manufacturing concerns that extended from the 30th to the 43d parallel. It had more than 500 connections and over 150 railroads. The states it served produced 85 percent of the nation's corn, 80 percent of its cotton, 76 percent of its wheat and 74 percent of its cattle. It was also one of the nation's chief coal roads and an important hauler of asphalt, gypsum, limestone, iron ore, oil, salt and sulfur.

This was the picture of the Illinois Central through most of the 20th century, including the calamitous Great Depression and World War II. Its *Green Diamond* served the Chicago to St Louis run, and the *Panama Limited* and *City of New Orleans* took passengers down

through the Mississippi River country, where so much of the Illinois Central's history had been written.

In 1951, the Illinois Central bought the Chicago, St Louis & New Orleans Railroad, and in 1953 the Alabama & Vicksburg, as well as the Vicksburg, Shreveport & Pacific, which had been leased by Illinois Central's Yazoo & Mississippi Valley subsidiary since 1926. In 1959, these roads were merged and the Illinois Central also purchased the Tremont & Gulf. The following year, Illinois Central took over the Peabody Short Line, and in 1968 acquired the portion of the Tennessee Central that ran from Nashville to Hopkinsville, Kentucky.

The 1960s were hard times for railroads and affected not just the small roads that the Illinois Central acquired, but larger roads as well—including the Illinois Central itself. By the end of the decade, the Illinois Central was ready to enter into a merger agreement with the Gulf, Mobile & Ohio, a road whose history and route structure paralleled—and often intersected—that of the Illinois Central. The merger became final on 10 August 1972, and the Illinois Central Gulf was born.

Above: The IC's Panama Limited *makes its 16¼-hour run between Chicago and New Orleans behind an EMD E6 passenger locomotive.*

Right: On the far track, the observation-lounge car of the Panama Limited *is visible as passengers board in Jackson, Mississippi.*

THE ILLINOIS CENTRAL GULF

By Bill Yenne

*T*here were a great many rail mergers in the 1970s and early 1980s. The Great Northern, Northern Pacific and Chicago, Burlington & Quincy joined to form the Burlington Northern in 1970. The Chesapeake & Ohio joined the Baltimore & Ohio, which in turn joined the Seaboard System to form CSX in 1980. The great Pennsylvania Railroad merged with its former competitor, the New York Central, in 1970 to form Penn Central, and they in turn merged with Erie Lackawanna (another amalgam) to make Conrail in 1976. The Norfolk & Western united with the vast Southern Railway system in 1982 to become Norfolk Southern.

Against this backdrop, the Illinois Central merger with the Gulf, Mobile & Ohio was of little surprise, especially given the fact that they served virtually identical regions. Indeed, the entire history of both roads, especially the Gulf, Mobile & Ohio, was full of acquisitions, mergers and takeovers.

To this last merger, Illinois Central brought 766 locomotives, 462 passenger cars (most of which would be sold to Amtrak or to scrapyards) and 49,709 freight cars. The Gulf, Mobile & Ohio contributed 258 locomotives, 92 passenger cars (also scrapped or sent to Amtrak) and 12,699 freight cars.

Illinois Central's 6760 miles of track in 1972 was virtually identical to the road's 1929 mileage. Meanwhile, the Gulf, Mobile & Ohio added 2734 miles, which compared to the 1762 miles operated by the Gulf, Mobile & Northern and the Chicago & Alton in the 1920s, and the 1786 miles operated by the Gulf, Mobile & Ohio and the Alton Railroad in the 1940s.

The Illinois Central Gulf Railroad, formed on 10 August 1972, was integrated into a new entity, a holding company known simply as the IC Corporation. This appellation was typical of an era dominated by a trend toward blandness in the naming of companies. Instead of giving a

company a name that identified what it did, corporate leaders favored names that obscured what they did, and consequently, company names were often simply initials. The Standard Oil Company of New Jersey, for instance, became Exxon, a word that means nothing except as a name for this company. This phenomenon was driven by a number of factors, not the least of which was a major upheaval in American business which took place between 1967 and 1974, a period that saw many old-line companies disappear or merge with others under umbrella holding companies that contained a wide spectrum of totally unrelated smaller companies.

Such was the case with IC Industries, which encompassed not only the Illinois Central Gulf Railroad (which it preferred to call ICG) but also Midas, the muffler company, and Hussman, a maker of large supermarket freezers, as well as Pet, a diversified food products company that began as an evaporated milk company, and a number of Pepsi Cola soft drink bottlers. Indeed, by 1982, Pet was a larger segment of IC Industries than was Illinois Central Gulf!

In the first decade after the merger, the Illinois Central Gulf accounted for roughly a quarter of the revenues of IC Industries, although the actual proportion obviously varied from year to year. In 1979, for example, Illinois Central Gulf earned $875 million of IC Industries' $3.4 billion in revenues.

The 1970s and early 1980s were hard times for railroads because freight levels were down and the accounting departments of the holding companies that held them didn't understand railroading. To them, railroading was 'archaic and got your hands dirty.' Gradually, IC Industries trimmed the Illinois Central Gulf rail network. By 1982, ten years after the merger, the entire network contained only 7196 miles of track, down from over 9600 miles at the time of the merger.

THE STORY OF CASEY JONES

John Luther 'Casey' Jones *(shown above, at the throttle)* was born on 14 March 1864 near Cayce, Kentucky from whence his nickname is probably derived. He went to work at 16 for the Mobile & Ohio and joined the Illinois Central as a fireman in 1888. He became an engineer two years later and served for a decade throughout the system, most notably aboard Illinois Central No 638, a Consolidation freight locomotive. He became a legend for his technique of 'quilling' the locomotive's whistle.

The popular engineer was transferred on 1 January 1900 to the *New Orleans Cannonball*, a Chicago to New Orleans passenger express. His segment of the run was between Memphis and Canton, Mississippi. On 30 April 1900, after just four months on the new run, Jones was killed—the only fatality of the wreck—when his locomotive, Illinois Central No 382, a McQueen 4-6-0, rammed the rear of a freight train. Jones is buried in Jackson, Tennessee.

The song *Casey Jones* was written by Wallace Saunders, a black Illinois Central roundhouse worker who had known Jones. A popular sheet music adaptation by T Lawrence Siebert and Eddie Newton was published in 1903.

Come all you rounden if you want to hear
The story of a brave engineer;
Casey Jones was the hogger's name,
On a big eight-wheeler, boys, he won his fame.
Caller called Casey at half-past four,
He kissed his wife at the station door,
Mounted to the cabin with orders in his hand,
And took his farewell trip to the promised land.
　　Casey Jones, he mounted to the cabin,
　　Casey Jones, with his orders in his hand!
　　Casey Jones, he mounted to the cabin,
　　Took his farewell trip to the promised land.
'Put in your water and shovel in your coal,
Put your head out the window, watch the drivers roll,
I'll run her till she leaves the rail,
'Cause we're eight hours late with the western mail!'
He looked at his watch and his watch was slow,
Looked at the water and the water was low,
Turned to his fireboy and said,
'We'll get to 'Frisco, but we'll all be dead!'
　　Casey Jones, he mounted to the cabin,
　　Casey Jones, with his orders in his hand!
　　Casey Jones, he mounted to the cabin,
　　Took his farewell trip to the promised land.
Casey pulled up Reno Hill,
Tooted for the crossing with an awful shrill,
Snakes all knew by the engine's moans
That the hogger at the throttle was Casey Jones.
He pulled up short two miles from the place,
Number Four stared him right in the face,
Turned to his fireboy, said, 'You'd better jump,
'Cause there's two locomotives that's going to bump.'
　　Casey Jones, he mounted to the cabin,
　　Casey Jones, with his orders in his hand!
　　Casey Jones, he mounted to the cabin,
　　Took his farewell trip to the promised land.

In 1983, revenues decreased three percent, to $907 million, while car and trailer loadings decreased two percent, compared with 1982. With traffic concentrated on fewer miles, system density increased from 6.5 million ton miles per route mile in 1982 to 6.8 in 1983. In early 1983, carloadings fell well below 1982 levels. However, in June, ICG loadings began a slow recovery, but it was insufficient to bring traffic levels up to those of the prior year.

In the face of depressed conditions in the agricultural and industrial markets it served, the Illinois Central Gulf implemented a major reorganization to streamline the system, reduce expenses and provide improved service. During 1983, the ICG terminated service on 226 miles of low-density branch line trackage, reducing total system mileage to 6970. This slow but steady upturn in traffic in the second half of 1983 continued into 1984. Through the first two months of 1984, car and trailer loadings were 14 percent ahead of 1983, and the Illinois Central Gulf's chemical, corn, soybeans, grain and lumber loadings all exceeded 1983 levels. The Illinois Central Gulf continued to streamline operations by employing technological advances in railroading, reducing service on additional uneconomical branch lines and by utilizing innovative operating and marketing techniques.

In its 1983 annual report, IC Industries stated that it intended to 'maintain the ICG as a strong and efficient railroad until it can be sold or merged with another railroad. Merger or sale of the ICG remains a corporate objective. Management believes that the ICG's best prospects for long-term growth are as part of one of the large railroad systems resulting from the current merger movement. The ICG originates about 65 percent of its traffic, providing an attractive base for potential merger partners.'

In 1984, the sale of real estate for the McCormick Place project in downtown Chicago helped give the Illinois Central Gulf a pre-tax income of $73 million—representing a profit swing of $84.7 million from the pre-tax loss of $11.7 million in 1983. Revenues in 1984 totaled $1.01 billion, up 12 percent over revenues of $907 million in 1983. The railroad reduced its break even from 114,000 carloads per month in 1982 to 98,000 in 1984. Productivity, as measured by revenue-per-dollar of labor expense, increased from a ratio of 2.6-to-1 in 1983 to 3-to-1 in 1984.

According to the IC Industries annual report—the report of a conglomerate that wanted to sell its railroad—the Illinois Central Gulf was being reshaped 'as a balanced transportation company serving the area between the Great Lakes and the Gulf of Mexico and beyond. The ICG now has a more efficient system of freight movement with expanded trucking services to complement its railroad operations. The company is serving customers through an expanded 32-state trucking authority with 15 rail hub centers and eight highway off-rail hub centers in major cities.'

In 1984, the ICG signed 977 freight contracts, and at year-end 1984, had 1053 contracts in effect, compared with 398 in 1983. Early in 1985, the ICG and three other railroads signed a 10-year contract with Mississippi Power Company to move 1.6 million tons of western low-sulfur coal annually from Colorado and Utah to Moss Point, Mississippi. The ICG expected to receive about $200 million in revenues over the life of this contract. By the end of 1985, the Illinois Central Gulf, now known as the IC (or Illinois Central) Railroad, had been trimmed to 4679 miles, and IC Industries had publicly stated its goal of reducing track mileage to roughly 3000 miles to make the road attractive to potential buyers. In 1986, nearly 1000 miles were sold, including a historic 418 miles of the old Yazoo & Mississippi Valley, to bring the track total down to 3719 miles. In the meantime, 12,636 cars were sold out of a stock of 28,616 that had been on hand at the beginning of the year.

In 1987, IC Industries earned $252 million in revenues of the company's total of $4 billion after a loss of $137 million for the previous year. The IC Railroad, now being referred to as the Illinois Central Railroad, contributed 14 percent of these total earnings, but only one percent of the profits of the corporation. The stage was now set for divestiture.

In 1987, half a decade after IC Industries had begun grooming the Illinois Central for sale, the corporation decided on a spin-off instead.

Since 1972, the Illinois Central Railroad (originally known as the Illinois Central Gulf Railroad) had been streamlined from a 9600 mile railroad to a core system of about 3000 miles, serving industrial and agricultural markets between the major freight gateways of Chicago, St Louis, Memphis and New Orleans. For 1987, the railroad had revenues of $554 million and operating earnings of almost $40 million, and had recently completed a $1.5 billion capital improvement program. Over the preceding five years, it had cut its break even point by one-third, and tripled its productivity.

It was against this backdrop that IC Industries adopted a plan to spin off the Illinois Central Railroad. Under this plan, the board of directors declared a dividend of the railroad's common stock to holders of IC Industries common stock after all legal and regulatory requirements were satisfied. The dividend action established the railroad as an independent company which was named the Illinois Central Transportation Company.

This spin-off was carried out during 1988 and completed on 1 January 1989, when IC Industries (now known as the Whitman Corpo-

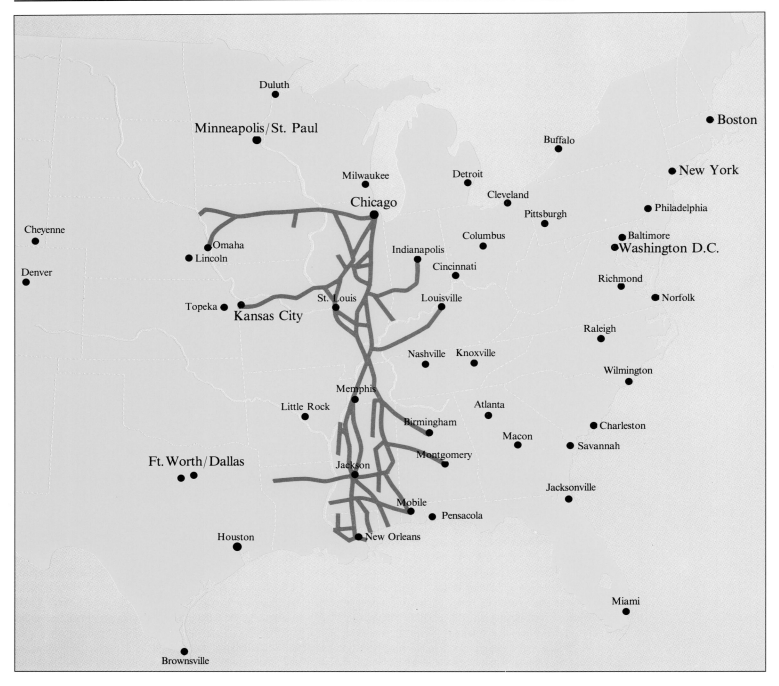

ration) transferred the common stock of the Illinois Central Railroad Company to the Illinois Central Transportation Company, which had been created for this purpose.

The Illinois Central Corporation was incorporated under the laws of Delaware on 27 January 1989. Illinois Central was formed by The Prospect Group, Inc for the purpose of acquiring the outstanding common stock of the Illinois Central Transportation Company. For that purpose, Prospect contributed to Illinois Central $59.5 million in cash and 1,026,800 shares of ICTC's common stock previously acquired for $12.7 million. In turn Illinois Central contributed this cash and Illinois Central Transportation Company common stock. On 16 March 1989, Illinois Central concluded its tender offer and the railroad was then a wholly-owned subsidiary and its only material asset.

The railroad's management team, led by Edward Moyers, who was an organizer, president and chief executive officer of MidSouth Corporation (another railroad holding company formerly owned by Prospect) proceeded to implement an operating plan designed to reduce operating expenses and capital requirements substantially over the next four years and to generate significant additional cash from sales of certain non-operating assets, the conversion of certain double main line tracks to single main line track, employment reductions and productivity improvements. The operating plan was based on cost reductions expected to be phased in over time and not dependent on increases in freight volume, although, absent an economic downturn, Illinois Central believed opportunities existed to increase freight volume in the 1990s. The pri-

Right: Nos 3041 and 3042 3000-hp GM-EMD GP40 model B-B locomotives were added to the Illinois Central fleet in the mid 1960s.

Left: A map of the Illinois Central Gulf railroad network.

mary element of the operating plan was the transformation of approximately 500 miles of double main line track to single main line track with a centralized traffic control system. Illinois Central believed that the double track was no longer required because of the significant 'downsizing' of the railroad over the preceding decade, which had resulted in lower traffic density. Illinois Central further believed that the extension of the existing centralized traffic control system, with two-mile sidings spaced approximately 15 to 20 miles apart, would permit efficient management of northbound and southbound trains at levels and frequencies more than adequate for expected traffic requirements.

Employment levels on the Illinois Central had been significantly reduced as a result of downsizing. Illinois Central continued this trend in conjunction with the conversion to a single main line. A total employment level of 3100 employees was contemplated by the Illinois Central's operating plan, a reduction from 3700 employees on 31 December 1988. The Illinois Central also disposed of non-operating assets, primarily real estate, as well as surplus rail and certain rolling stock not essential for the railroad's opertions. An agreement was reached for the sale of Chicago real estate for $16.2 million in cash. The railroad entered into contracts to sell a line of railroad and certain trackage rights in Indiana and Illinois for $5 million in cash and, as of 28 February 1990, had entered into various agreements to sell in excess of $12 million of surplus rail and rolling stock. In addition, the railroad sold for $13 million in cash approximatley 75 percent of its interest in Trailer Train Company, a railroad

equipment company. The Illinois Central also held a minority investment in other companies, including a 46 percent ownership share of the Peoria & Pekin Union Railroad. In addition, surplus and bad order locomotives and rail cars were disposed of, along with the intermodal terminal facilities located at Chicago, Memphis, Jackson, Mississippi and New Orleans. Proceeds from these transactions were to be applied to reduce Illinois Central's long-term debt.

As it entered the 1990s, the 15th decade since the original land grant, the new Illinois Central Railroad operated as a major rail freight carrier over 2900 route miles in seven cities. The railroad's principal yard facilities are located in Markham near Chicago, Illinois; Memphis, Tennessee; and Jackson, Mississippi. Other yard facilities are located in New Orleans and Baton Rouge, Louisiana. Approximately one-quarter of the railroad's $547 million in revenues during 1989 were derived from chemical shipments, primarily petrochemicals produced on the Louisiana Gulf coast. Coal was the second largest commodity group shipped by the railroad, ranked by revenues; most of this coal was mined in the southern Illinois coal fields and transported to electric utilities, primarily in the Midwest. Paper is also a major commodity, as are grain and grain products.

After those 15 decades of ups and downs, the Illinois Central stood as originally envisioned, the true Main Line of Mid-America, a railroad that paralleled the Mississippi River through America's heartland, from the great hub, Chicago, down to the great Gulf ports of Mobile and New Orleans.

THE NEW YORK CENTRAL

By Aaron E Klein

*T*he earliest origins of the New York Central stem from a man who was more of a dreamer than a speculator. George Featherstonaugh, a New York gentleman farmer from Duanesburgh, had been fascinated by news of steam railways in England—so much so that he became determined to build one in his home state of New York. If any of Featherstonaugh's neighbors laughed at him, their merriment was not unjustified. In the 1820s, when Featherstonaugh started to formulate his plans, New York was practically the last place in the country—or in the world, for that matter—to make a success of a major railroad, due in large part to the Erie Canal, which was opened to traffic in 1825. This great ditch, running from Albany to Buffalo, was the largest and most ambitious engineering project that had yet been completed in the young nation. Connecting New York City with the Great Lakes via the Hudson River, the canal brought a new era of prosperity to New York. Many of the most powerful politicians in the state had a financial interest in the canal, and they were not about to let anything or anybody emerge as serious competition. In order to build his railroad, Featherstonaugh had to get a charger from the state legislature, and that seemed to doom the enterprise from the start.

Featherstonaugh was realistic enough to know that he would have to present his idea to the legislature in such a way it was not perceived as a threat to the canal. He also knew that he would need help from someone who had political power. To this end, he traveled 20 miles to the seat of power in Albany to talk with Stephen Van Rensselaer, the grand old man of the Upstate aristocracy.

Van Rensselaer and Featherstonaugh had every reason to believe that the 16-mile Mohawk & Hudson Rail Road that they proposed would be sufficiently nonthreatening to get by the canal interests, which were backed

up by a powerful group of politicians, merchants and financiers generally known as the Albany Regency. However, the modest proposal initially encountered fierce opposition in the legislature. Many Albanians—as residents of Albany were called—feared that the railroad would bring economic ruin to their city.

The railroad was also understandably opposed by the Albany and Schenectady Turnpike Company, a rather badly constructed toll road that was not doing well. Van Rensselaer became so pressured by opponents he told Featherstonaugh he might have to withdraw his support. Then, much to the two men's surprise, the charter passed the legislature only a few months after it was introduced and was granted on 17 April 1826. The Mohawk & Hudson, the first of the small lines that eventually became part of the New York Central, was now

a reality. It opened for business on 9 August 1831.

The Lockport & Niagara Falls Railroad, incorporated in 1834, most likely opened for traffic in 1838; most of the records of this railroad have been lost. The line was later extended to Batavia and Rochester, becoming the Rochester, Lockport & Niagara Falls Railroad in the process. The Buffalo & Lockport Railroad, completed in the early 1850s, provided a more or less direct route between Buffalo and Niagara Falls. The intention of the Syracuse and Utica Direct Railroad, incorporated in 1852, is implicit in its name. This line covered a considerably shorter distance between these two cities than the previous route, which curved to take in the city of Rome.

The Mohawk Valley Railroad, incorporated in 1851, also became part of the New York

Below: The DeWitt Clinton, *the first locomotive to be operated in New York State, was built at West Point Foundry. On 9 August 1831, this engine, with passenger cars resembling stagecoaches, made its initial run from Albany to Schenectady, New York, on the Mohawk & Hudson Railroad.*

Right: A lithograph of the Roebling suspension bridge over the Niagara River, engraved by William Edgar (1876).

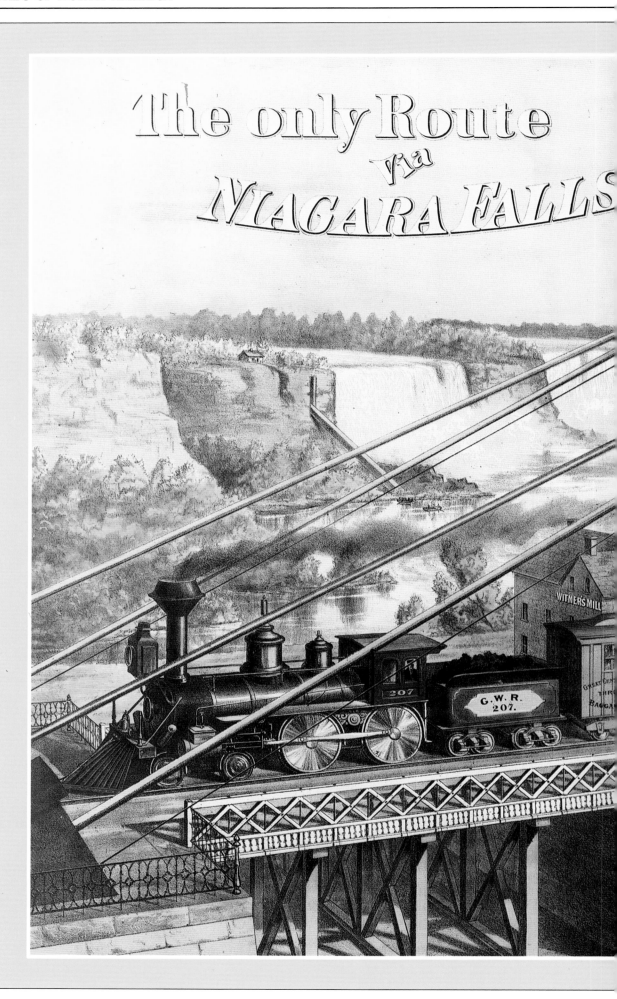

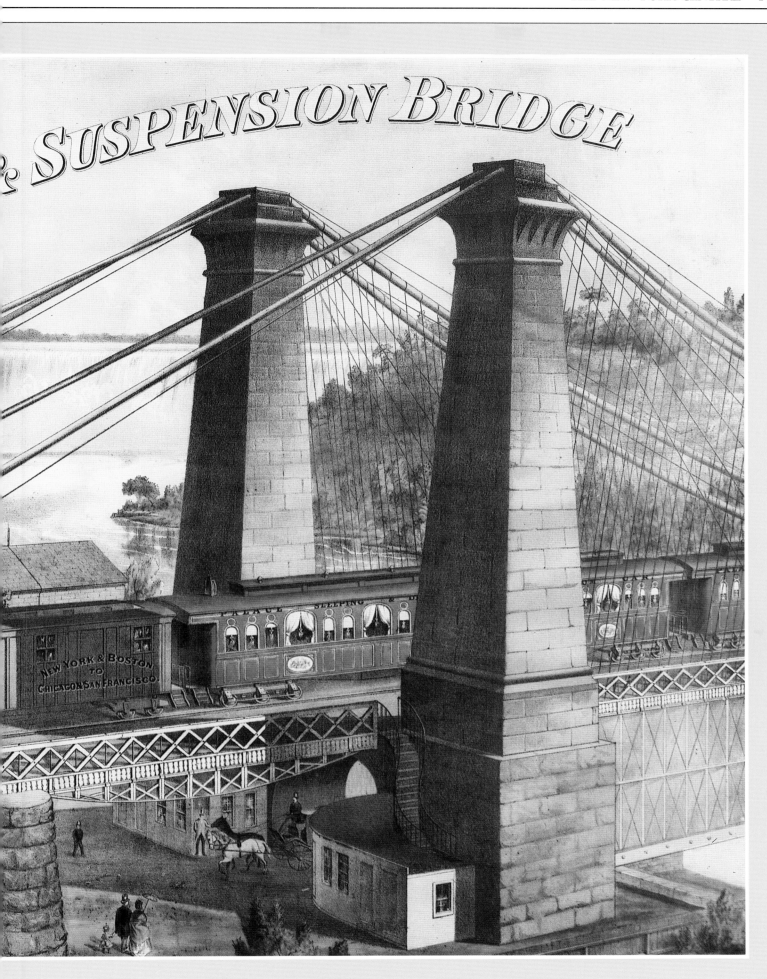

Left: Shipping, and later railroad, tycoon Cornelius Vanderbilt.

Below: The Stourbridge Lion *was the first commercial locomotive in North America. It was brought over from England in 1828 by Horatio Allen for the Delaware & Hudson Canal Company.*

Right: Ten lines with over 600 miles of track were consolidated in 1853 to form the New York Central.

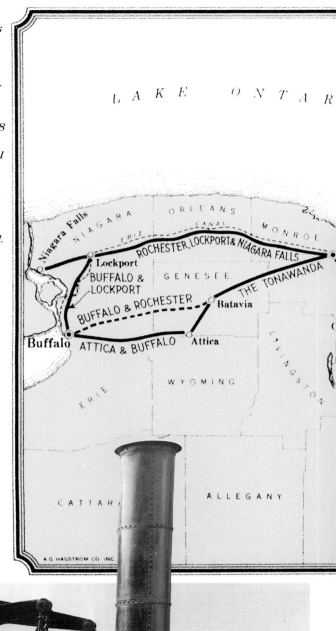

Central. However, when it was absorbed by the Central, it existed only as stockholders and a rather distinguished group of directors; although the route had been surveyed, no track had ever been laid.

Completion of the Attica & Buffalo Railroad in 1843 made it possible to travel by rail all the way from Albany to Buffalo, a trip not undertaken lightly. There were few attempts to coordinate the schedules of the various lines, particularly in the salad days of the 1830s and 1840s. Such conveniences as the ability to buy one ticket for the entire trip and through baggage checking were slow in coming. However, by the time the final link in the chain was finished, the management of most of the rail-

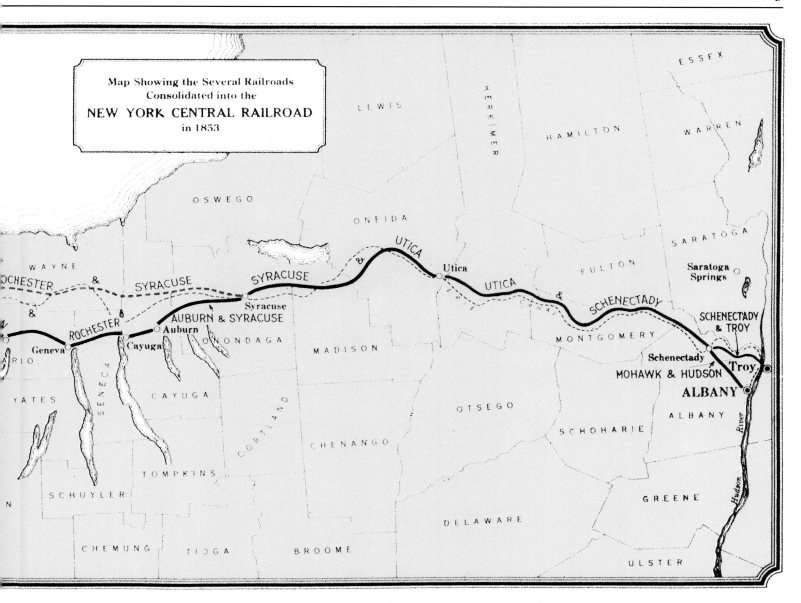

Map Showing the Several Railroads
Consolidated into the
NEW YORK CENTRAL RAILROAD
in 1853

roads had come to the rather obvious conclusion that coordinating their services would benefit all of them.

By the early 1850s, the unification of the railroads stretching across New York seemed logical, if not inevitable. In February 1851, representatives of 10 New York railroads met in Albany to discuss the possibility of consolidation, although, in a sense, partial consolidation had already taken place.

On 12 April 1853, representatives from the 10 railroads met in Syracuse. The 10 lines in attendance, in more or less east-to-west order, were: Albany & Schenectady; Schenectady & Troy; Utica & Schenectady; Mohawk Valley; Syracuse & Utica; Syracuse & Utica Direct; Rochester & Syracuse; Buffalo & Rochester; Buffalo & Lockport; and Rochester, Lockport & Niagara Falls.

The total main line length of these railroads was 298 miles. When the branch lines in existence and under construction were added, the proposed line totaled some 600 plus miles. The New York Central was capitalized at over $23 million. That seems like a piggy bank collection

by today's standards, but in 1853 it was an enormous amount. Indeed, it was almost half the 1853 budget of the United States!

The history of the modern New York Central Railroad and the Vanderbilt family saga are practically the same story. Yet in the 1830s, when the rail links that later became the New York Central were being forged, Cornelius Vanderbilt, founder and patriarch of the Vanderbilt clan, had no interest at all in railroads. Prophetically enough, however, he was already in conflict with Daniel Drew, the man who for years was to be his chief railroad adversary.

Cornelius Vanderbilt, born in Port Richmond on Staten Island in 1794, was the personification of the American poor-boy-makes-good success story. His paternal ancestors, Dutch settlers who came to Long Island in the late seventeenth century, spelled the family name van der Bilt. His father, who was a farmer, earned a little extra money from time to time transporting goods and people around New York Harbor in a small boat.

Vanderbilt—now known as 'The Commodore'—turned his attention to Long Island

Sound, establishing steamer service to Providence and Boston. By the mid-1840s he was a millionaire and anxious to gain a place for himself and his family in New York society.

Vanderbilt was also interested in the Hudson River Railroad, and by 1863 had obtained a few shares in this line, which ran along the east bank of the river. It was organized by a group of Poughkeepsie businessmen in 1842, largely in response to the need for transportation during the winter months when the Hudson was frozen over. Construction problems were formi-

vants with verbal and other, more tangible, inducements. The word got around Wall Street, and Hudson River Railroad stock moved up from $25 toward $150.

The Commodore was now ready to take on the New York Central. However, Central president Erastus Corning and the Albany Old Guard were not about to just hand over the Central to the man from Staten Island without a fight. Vanderbilt had held a few shares of Central stock since 1863, and made it quite clear that he would like a seat on the board; Corning

Left: One of the last Mohawk & Hudson posters, before the name change to Albany & Schenectady.

Right: The Lake Shore Railroad, bordering Lake Erie, gave access to the Middle West.

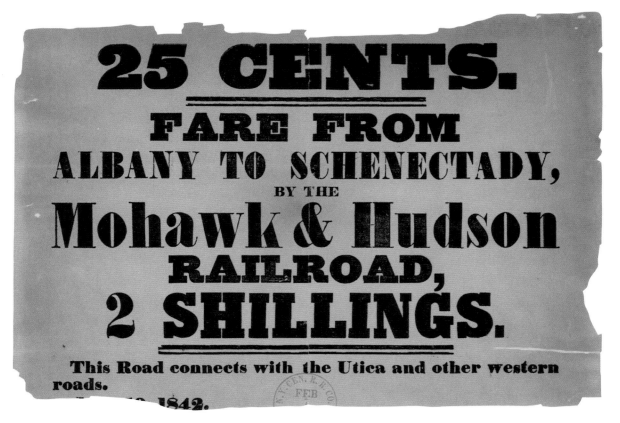

25 CENTS.
FARE FROM
ALBANY TO SCHENECTADY,
BY THE
Mohawk & Hudson
RAILROAD,
2 SHILLINGS.

This Road connects with the Utica and other western roads.
1842.

dable, and the first section between New York and Peeksill was not opened until 1849. Service to Albany, via Hudson River ferry, was available by 1851. The line did not prosper, and by the time Vanderbilt started to buy shares, its track was in disrepair and the company near bankruptcy.

Once Vanderbilt took an interest in railroads, he went after what he wanted with zeal and ruthlessness. He bought New York & Harlem stock at $9 a share and through skillful manipulation, the price soared to $50. At this point, he bribed members of the New York Common Council, then under the control of William March ('Boss') Tweed, to extend the New York & Harlem southward as a street car line from 42nd Street to the Battery. The stock shot up again to more than 10 times its original value.

Next on Vanderbilt's agenda was a merger of the New York & Harlem with the Hudson River Railroad. For this he needed permission from the New York State Legislature. Accordingly, he traveled to Albany to persuade the public ser-

made it equally clear that he did not want the Commodore in any situation that would make it easier for him to assume control. However, although they were business rivals, there was no animosity between the two men.

Representatives from the Hudson and the New York Central met in 1866 to discuss ways of increasing cooperation between the lines. The boards were unable to reach an agreement, but the two principals reportedly agreed that it would have been possible had no third party been involved. Once it was clear, however, that the Central was not going to cooperate with him, Vanderbilt went after the line in his own style.

Vanderbilt quietly bought the stock while the price was down, and by 1867, a group that held almost half of the New York Central's stock petitioned Vanderbilt to become the president. He accepted, and soon almost all of the Old Guard were gone, replaced by Vanderbilt men, including William H Vanderbilt as vice president.

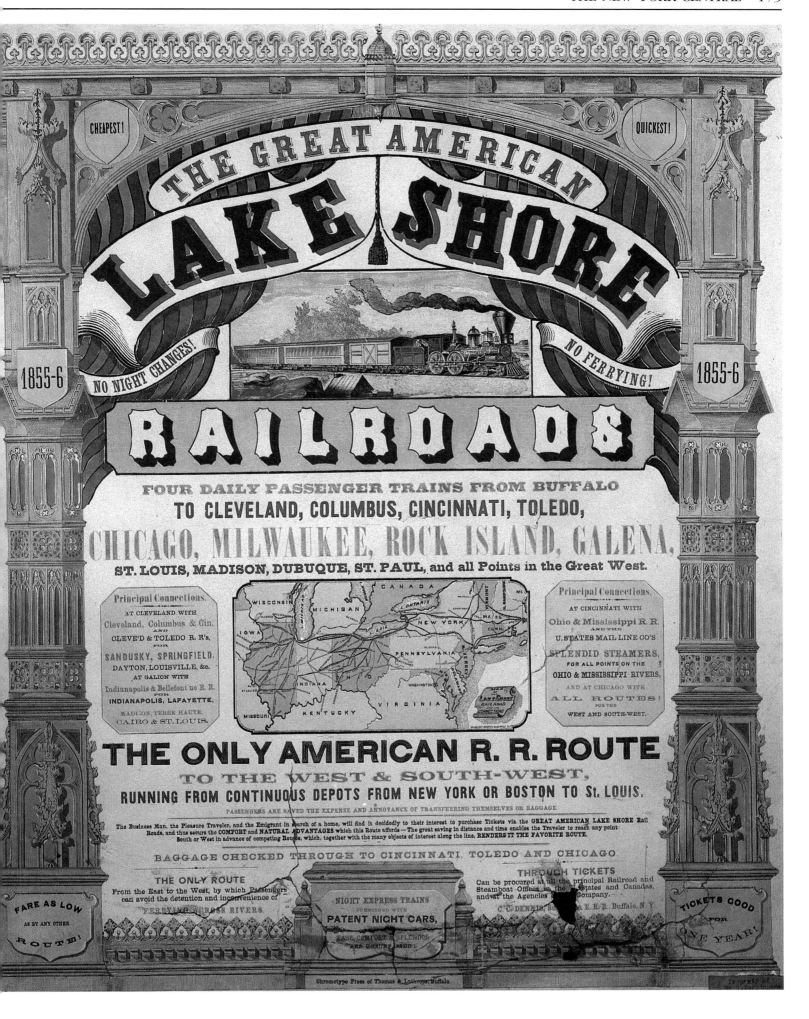

Vanderbilt's ultimate objective was a merger of the New York Central, the Hudson River and the New York & Harlem. He also had ideas of bringing in the Erie, but this prize eluded him. His failure to capture the Erie was one of the few cases in which his adversaries—Jim Gould and Jim Fisk—got the best of him, and one of the most spectacular battles of the 'Erie Wars.'

Recovering quickly from the Erie debacle, the Commodore turned his attention to the merger of the New York Central and the Hudson River Railroad, which was completed in 1869. The result of this merger was called the New York Central & Hudson River Railroad. A huge stock-watering scheme, engineered by Vanderbilt, increased the paper value of the stock until the NYC & HR was capitalized at $45 million. (The term 'stock watering' probably originated from one of Daniel Drew's favorite tricks during his days as a cattle dealer. Just before sale, he would give the stock salt blocks to lick. This made them drink large quantities of water, increasing their apparent weight.)

Vanderbilt, always a lover of the grand and magnificent, then started construction of the grandest and most magnificent railroad depot the great city of New York had ever seen. Grand Central Depot, as it was first called, started to go up at Fourth Avenue (later Park) and 42nd Street in 1869, the site of the New York & Harlem Railroad's steam locomotive terminal. Critics said the 42nd Street location was too far north of the business district. However, the city was rapidly expanding northward, 42nd Street was a wide thoroughfare, newly paved with cobblestones, and it was the route of the new cross-town horse car. The decision was sealed by the city's prohibition against the operation of steam locomotives south of 42nd Street.

Three railroads used Grand Central Depot: the New York Central & Hudson, the New York & Harlem and the New York & New Haven. The latter was a tenant, and relations between railroads and landlord were not always amiable. The Vanderbilt railroads began to use the new terminal in 1871, but the New Haven, unhappy about the rental fees, continued to move its trains south by horse to 27th Street for another year until the dispute was resolved. (The old 27th Street Station was later bought by P T Barnum, who converted it into the first arena to be called Madison Square Garden. It is no small irony that the present Madison Square Garden is built on the site of Pennsylvania Station, the other great New York City terminal built by the Pennsylvania Railroad.) As the New York Central grew so did its depot, which in later years came to be known as Grand Central Station.

William Vanderbilt's zeal to extend the Central to Chicago was not shared by the Commodore. Eventually, however, the elder Vanderbilt went along with his son's plans, carrying out

Above: The north end of the Grand Central Depot as viewed from the railroad yards in 1883.

Right: The imposing exterior of the Grand Central Depot, at 42d Street and Fourth Avenue in New York City.

the necessary financial manipulations at which he was so much more adept than William. The first step was to patch up the community of interests that Erastus Corning had arranged with the Lake Shore and the Michigan Central. The latter proved to be no problem since its chairman, James Joy, who was on the Central board, was amendable to cooperation and indicated that he would at least talk about a merger. The Lake Shore & Michigan Southern (formerly the Lake Shore), however, was quite another story. Acquiring this line was vital to establishing a Chicago connection, but it was run by men not at all friendly to the Vanderbilts, including LeGrand Lockwood, who controlled the line, and Henry Keep, who was a major stockholder.

The Commodore tested the waters by buying a few shares and waited for the right time to make his move. He was inadvertently helped by Jay Gould and Jim Fisk, who, in their attempt to corner the gold market, caused the financial ruin of thousands, including LeGrand Lockwood. In order to raise cash quickly, Lockwood sold his railroad to Vanderbilt for the bargain price of $10 million. Vanderbilt's son-in-law, Horace Clark, was made president of the Lake Shore & Michigan Southern.

The old Commodore did not live long enough to see the New York Central extend to Chicago. He died in 1877.

Starting in 1882, William Vanderbilt expanded the New York Central westward. He leased the bankrupt Canada Southern and merged it with the Michigan Central. Then he moved southward into the Pennsylvania Railroad's territory through acquisitions of the Pittsburgh & Lake Erie and a number of small lines. The biggest event of that year for William was acquiring the New York, Chicago & St Louis Railroad, a move that extended the Central to St Louis. William was on the Union Pacific board, and for a while he gave some thought to acquiring that line. Had he done so, the United States would have had a coast-to-coast railroad. Of course, the Pennsylvania did not sit back and let William have his way. They responded by moving into Central territory and cutting their rates, thus starting a chaotic period in American railroad history.

Below: The Putnam, *a 4-4-0 locomotive of the post-Civil War era.*

Right: The New York & Harlem Railroad trestle, circa 1875.

William resigned from the presidency in 1883 but retained his seats on the boards of various constituent lines. He made his son, Cornelius II, Chairman of the New York Central and Michigan Central, while another son, William K, was given the chairmanship of the Lake Shore & Michigan Southern. The elder Vanderbilt was well aware of his offsprings' limitations, so he named James Rutter as the president and chief operating officer of the New York Central (Rutter had previously been general traffic manager). When he died soon after taking office, Vanderbilt, who had suffered a stroke, named Chauncey M Depew as the Central's chief executive officer. Depew did not know a great deal about railroads, but was a skillful politician and on good terms with the powers in Washington, who left the actual running of the railroad to qualified technicians.

From the time it was first created in the mid-1850s, the New York Central had no serious competition in New York. The Erie tried, but was never able to mount a challenge of any consequence. Through the 1860s and 1870s, various groups of entrepreneurs tried to organize competing lines. While many of these obtained charters, their progress was limited to surveying routes and laying a few miles of track before they went bust.

The situation changed in the 1880s when the Central found itself in fierce competition with the Pennsylvania. For the first time, the prospect of a rival line in New York was very real indeed. In 1880, a strongly financed group took over the assets of the New York, West Shore & Chicago, one of the failed would-be competitors of the Central, renaming it the New York, West Shore & Buffalo. Among the investors was George Pullman, still seething over Central's decision to use Webster Wagner's sleeping cars instead of his, and intent on revenge. Closely allied with a group of bankers who had organized the North Shore Railroad, the new operation was generally called the West Shore because it was projected to run along the west shore of the Hudson River. By 1883, the West Shore had constructed tracks from Jersey City to Newburgh, then on to Albany and Syracuse, and limited operations started that same year. The Central immediately put on the pressure by cutting its rates, and the West Shore was soon in deep financial trouble, declaring bankruptcy in 1884.

Wall Street brokers were quite surprised when sales of the bankrupt West Shore's stock continued to be brisk. The buyer was George Roberts, president of the Pennsylvania Railroad, who hoped to revive the West Shore and

Below: This Buffalo switcher was built circa 1865.

Right: The New York Central Station at 138th Street, New York City.

show the Central what it was like to have real competition. This plunged the two railroad giants into a rate war that came in the middle of an economic depression, a move which would have been disastrous had it continued. J P Morgan was deeply disturbed by this corporate mayhem, fearing that the entire structure of American capitalism could be irreversibly damaged. He wanted what amounted to a peace conference, but Chauncey Depew would do nothing without the approval of Vanderbilt, who was then on an extended vacation in Europe. So Morgan went to Europe to fetch Vanderbilt, and they returned on the same ship.

The peace conference was held in July of 1885 aboard Morgan's yacht *Corsair*. It was reported that Morgan chose the yacht as the site so no one could storm out in anger. In attendance were George Roberts, Frank Thomson (who would become president of the Pennsylvania in 1897), Chauncey Depew and Morgan. The four men settled down in deck chairs, and as the *Corsair* sailed up and down the Hudson, they drank Morgan's whiskey and

hammered out an agreement. The Pennsylvania agreed to sell off its West Shore stock, which would be bought by a group headed by Morgan and Depew, who would lease the line to the New York Central. Vanderbilt agreed to sell his shares in the South Pennsylvania Railroad, a line that he had started to compete with the Pennsylvania. He also agreed to give up his interest in the Reading Railroad, which competed sharply with the Pennsylvania for coal-hauling business.

With the *Corsair* agreement, Morgan consolidated his position as the most powerful financier in the country and the enforcer of order in the railroad industry. The Central and the Pennsylvania continued to be rivals, but they found that with Morgan tightly in control of the purse, there was little they could to without his tacit approval. The Interstate Commerce Commission (ICC) had been established in 1877 to enforce various federal railroad regulations, which were largely ignored in the late nineteenth century; the real regulating force was Morgan. For example, in 1894, the Central and

Pennsylvania worked out an agreement for pooling freight business and for consultation on rates and matters of expansion into each other's territory, in violation of several federal regulations. However, because Morgan approved of the agreement, the ICC did nothing.

In the last 20 years of the nineteenth century, William H Vanderbilt actively sought to expand the Central through the acquisition of other lines. Shortly after the West Shore threat was removed, Vanderbilt bought the Cleveland, Cincinnati, Chicago & St Louis, and the Rome, Watertown & Ogdensburg was added in 1891. Prior to this purchase, the Central had made plans for expanding into Watertown, New York; surveyors had already been sent out. This line enabled the Central to connect with Canada's Grand Trunk Railway for access to Montreal.

The biggest addition of the late nineteenth century was the Boston & Albany. Although the line was not purchased outright, it came under total control of the Central in 1894. New Englanders were not at all happy about the loss

Above, right: The Lake Shore and Michigan Southern Ticonderoga—a 4-4-0 type used for mixed traffic.

of 'their' railroad to the New Yorkers. William H Vanderbilt was not noted for his tact, and he promptly added outrage to the New Englander's indignation by having New York Central logos painted on the Boston & Albany rolling stock.

It was now clear to the people who ran the New York Central that the age of public relations had arrived. They needed someone to help improve the Central's public image, and that someone was George H Daniels, the Central's passenger agent. A short, plump man sporting a white goatee, Daniels bombarded the Central management with ideas from the moment he was hired. Daniels convinced the Central managers to run a special New York-Buffalo train called the *Empire State Express*. A special big-wheeled, Atlantic-type locomotive was constructed just to haul the train. On 14 September 1891, the 436-mile run from New York to Buffalo was made in seven hours and six minutes, including stops, at an average speed of 61.4 mph, a new record. Daniels' tour-de-force

came at the opening of the new century. He wanted to run the fastest, most luxurious train in the country on the Central's New York-Chicago route. He could have continued to call the train the *Empire State Express*, but he wanted a new name to evoke the idea of continuing progress into the new century, so he chose to call it the *Twentieth Century*. Shortly thereafter, when it was decided to limit the number of stops, the name was altered to the *Twentieth Century Limited*. Service on the new train started in 1902, and was scheduled to make the 960-mile run to Chicago in 20 hours, for an average speed of 80 mph.

Daniels planned the *Twentieth Century* as a train for wealthy and important people who required speed, demanded luxury and could pay for both. The train was due to arrive in New York at 9:30 am, allowing businessmen a full day's work and pleasure travelers time for a taxi to the docks to board transatlantic liners. The train was to be all-Pullman. By the turn of the century, the Wagner Palace Car Company,

Below: The Vanderbilt name was synonymous with American railroading by the 1880s.

Left: A double-end type 2-4-4-T in suburban service, 1910.

Below: Some 11,000 of these 2-6-0 steam locomotives were built in the United States.

which had been closely allied with the Vanderbilts, had been absorbed by Pullman. The use of his cars on the crack train of the railroad that had snubbed him for so many years must have been a source of gloating satisfaction to Pullman. Passengers could sleep in their own roomettes and dine in the recently introduced dining car. They could avail themselves of a barber shop, a beauty salon, secretarial services, telephone and telegraph.

The Pennsylvania Railroad had been running its own fast train from New York to Chicago, the *Pennsylvania Limited*, for several years when Daniels initiated the *Twentieth Century*. The Pennsylvania Railroad immediately upgraded its New York-Chicago service to make it competitive with the Central's, inaugurating a luxury, high-speed train between these two great cities they named the *Broadway Limited*.

The competition between the *Twentieth Century* and the *Broadway Limited* became the most celebrated rivalry in the history of North American railroads. They kept pace with each other in matters of service, speed and

luxury, with the major difference lying in the nature of the route. The *Broadway*'s route was more direct, but went through some fairly mountainous terrain. The New York Central's route formed a 90-degree angle—due north to Albany, then due west to Chicago—with the main line going through the relatively flat terrain of the Hudson and Mohawk Valleys and the Great Lakes shore, a circumstance that fostered use of the term 'Water Level Route' in New York Central's advertising. The implication was that the Central's level route would provide passengers with a more comfortable ride and a better night's sleep.

Competition between the two trains was keen but not cutthroat. Both railroads considered their crack trains a source of pride, prestige and publicity. For a while, the schedules of the two trains were such that they were on parallel tracks a few miles outside of Chicago. This juxtaposition gave every appearance of a race, and many excited passengers believed the trains were indeed racing. Actually, their running times were kept equal by agreement between the competitors. As the Central and

EASTWARD, WESTWARD
The Centuries at Buffalo Central Terminal
THE NEW YORK CENTRAL LINES

the Pennsylvania poured more money into these trains, they ceased to be moneymakers, but management justified their continuance as the best advertising money could buy.

Over the years, both the speed and the amenities of the *Twentieth Century Limited* were constantly improved. The original train consisted of three sleepers, a diner and a library-buffet car. Later versions included cars with drawing rooms. The train became so popular that it was run in several sections, the wooden cars being replaced by all-steel equipment between 1910 and 1912. By the mid-1920s, the Central was calling the train a 'national institution,' and it had, in fact, become a source of patriotic pride. In 1912, the Pennsylvania and the Central agreed to a running time of 20 hours (the Central had previously made the run in 18 hours). In 1932, the two roads agreed to a time of 18 hours, and in 1935 it was reduced to 16.5 hours. The 18-hour time was cause for a celebration on the departure platform, and was attended by Jimmy Walker, the flamboyant mayor of New York City, and William K Vanderbilt.

In the 1920s, the Atlantics were replaced by big 4-6-4 locomotives called Hudsons, which hauled the *Twentieth Century* until they were replaced by diesels in the 1950s. Modified over the years, the most powerful versions of the Hudson developed more than 4700 horsepower at 75 mph. The most noticeable change came in 1938 with the streamlined Hudson designed by Henry Dreyfuss. Actually, this locomotive was essentially the same old Hudson covered with what one observer called 'an upside-down bathtub.' Streamlining was supposed to cut down on air resistance and evoke an image of progress. The only certain thing about streamlining steam locomotives was that it covered many of the parts, making maintenance more difficult.

Arrivals and departures of the *Twentieth Century Limited* came to be as exciting as those of transatlantic liners. A red carpet rolled out from the gate to the platform was the Central's way of telling passengers they were special and could look forward to regal treatment in exchange for their extra fare. Many of the passengers were very special indeed. Celebrity

Above: Eastward, Westward *by Walter L Greene shows the great Buffalo terminal.*

Right: Greene paintings conveyed the power and pride of the NYC's halcyon days.

hounds haunted the departure gate area hoping to see such notables of the day as Kate Smith, Gloria Swanson and other movie stars, politicians, sports figures and others.

Twentieth Century passengers could enjoy such luxuries as fresh sole and strawberries for breakfast. Before breakfast, a newspaper appeared under their doors, and as they entered the dining car a boutonniere was presented to them. Wrinkled trousers or skirts were pressed by the valet, who also served as the train secretary. The *Twentieth Century Limited* was the inspiration for songs, plays and radio shows. The Columbia Broadcasting System's 'Grand Central Station' was one of the most successful radio shows ever produced for more than 20 years. There was a small group of

aficionados who regularly rode the *Twentieth Century* just to get a shave and a haircut—a form of dandyism that entered popular legend.

By the turn of the century, the New York Central and the City of New York had spent millions on sinking the Park Avenue tracks below street level and on other improvements. However, many New Yorkers still felt that the railroad was an unbearable intrusion into their lives. The yards still existed at ground level from 42nd to 56th Street, creating not only a safety hazard but a smoky, grimy eyesore that was retarding the city's development. Existing tracks and switches in the yard and trainshed could not handle the volume of traffic. Trains often had to wait in the Park Avenue beam tunnel, spewing smoke on citizens taking their

Below: Hudson locomotives like this 4-6-4 hauled the *Century* until they were replaced by diesels in the 1950s.

Right: The Pennsy and the New York Central were in constant competition with one another, even racing their locomotives on the stretches of track that ran parallel.

THE *New* 20ᵀᴴ CENTURY LIMITED

NEW YORK – *16 hours* – CHICAGO

NEW YORK CENTRAL SYSTEM

Left: Twentieth Century Limited, *NYC's super-train photographed along the Hudson River. The streamliner, running at about 80 miles per hour, is drawn by a 4700 hp streamlined Hudson locomotive.*

Below, left: The Twentieth Century Limited *arrives in Chicago on 22 July 1965.*

Above: The streamlined, aerodynamic design of the Limited *is highlighted in this illustration.*

strolls or carriage rides and covering buildings in a film of soot.

The Central managers were also concerned about the effect of smoke and fumes on their operations. Often the fumes were so thick that signals were obscured. The inevitable happened on 8 January 1902, when a New York Central train ran past a red signal and crashed into the rear of a standing New Haven train, killing 15 passengers. The need to do something about this situation was made all the more imperative by the response of the New York State Legislature to this tragedy. An act was passed prohibiting operation of steam locomotives south of the Harlem River after 1 July 1908. It was now up to the Central to figure out how they were going to get their trains into Grand Central Station after that date. The answer was electrification of the lines and locomotives.

The current Grand Central Terminal was completed in 1913. In that same year, the New York Central and Hudson Railroad was reorganized. The various constituent roads such as the Hudson River Railroad and the Lake Shore and Michigan Southern were abolished as separate entities and completely absorbed into the parent organization, now called simply the New York Central Railroad. The 34-story New York Central Building was constructed in 1929. Now called the Vanderbilt Building, it stands right at the Park Avenue centerline between 45th and 46th streets. The five-story Pan Am Building, completed in 1964, completely changed the Park Avenue view.

Although Grand Central Station is still one of the major railroad stations of the world, someone seeing it today for the first time in 20 or 30 years could not fail to notice obvious signs of decay that are in many ways a monument to the rapid decline suffered by railroads in general since the end of World War II.

The post-World War II version of the *Twentieth Century Limited* was inaugurated in 1948 with a ceremony featuring the presence of Dwight D Eisenhower (not yet President) and singer Beatrice Lillie. The champagne bottle Miss Lillie smashed against the observation car was filled not with champagne but with waters from the Mohawk and Hudson Rivers and from the Great Lakes. The observation car no longer had an open platform. Like the rest of the train, it was streamlined and featured an aerodynamically designed, curved rear end.

The ceremony around the newly modernized *Twentieth Century Limited* was supposed to herald a postwar era of prosperity for the New York Central. While the train was bright and new, those who rode ordinary Central trains could see the unmistakable signs of trouble. The paint on the cars was peeling, windows were dirty and seat upholstery was likely to have unrepaired rips.

After the war, Americans hungered to get back into their automobiles, and the airlines surged into war-postponed expansion. Both the airlines and the automobile makers were helped by the government—at taxpayers' expense. Federally funded programs sped construction of highways and airports, while taxpaying railroads continued to be hobbled by thousands of ICC regulations.

Of course, the New York Central was not alone in its woes; all American railroads suffered to some degree from competition with automobiles and airplanes. However, the New York Central was particularly vulnerable to competition from automobiles, buses and trucks. Its routes were short compared to those of such Western lines as the Union Pacific. Shippers generally found it more expedient and economical to use trucks rather than the railroad for short hauls.

Through the late 1950s and the early 1960s, New York Central Chief Executive Officer Alfred Perlman approached a number of roads to talk merger. Of course, the Central was not the only line to seek salvation by this means. It seemed that merger fever had descended on the American railroad scene. However, few roads seemed interested in the New York Central. Perlman was snubbed by the B&O, the C&O and several others. The New York Central's archrival, the Pennsylvania Railroad, had also been looking into mergers without much success. It slowly dawned on these two roads that about the only option left was the unthinkable. To many observers, a political union between the United States and the Soviet Union seemed a more likely possibility than a merger of the New York Central and the Pennsylvania. Nevertheless, Perlman had several meetings with James Symes, chairman of the Pennsylvania, although the two men did not particularly like each other.

The merger agreement was finally worked out in 1961. However, the necessary ICC approvals and the resolution of all the court cases instituted to stop it delayed the actual merger until 1968. The deal was also delayed by the ICC's insistence that the bankrupt New York, New Haven & Hartford be included. Neither the Central nor the Pennsylvania wanted to take in the New Haven. This once-great road was now a shambles, the victim of stock raiders and the Connecticut Turnpike, which was saddled with an unprofitable but essential commuter service to New York City. Central and Pennsylvania executives knew they would have to include the New Haven if their merger was to be approved, and so they reluctantly agreed.

Perlman was not happy with the deal, knowing that it was more of an absorption of the Central by the Pennsylvania than a true merger. In 1963, Symes retired and was replaced by Stuart Saunders, who disliked Perlman even more than Symes did. The outlook for the newly formed Pennsylvania New York Central Transportation Company, better know as Penn Central, did not seem bright.

Below: This American Locomotive Company (ALCO) diesel passenger locomotive (PA-2) with a 16-cylinder, 4-stroke engine, was built in 1959.

Right: An RS-11 switcher of the late 1950s, when diesel power had come into its own.

The Penn Central was in financial distress almost from its inception. The organization of the company created a New York-Philadelphia dichotomy that made it even more difficult for the Central and Pennsylvania people to work together. Transportation operations were run mainly from New York by ex-Central executives, while the other interests, like real estate and amusement parks, were directed from the Philadelphia office.

Confusion was rampant. Freight trains were actually 'lost,' only to turn up hundreds of miles from their appointed destinations. Of course, shippers would not tolerate this kind of thing, and many gave their business to trucks. It seems there were basic differences in operating philosophy between New York Central and Pennsylvania people that prevented a smooth combined operation.

In the first quarter of 1970, losses in the transportation division of Penn Central exceeded $300 million. However, through fund transfers and various paper shufflings, the loss was made to appear minimal. The Penn Central started to look around for funds, but couldn't have picked a worse time; the country was in a double bind of recession and inflation. The stock market plunged.

The final outcome seemed assured when the same banks that the Penn Central was begging for loans started to sell their Penn Central stock. The Penn Central had nothing left to do but declare bankruptcy.

Amtrak came into existence on 1 May 1971, and under the provisions of the act that created it, railroads could give up their best passenger equipment to Amtrak in exchange for permission to discontinue their long-distance passenger service. The Penn Central certainly agreed. No one dared to say it out loud, but it seemed that the United States now had a national railroad, for without massive federal subsidies, Amtrak could not survive.

The Penn Central was almost abolished completely when in 1973, the trustees said that unless financial aid was forthcoming, the railroad would be ordered to stop all operations by 1 October. The ultimatum stirred action in Congress, and the word 'nationalization' was actually heard in serious tones. The Congressional action was the Rail Revitalization and Regulatory Reform Act, whose ultimate result was the Consolidated Rail Corporation, or Conrail. A precursor creature of the Act, the United States Railway Association, proceeded to cut some 12,000 miles of track from Penn Central's operation. In accordance with the Act's provisions for bankrupt railroads to turn over their assets to Conrail, what was left went to that organization. By 1976, Penn Central was no more, as Conrail took over the Penn Central offices in Philadelphia.

THE NORTHERN PACIFIC

By Bill Yenne

*T*he idea of building a transcontinental, or 'Pacific,' railroad was first seriously promoted by Dr Samuel Bancroft Barlow in 1834 and by John Plumb in 1836. In 1845, Asa Whitney surveyed a possible rail following the trail blazed by the explorers Lewis and Clark in 1805. After sailing north on the Mississippi River and west on the Missouri, Lewis and Clark had traveled overland across the Continental Divide in Montana and down the Columbia River, finally reaching the Pacific Ocean in December 1805.

Senator Thomas Hart Benton of Missouri introduced the idea of a railroad to Congress in 1849, and Pacific Railroad conventions were held in Memphis, New Orleans and Boston that same year. It seemed as though the California Gold Rush had won many converts to the dream of a railroad link to the West.

The only question, apparently, was that of what route the new road would take. The central route to the Pacific followed the major overland routes of the day and was the shortest, straight-line distance between San Francisco and chief western embarkation points like St Louis and Kansas City. Advocates of a northern route—the Lewis and Clark route—pointed out that the nature of the navigable Mississippi/Missouri River network made the Puget Sound 700 miles closer than San Francisco in terms of track that would have to be laid.

The southern route, too, had many advocates. In 1853 Secretary of War (and later President of the Confederacy) Jefferson Davis of Mississippi presented a 13-volume study of nine possible southern routes, which, it was pointed out, were largely free of snow and high mountain passes. The Gadsden Purchase of 1854, which added portions of present-day New Mexico and Arizona to the United States, made these routes all the more attractive.

When the Civil War began, the idea of a transcontinental railroad became an issue vital

to the national security—the California gold fields *had* to remain under the control of the Union. For obvious reasons, the southern route was now impossible, and, of the two remaining choices, the central route seemed the most expeditious.

Signed into law in 1862 by President Abraham Lincoln, the Pacific Railroad Act called for *two* companies to undertake the task of constructing the new line. In the West was the Central Pacific Railroad, founded independently in 1861 by Leland Stanford, Collis Huntington, Charles Crocker and Mark Hopkins— the 'Big Four'—to build a rail line across the Sierra Nevada to connect with the rails from the East, that they correctly assumed would soon be completed. From the East these tracks would be built by the federally chartered Union Pacific.

In terms of hands-on development of the 'Pacific' railroad, the first principal player was Theodore Dehone Judah, who had engineered the first railroad in California (the Sacramento Valley Rail Road of 1856), and who had lobbied hard in Congress for construction of a road on the central route. Judah had already surveyed the route through the Sierra Nevada, and before the Pacific Railroad Act was signed in 1862, he and the 'Big Four' were already building their railroads. Judah's counterpart at Union Pacific was Major General Grenville Mellon Dodge. Dodge, who was granted an indefinite leave from the Army, was named chief engineer for Union Pacific.

The construction of the Union Pacific line from Omaha really didn't begin until 1866, after the Civil War had ended, but in the West, the Central Pacific was having a great deal of

Below: This Northern Pacific 4-4-0 operated on the St Paul to Portland run. It is shown here in 1883 at the Last Spike Celebration at Gold Creek, Montana. NP financier Henry Villard is standing with his hat off.

difficulty getting through the rugged Sierra Nevada. Once it finally began construction, the Union Pacific made rapid progress building its line across the plains—despite attacks from Indians. By the time the Central Pacific had surmounted the Sierra Nevada Mountains and was into Nevada in July 1868, the Union Pacific had already reached Wyoming. Since no site for a meeting point had been specified, a competition between the two began, which culminated with their meeting at Promontory, Utah, north of the Great Salt Lake, on 10 May 1869. The nation torn apart North and South by the Civil War was now bound together East and West by bands of steel.

The *central* route to the Pacific had been inspired, in part, by the necessity of expedience brought about by the Civil War, but even before the conflict ended, the government made a commitment to completing the *northern* route as well.

Land surveys, beginning with that of Asa Whitney in 1845, already existed. Edwin F Johnson, an eminent engineer, made further in-depth studies in the early 1850s, and published a widely circulated book advocating a northern transcontinental line. In 1853, after consid-

Left: Emigration to the Northwest was encouraged in the United States and abroad, as seen in this pamphlet from the railroad's European agency.

Below: The NP employed imported Chinese labor for much of the construction of their northern route.

Right: The famous Northern Pacific locomotive, Minnetonka, *was purchased 18 July 1870 and used for early construction work in northern Minnesota.*

erable debate over competing routes, the United States Congress voted an appropriation to commission another survey of the northernmost route by Issac I Stevens, an experienced Army officer who had also been the first governor of the Washington Territory. His comprehensive, two-volume report showed the route to be a very favorable one, and one that was rich in natural resources and potentially of great economic importance to the growing nation. Meanwhile, Josiah Perham of Massachusetts made intensive efforts to persuade Congress to authorize construction of the Northern Pacific, and he later coincidentally became the company's first president.

Finally, on 2 July 1874, just two years after he had signed the original Pacific Railroad Act and five years before the rails would link at Promontory, Utah, Abraham Lincoln signed an Act of Congress creating the Northern Pacific Railroad Company. Its eastern terminus would be on Lake Superior and its western terminus on Puget Sound, and much of its route would follow the trail originally blazed by Lewis and Clark on their expedition in 1804-1806.

The Act provided for a right-of-way through public lands 200 feet on either side of the tracks, as well as ground for station buildings and other railroad facilities. In providing federal lands to make possible the building of the

Northern Pacific, Congress was concerned not only with opening the Northwest to settlement. It also wanted military security in the West and ready access to the North Pacific coast for troops and supplies. Furthermore, it wanted to provide employment for thousands of soldiers returning home from the war. Finally, the federal government wanted to increase the value of adjoining government lands for the profit of the United States Treasury. While the United States had abundant land in the West, its cash resources were painfully limited.

The Act creating the Northern Pacific also provided grants of land, which could be sold by the railroad company to finance construction through the largely unsettled and unproductive territory. However, the land was of little or no value without the railroad, nor did it serve as a stimulus to the selling of stock, as had been hoped and as had been the case with the Union Pacific. Furthermore, the Act specifically forbade the company from issuing bonds or imposing mortgages on its property. As a result, the pioneer incorporators, with all of their enthusiasm and energy, were faced with almost insurmountable obstacles in going forward with their ambitious project. The Northern Pacific charter had enjoined the company from mortgaging its grant, in the belief that land sales

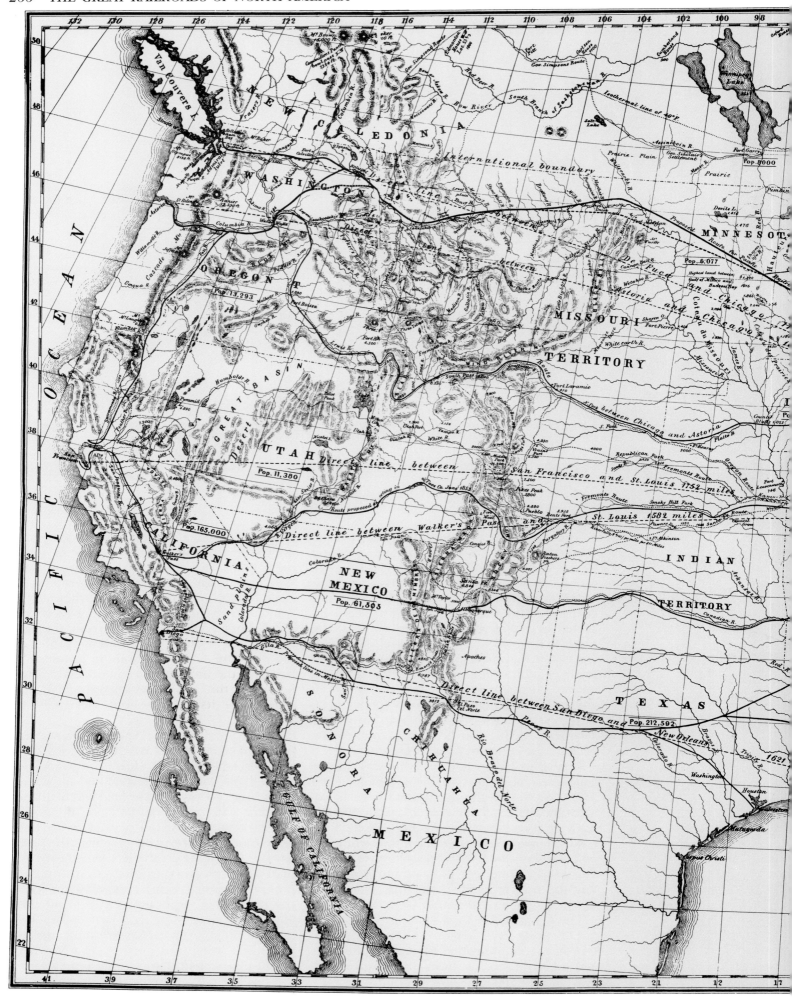

Long. West from Greenwich

NEW BRITAIN

James Bay

Gulf of St. Lawrence

I. Anticosti

NEW BRUNSWICK

NOVA SCOTIA

Halifax

Lake Superior

Thunder Bay

Copper

Iron

Michipicoten

Hills Rocky Steep

Sault Marie

CANADA WEST

Isothermal line of 40°

CANADA EAST

Quebec

Ottawa R.

St. Lawrence R.

Montreal

St. Johns

MAINE
Pop. 583,088

VERMONT

N. HAMPSHIRE
Pop. 317,964

MICHIGAN

L. Huron

Georgian Bay

Green Bay

L. St. Clair

WISCONSIN
Pop. 305,191

Wisconsin R.

Milwaukee

Janesville

Lake Michigan

MICHIGAN
Pop. 397,654

Detroit

L. Ontario

Toronto

Buffalo

Oswego

Utica

Erie Canal

NEW YORK
Pop. 3,097,394

MASSACHUSETTS
Pop. 994,499

R.I.

CONNECTICUT
Pop. 370,791

ATLANTIC OCEAN

Long. E. from Washington

Dubuque

Rock I.

Chicago

L. Erie

Erie

Dunkirk

Toledo

Sandusky

Cleveland

Wheeling

PENNSYLVANIA
Pop. 2,311,786

Pittsburgh

Harrisburg

N. JERSEY

Philadelphia
Pop. 489,555

ILLINOIS
Pop. 851,470

INDIANA
Pop. 988,416

OHIO
Pop. 1,980,408

Columbus

Cincinnati

Ohio R.

MARYLAND

Baltimore

Washington

DELAWARE

Illinois R.

Alton 380 above tide in Hudson

St. Louis

All points in this line equidistant from St. Louis and Chicago

VIRGINIA
Pop. 1,421,661

MISSOURI
1043.

Cairo 275 above Gulf of Mexico

Louisville

KENTUCKY
Pop. 982,405

Cumberland R.

Norfolk

White R.

Mississippi R.

Memphis

Tennessee R.

TENNESSEE
Pop. 1,002,625

N. CAROLINA
Pop. 866,903

Blairsville

Wilmington

Arkansas

S. CAROLINA

Columbia
Pop. 668,507

Charleston

Natchez

Yazoo R.

MISSISSIPPI
Pop. 606,555

ALABAMA
Pop. 771,671

GEORGIA
Pop. 905,999

Savannah

Mobile

Pensacola

St. Augustine

FLORIDA
Pop. 87,401

BAHAMAS

GULF OF MEXICO

Long. West from Washington

Map
OF THE
Proposed **NORTHERN ROUTE** for a
Railroad to the
PACIFIC,
by Edwin F. Johnson, C.E.
1853.

Scale in Statute Miles

Lith. of E. C. Kellogg & Co., Hartford, Conn.

would be adequate to finance construction. Without the railroad, however, sales were sluggish.

The impasse wasn't resolved until 1870, when Congress authorized the Northern Pacific to issue bonds to aid in construction, and to secure the bonds by a mortgage on all of its property and rights of property, including its franchise as a corporation. Bonds were issued, and the banking house of Jay Cooke & Company was appointed to sell the bonds and handle the company's finances.

To build the original transcontinental, the Union Pacific had received a federal subsidy of $27,226,512 in government bonds and the Central Pacific a subsidy of $27,855,680. Each road had a grant of public lands of 12,800 acres per mile of road. The Northern Pacific was given a land grant of 20 sections per mile of road in Minnesota and Oregon and double this in the intervening Dakota, Montana, Idaho and Washington territories. It did not get a subsidy, but the directors continued to solicit Congress.

A formal ground-breaking ceremony on 15 February 1870 near the present town of Carleton, Minnesota, a few miles west of Duluth, marked the start of the Minnesota Division of the Northern Pacific Railroad. Actual construction began in July, with adequate financing assured.

In 1872 Northern Pacific leased the Lake Superior & Mississippi River Railroad, giving it a line between Duluth and St Paul. A year later, construction of the rail line had reached Bismarck and the Missouri River in Dakota Territory.

Previous pages: An 1853 map of Edwin Johnson's proposed northern transcontinental route with the eastern terminus at Chicago.

Above: In March 1879, No 57 led the first train over the Missouri River on tracks laid on the ice.

Left: In this 1883 portrait by F Jay Haynes, Henry Villard is seated in the center of a group of railroad men.

The first stirrings of activity on the west end of the projected transcontinental line came in 1870, with the initial goal being to link Portland and Tacoma, Washington. Completion of the segment between Kalama, on the north bank of the Columbia River, and Tacoma came in 1873, with much of the material and equipment shipped around Cape Horn from the Atlantic seaboard. This segment was the first standard-gauge railway to be built in Washington state.

Later in the year, however, construction ground almost to a halt as the Great Panic of 1873 brought failure to Jay Cooke & Company and bankruptcy to the railroad itself. Five years would pass before new financing could be obtained and progress resumed. Reorganization and refinancing under the presidency of Frederick Billings breathed new life into the Northern Pacific, and in 1879 the westward march began anew. Later, the town of Billings, Montana, now the Big Sky State's largest city, was named for him.

Frederick Billings was succeeded as president in 1881 by Henry Villard, an important nineteenth century industrialist and the figure who would preside over the completion of the Northern Pacific line. He had emigrated from Germany in 1853 at the age of 18, studied law and subsequently became a distinguished journalist. He reported the Lincoln-Douglas debates and the Chicago convention where Lincoln was nominated for President. In Washington he covered the political front for a syndicate of newspapers, and as a war correspondent he chronicled important engagements of the Civil War.

Villard's entry into the transportation field came on a visit to Germany, where a group of European financiers persuaded him to represent them in protecting their investments in American railroads. He not only served his clients well, but soon organized his own company, which eventually led to control of the Northern Pacific.

Construction on the Northern Pacific in the Yellowstone Valley from Glendive proceeded rapidly during 1882, with the season's work ending at Livingston, Montana in November. During this period the company was faced with acute shortages of both labor and materials. The first was resolved by importing from

Left, top: Northern Pacific No 225 4-4-0 photographed in Portland in 1883.

Above: This NP 2-8-0 Consolidation locomotive was built by Baldwin in 1889.

Left: A photographic record of the first passenger train to arrive in Minnewaukon, North Dakota, on 10 August 1885.

China 15,000 of the required 25,000 laborers. Chinese laborers had been employed earlier to great advantage by the Central Pacific on the Sacramento-to-Promontory route in 1862-1869. Because of a domestic steel shortage, it was also necessary to import rails, tie plates and spikes from France and England.

Meanwhile, taking advantage of trackage completed by the Oregon Railroad & Navigation Company between Portland and Wallula, in southeastern Washington, the Northern Pacific rapidly pushed its eastward construction from that point. By the spring of 1883 only 300 miles remained between the two rail heads.

The completion of the Northern Pacific came on 8 September 1883 at Gold Creek, Montana, before an audience that included distinguished guests from the United States, Germany, England and the Scandinavian countries. Witnessing the ceremony were cabinet officials; 10 United States senators and three former senators; 20 congressmen and four former congressmen; nine governors of states and four ex-governors; 25 of the nation's top railroad executives; judges; mayors; and 50 journalists.

After the oratory, 300 men quickly laid the rail and drove the spikes on the last thousand feet of track. The ceremonial 'last spike' was driven by Henry Villard and former United States President Ulysses S Grant. It was not a gold spike, but rather the same steel spike used 13 years earlier to mark the beginning of construction near Carleton, Minnesota.

The joining of the rails at Gold Creek marked the first through route from Lake Superior to the Pacific coast, but not the end of construction. It was still necessary for Northern Pacific trains to run over the rails of the Oregon Railroad & Navigation Company from Wallula to

Portland. To comply with its charter requirements, the Northern Pacific had to build a line from Wallula to Tacoma.

The last remaining segment of the Pacific coast line was completed with the opening of service between Seattle and the Columbia River in July 1884.

Crossing the rugged and heavily forested Cascade Mountains took from 1883 to 1887, and was fraught with engineering and construction problems. The line ascended the steep mountain grades on switchbacks until completion of the 1.8-mile Stampede Tunnel in 1888.

Less than seven years after the link-up of Northern Pacific rail lines at Gold Creek, and within three years of the Cascade line completion, the entire tier of Pacific 'Northwest' territories had sufficient population to join the Union. North Dakota entered on 2 November 1889; South Dakota, which derived much of its population through immigration over the Northern Pacific, came in the same day. Six days later, on 8 November, Montana achieved statehood, followed by Washington on 11 November. Idaho joined on 3 July 1890.

The growth and ultimate admission of these states into the Union tell a graphic story of the part played by Northern Pacific in the settlement and development of the Northwest.

In December 1945, Congress repealed the land grant rate provision, which had made construction of the Northern Pacific and many other western railroads possible. The repeal took effect on 1 October 1946.

By 1850, the year of the first railroad land grant act, the federal government owned nearly 1.4 billion acres of wild land in the West and the South. For a generation the government had offered its lands to settlers at low

Left: NP passenger and freight trains rumbled through Castle Rock, Washington, in the 1880s putting the small town on the map.

Below: NP class W-5 2-8-2. Baldwin referred to this locomotive type as the Mikado because the first ones were built for export to Japan.

prices, but there were few takers because of the lack of transportation. Between 1850 and 1871 the government made grants of land to 12 states and 14 companies to promote the construction of pioneer railroads through sparsely settled, or unsettled, areas of the public domain.

A precedent for utilizing federal land to promote public transportation was established as early as 1827, three years before the *Best Friend of Charleston* became the first locomotive to haul a train of cars in regular service on a common carrier railroad in the United States. The initial grant helped facilitate construction of the Wabash & Erie Canal. Earlier, wagon roads similarly benefited.

In the 1890s the Northern Pacific had embarked on an aggressive campaign to attract settlers to its agricultural lands, and by 1921 it had disposed of more than 35 million acres to United States and European immigrants. The influx of new population, bringing with it both

increased production and consumption, fulfilled the most expansive hopes for development of the western frontier.

In all, land grants that the railroads received from the federal government totaled upwards of 131 million acres, whose estimated value at the time of transfer was approximately 94 cents an acre, or $123 million.

In return, the roads—including the non-land grant lines competing with them—carried government troops and all government property used for military purposes during World War II for one-half of the standard rates, until as late as October 1946. Until 1941 the land grant railroads and competing lines also carried government property used for non-military purposes for one-half of the established rates. In addition, the land grant railroads carried United States mail for four-fifths of the standard rate until 1941.

In March 1945 the Interstate Commerce Committee of the House of Representatives

Above: *Northern Pacific's passenger train the* North Coast Limited *leaving Easton, Washington, headed east. In the foreground is an EMD FT diesel freight locomotive.*

Right: *No 5000 is an ALCO-Schenectady 2-8-8-4 built in 1928.*

reported that the railroads 'had already contributed over $900 million in payment of the lands that were transferred to them under the Land Grant Act.' Between the time of that report and the end of land grant deductions in government rates, there were further payments estimated at not less than $350 million.

Thus, the total contributions of the railroads to the government through rate deductions due to land grants were approximately ten times the value of the lands at the time they had been granted.

Meanwhile, the Northern Pacific and other railroads built under the government's land policy created billions of dollars in wealth for the states and populations they served; increased the value of public and privately-owned lands; converted vast, non-taxable areas into taxable properties; gave impetus to agricultural and industrial development; and knitted a nation together at a most critical point in its history.

By 1970 the Northern Pacific had disposed of 37,231,057 acres of its land grant properties. The remaining acreage, not including mineral rights retained by the Northern Pacific, was comprised, for the most part, of timber and grazing lands, which went unsold in the early days of development because they were not well suited to agricultural purposes.

In the decade following completion of the transcontinental line, Northern Pacific, under presidents Thomas Oakes and Brayton Ives, had turned its energies to constructing branch lines and expanding its operating and other facilities. As the Northwest Territory prospered, so did the railroad. However, the financial crisis which swept the country in 1893 had

forced a number of lines into receivership, among them the Northern Pacific. The receivership finally ended in 1896, when the property of the railroad was sold to a new corporation called the Northern Pacific Railway Company. Edward Adams served briefly as president, followed in the same year by Edwin Winter, who successfully reorganized the company on a sound financial basis. With overall business conditions continuing to improve, the future brightened for the new company.

In 1901, four years after Charles S Mellen succeeded Edwin Winter as Northern Pacific president, the Northern Pacific and Great Northern, which had completed its own transcontinental line in 1893, jointly purchased nearly all of the outstanding stock of the Chicago, Burlington & Quincy Railroad, providing the two lines with direct access to Chicago and the markets of the Midwest and South.

Soon after the Northern Pacific and Great Northern acquired the Chicago, Burlington & Quincy, the two 'Northerns' began joint development of a new rail system to serve the natural resource areas of Washington and Oregon. Built between 1905 and 1909, the Spokane, Portland & Seattle Railway had 1000 miles of main line. By 1929 the Northern Pacific itself had 1087 locomotives, 933 passenger cars and 50,960 freight cars operating over 6784 miles of main line track.

In 1932, under president Charles Donnelly, Northern Pacific formed a wholly-owned subsidiary, the Northern Pacific Transport Company, to provide highway freight and passenger service as a motor common carrier, and to supplement its rail service. Northern Pacific Transport was authorized to operate in the

states of Washington, Montana, Idaho, Wyoming, North Dakota and Minnesota.

During World War II, under president Charles E Denney, Northern Pacific began a major, decade-long rehabilitation program, reballasting and laying heavier rail on 2000 miles of lines. More than 300 main line curves were eliminated or reduced, bridges and tunnels replaced and new shops and freight houses built.

As part of its continuing effort to streamline operations and expedite the movement of traffic, Northern Pacific introduced train radio, continuous welded rail, centralized traffic control and many other technological innovations. The replacement of its steam fleet with efficient diesel-electric locomotives was begun in 1938 under president Charles Donnelly and completed in 1958 under Robert Macfarlane. Many more millions of dollars were invested in new freight and passenger equipment.

At Pasco, Washington the company constructed the first modern electronic freight classification yard in the Pacific Northwest. Completed in 1955, it provided more expeditious handling of the increased traffic from the vast Columbia Basin agricultural region.

In 1957, during the presidency of Robert

Below: NP No 5410 is an example of the EMD 1350 hp 'Bulldog' FT series with four portholes intact and dynamic brakes.

Macfarlane, Northern Pacific installed its first computer in 1957, heralding a new era of efficiency in operations and management. The vital need for a speedy, dependable system to handle the increasing amount of transmitted computer data, as well as telephone communications, prompted the company to begin construction of a microwave system linking St Paul, Seattle and Portland. The installation between Seattle and Portland was completed in 1964. Five years later the last microwave tower between Seattle and St Paul was erected, completing the system and ending Northern Pacific's dependence on wire transmission, which is vulnerable to winds, storms, snow and sleet.

On 2 March 1970, four years after Louis Menk succeeded Robert Macfarlane as Northern Pacific president, Burlington Northern was formed, merging the Northern Pacific and Great Northern, along with the Spokane, Portland & Seattle, together with the Chicago, Burlington & Quincy. To the new company, Northern Pacific contributed Louis W Menk, its president, as the new firm's first chariman, as well as 6771 miles of track, over which ran 604 locomotives, pulling 34,961 freight cars and 192 passenger cars.

THE PENNSYLVANIA

By Timothy Jacobs

*T*he railroad with the familiar keystone logo is all but a memory now. The largest railroad in the world for most of its 124 years, the rails of the Pennsy now form the foundation for a modern titan, ConRail. Comprising over 10,000 miles of track at its height, the Pennsy moved more freight and more passengers than any other railroad in the world. From the *John Bull* to the *Metroliner*; from wood to coal to electric to diesel fuel; from the luxury of the Pennsy's famous *Broadway Limited* to the clank of an old time handcar—the Pennsy was this and much more.

In 1830, Robert L Stevens, son of shipping and horse-railroad baron John Stevens, set sail for England to buy a locomotive and rails for his father's Camden & Amboy Railroad. The rails in use in America at the time—wooden slats topped with strips of iron—were dangerous, coming loose and derailing trains, or punching through the car bottoms and injuring passengers, or injuring the horses used to draw the cars. Stevens designed the iron 'T' configuration on his trip, which became the standard in the US upon his return.

Stevens brought back something else from England: a locomotive he named *John Bull*. Shipped in one piece, except for rods, pistons, wheels and other vital parts, there were no instructions for assembly. A steamboat mechanic named Isaac Dripps put the *Bull* together.

Stevens enlisted Matthias Baldwin, a former watchmaker, to build some locomotives domestically. The first, *Old Ironsides,* ran on 23 November 1832, for the Philadelphia, Germantown & Norristown Railroad. In 1833, *John Bull* became the first passenger steam engine on the Camden & Amboy line. The wheels of industrial commerce and relatively fast nationwide travel were set in motion.

Stevens' dream was to build a railroad from New York to the Great Lakes. The state legisla-

ture, afraid of losing its power as the shipping trade portal to New York, was intent upon building a state-commissioned railroad and revoked Stevens' charter. On 24 March 1828, with two million dollars appropriated, the state began to build the Philadelphia & Columbia Railroad. The 40 miles completed by 20 September 1832 were used as feeder lines to supply materials for the State Road's completion.

Meanwhile, Matthias Baldwin was busy building much-acclaimed locomotives such as *Lancaster* and *Columbia*. The *Lancaster* hauled 19 fully-loaded cars over the steepest, highest grades, spelling the beginning of the end for horses as the nation's prime movers. The inclined planes on this road were equipped with a heavy rope, which was attached to the rail cars at the beginning of the grades. This rope then 'reeled 'em in' by a 60 hp engine

situated at the top of the grade. Rope was let out at a measured pace to lower cars down the grade. The danger and expense of this method caused a worried State Road to build alternate routes on flatter ground.

Between 1830 and 1835, more railroad building was done in Pennsylvania than in any other state. Investors and legislatures took an increasing interest in railroads, which soon became emblems of power and prestige. Though no one knew it at the time, these roads were forming the nucleus for what would become the world's largest railroad, a paragon of efficiency, luxury and engineering acumen: the Pennsylvania.

The Pennsylvania Railroad was incorporated on 13 April 1846, at a time when the intense competition between New York and Philadelphia was matched by the competition

Below: John Bull *on the Camden & Amboy Railroad.*

among Pennsylvania railroads. The Baltimore & Ohio was petitioning to build a line into Pittsburgh, and the Pennsy had to fulfill three conditions or the B&O would swallow up Pennsylvania's western trade routes. By July 1847, $3 million in investor subscriptions were firm—$1 million was in the treasury, and 35 miles of road bed were under contract. The B&O's rights were voided in August of that year.

Samuel Merrick became the first president of the thirteen-man Board of Directors on 31 March 1847. Not being engineers themselves, Merrick and his successor, WC Patterson, had some difficulty commanding the respect of the stockholders and many of the personnel. Chief Engineer John Edgar Thomson's leadership qualities began to shine under president Patterson, when Thomson lobbied tirelessly to push construction west against competition from New York and Maryland. Thomson assumed Patterson's office on 2 February 1852, instituting a policy of Pennsy officers 'working

Left: Robert Livingston Stevenson, president of the Camden & Amboy, was so impressed by the British-built Stephenson locomotives that he bought the John Bull.

Left, below: The John Bull *was shipped from England in 1831.*

Right: *This Currier & Ives print celebrates the wonder of the express train.*

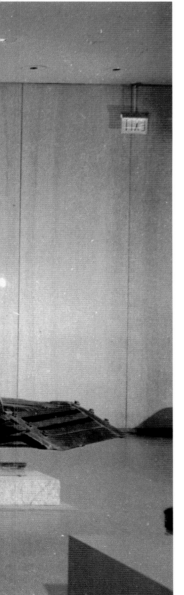

their way to the top'. Thomson was the first of five presidents in what would later be viewed as the Pennsy's glory days.

Thomson both built the lines and organized the Pennsy's foundation. The first Pennsy track section opened on 1 September 1849, rolling from Harrisburg to Lewistown. By 10 December 1852, the first through train made its run from Philadelphia to Pittsburgh, using the tracks of both the Allegheny Portage and the Philadelphia & Columbia; the trip took a mere 13 to 17 hours. And the first Pennsylvania Railroad train rode company tracks all the way from Philadelphia to Pittsburgh on 18 July 1858.

The State Works System was now clearly outdated, and a financial burden to the Commonwealth. The canal segments froze solid in the winter, halting operations and generating heavy debts. The state offered the canal system to the Pennsy for $9 million. To sweeten an obviously sour deal, the purchaser of the canals would never again have to pay the kind of freight tonnage taxes that were regularly levied against transport companies in Pennsylvania. Pennsy bought the State Works on 27 June 1857.

Due to merchants' and the public's demand for speed, reliability and ready access, the days of the small railroad were numbered. The year 1850 saw the rapid merging of many small railroads into longer roads under one management. Consolidations, mergers and buyouts were the means of growth for larger railroads such as the Pennsy.

Probably the first privately built railroad acquired was the Harrisburg, Portsmouth, Mt Joy & Lancaster Railroad, whose first president was James Buchanan. On 1 November 1848, the Pennsy leased the road from Harrisburg to Dil-lersville for 20 years, later extending the lease to 999 years.

With the onset of the Civil War, trains were needed desperately to move troops and supplies to the front; Thomson's second-in-command, Thomas A Scott, was summoned by President Lincoln to oversee this operation as well as the repair of bridges burned by Confederate forces. Scott effectively rescued General Hooker, boxed in by Confederate Troops on Lookout Mountain in Tennessee, helping deliver Chattanooga into the North's power. He also instituted the wartime practice of protecting the President from possible assassination by providing decoy trains and coaches to lure would-be malefactors from the actual travel route. He performed his duties with such alacrity that Lincoln appointed him Assistant Secretary of War, and gave Scott command of all government railroad activity. By the end of the war, railroads had replaced canals as the American mode of shipping.

During an investigation into the finances of Credit Mobilier, Congress discovered a Union Pacific kickback scheme. News of the scam caused stocks to fall, all types of businesses to fail, and a reduction in wages for the workers who didn't lose their jobs. Thousands did. Railroads then had to resort to rate wars to recoup losses created by the Panic. Another wage reduction was implemented, this time 10 percent across the board, from executives to apprentices.

On 27 May 1874, J Edgar Thomson died of a heart attack. The strain of bringing the Pennsy through the Panic of 1873 had worsened his already poor health. However, the future would dawn more brightly when the brilliant Thomas Scott succeeded him at the helm of the Pennsy.

R.R. Feb 1861   M.W. Baldwin's 1000th Locomotive

Rockefeller's Standard Oil, the largest refinery in the eastern US, shipped 65 percent of its barrels over Pennsy rails. Pennsy, in turn, paid Standard up to $10 million in rebates in one 18 month period. The Pennsy moved its oil shipments via the Empire Transportation Company. Empire's president, Joseph Potts, in a naive and unbelievably self-destructive move, announced a scheme whereby Empire and Pennsy would get Standard over a barrel: they would go into the oil business themselves. Rockefeller simply said that Standard was not going to use a a shipper who was in competition in the oil business with them, thereby cutting off huge revenues for Pennsy. In June 1877, Scott cut wages for the workers, who in turn struck in Pittsburgh. By August, Scott was shaken to learn that his railroad could not pay its dividend to stockholders. Standard then bought Empire's cars, pipeline system and refineries, gaining a complete monopoly on oil gathering facilities in the East. Scott, much to the dismay of third vice president (and future Pennsy president) Alexander Cassatt, went to Rockerfeller to accept his terms.

Rockerfeller himself described Scott's signing of the new contract allocating only 47 percent of Standard's business to the Pennsy: 'I can see him now, with his big, soft hat, marching into the room in that little hotel to meet us; not to sweep us away as he had always done, but coming in with a smile, walking right up to the cannon's mouth.' Pennsy would now have to pay the rebates for Standard's business, plus rebates *for any oil shipped by any of Standard's competitors.*

Tycoons, labor unions and government legislation were not the only dangers to the Pennsy. On 31 May 1889, the Conemaugh River dam burst, releasing a 20 foot high wall of water. The resulting 'Johnstown Flood' drowned 30 passengers, and destroyed 34 locomotives, 24 passenger cars and 561 freight cars. Some locomotives were carried as much as a mile downstream. Full service was restored within six weeks, but at a cost of millions of dollars.

Despite whatever difficulties it faced, the Pennsy continued to pioneer in both luxury and technology. Pennsy incorporated many modern conveniences for coordinating switchyard operations: loudspeaker systems, telephones installed in engine cabs and teletype machines. Perhaps most importantly, the Janney automatic coupling system replaced the time-consuming and dangerous manual link-and-pin, thus lowering the number of switching yard casualities. The development of Westinghouse air brakes were testament to the fact that stopping a train was at least as important as moving one.

George Pullman's creations of 1867 were the first luxury accomodations on the Pennsy. His

Right: The Great American Tea Company produced this rather egocentric view of a hasty stop for refreshments.

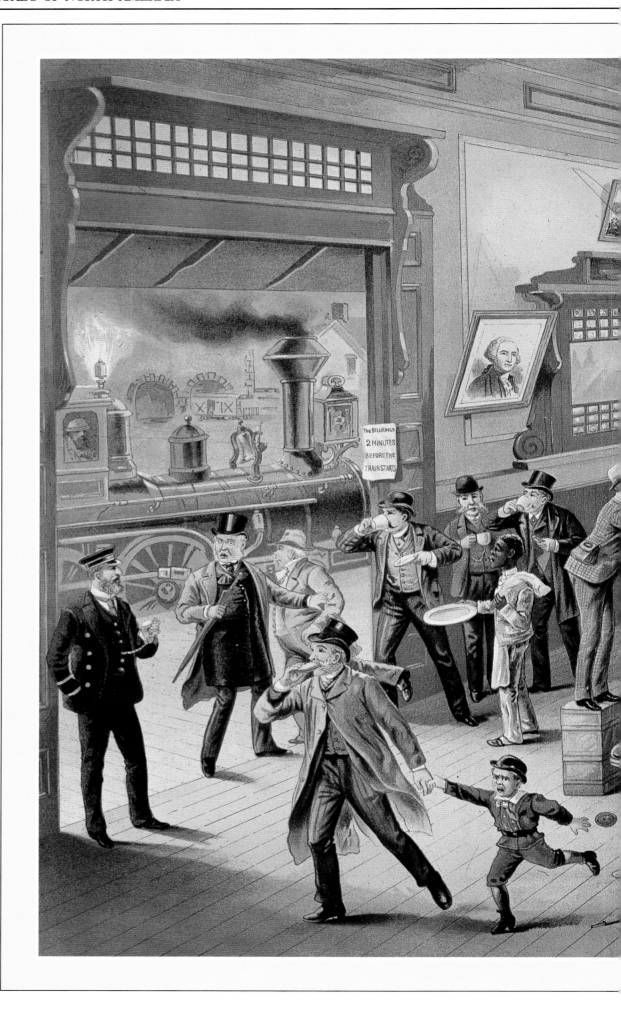

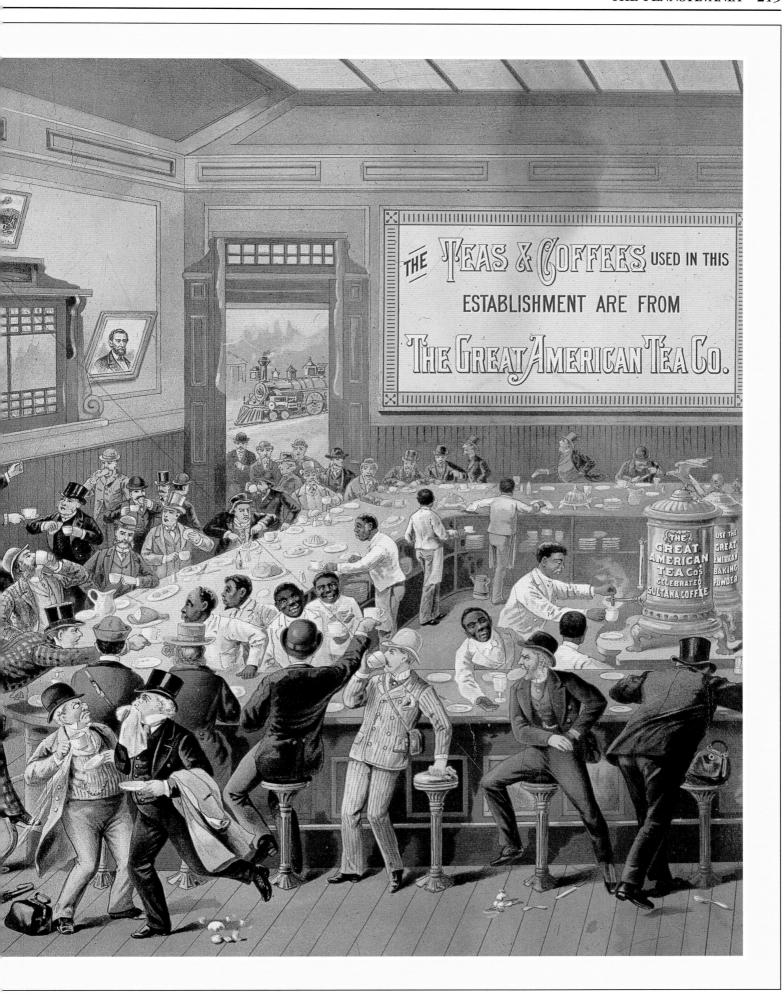

'Silver Palace Sleeping Cars' included diners with full kitchens, smoking lounges, card rooms, barber shops, beauty salons, libraries, and of course, well-appointed sleepers. Steam heating was introduced in 1881. A Pennsy employee designed a car appointed with stained-glass, mahoghany, velvet and silver chandeliers. Other major design changes came in 1938, with electro-mechanically air conditioned cars, lit by the then-revolutionary fluorescent light, and featuring men's and ladies' rooms, a wine closet and 4 silver chandeliers.

The Pennsy was the first railroad to run a 'limited' passenger train, in 1876, between Jersey City and Chicago. The route was upgraded in 1881, and the New York to Chicago record was broken with a time of 26 hours and 40 minutes. The *Pennsylvania Limited* was remarkable for its punctuality, and the New York Central's *20th Century Limited* adopted a similar schedule. The two competing trains 'raced' from Chicago to New York City, over parallel tracks for the first leg of the journey. Literally within a stone's throw of one another, the trains' crews and passengers cheered their locomotives on.

Frequent loss of luggage resulted from the 'help yourself' baggage handling of the early days, until Pennsy instituted the baggage check plan which is still in use today. Baggagemen in the 1860s were usually serving double or triple duty, keeping passenger lamps lit and often serving as brakemen. Brakes had to be appplied uniformly throughout the train before the advent of air brakes. All passenger locomotives on the Pennsy were equipped with automatic air brakes by 1 July 1879. The Pennsy was the first railroad to adopt them as the standard.

Improvements were constantly being implemented. The shape of the passenger cars had originally been something like a carriage. George Pullman made the cars longer, more lozenge-shaped, with more head room. Raymond Loewy, the designer responsible for the distinctive Studebaker in the late 1940s, brought an aerodynamic bullet-like look to passenger locomotives in the 1930s. Working with the Pennsy's Engineering Department, Loewy set the streamlined standard for other railroads to follow.

The first steam turbine loco saw service on the Pennsy in 1944. This loco eliminated the outside driving apparatus of traditional steam power. With no pushrods or cylinders, it was powered by steam pressure against turbine blades, and developed a respectable tractive force of 65,000 pounds. Jointly designed by Baldwin and Westinghouse and Pennsy engineers, this loco was seen by many as an effort to avoid dieselization.

The opening of Broad Street Station in Philadelphia and the extensive electrification which

Above: The Philadelphia Limited *crosses Rockville Bridge in the 1880s.*

Left: Red plush was de rigueur in the luxuriously appointed cars.

Right: Pennsy instituted the baggage check system which is still in use today.

Left: Design precursors to the E6s 4-4-2, two vintage E3s hustle a passenger train through the Carpenters, Pennsylvania landscape on a museum exhibition run in 1983.

took place in that area produced the usage of the 11,000 volt overhead electrical system. By 1924, there were 286 motor cars in use. The most powerful of them all was the experimental 2-8-8-2 FF-1 loco, a side rod type developing 140,000 pounds of tractive force.

Soon, however, Pennsy was experimenting with gasoline-fueled switchers. In 1929, these had 400 hp internal combustion engines. By 1945, the Pennsy purchased an EMD (General Motors' Electro-Motive Division) 6000 hp diesel locomotive. Diesels were hardy, and like the famed C-47 flying boxcar, would 'fly with a wing shot off and a tail missing.' They also used cheap fuel. In 1947, Pennsy ordered 77 EMD diesels for freight and passenger service. Steam engines were out of steam. Thousands of steam locos were scrapped.

The ALCO RS-3 saw service on lines that would become part of the ConRail network. It was a breakthrough with its cab placed such that engineers could actually see the road ahead, making for a more versatile locomotive, and for more road safety. The early seventies saw the use of modularized loco electronics, such as are found on the General Electric U23-B 2300 hp road switcher.

Alexander Cassatt, president of the Pennsy from 1899 to 1906, had admitted what most Pennsy officials refused to recognize: New York

City had stolen Philadelphia's crown as the nation's hub of trade, and the Pennsy must develop an alternative to ferrying their passengers across the river. Building a bridge would require the cooperation of several railroads, and the Pennsy found itself at the turn of the century standing alone. The first proposed substitute was a tunnel under the Hudson, although the officials of the pre-electric Pennsy didn't want steam locos in submarine tunnels.

Despite these drawbacks, DeWitt Haskin organized the Hudson River Tunnel Company in 1874. Haskin's experience with tunneling involved hard rock mining in the West. He was not prepared to deal with the Hudson's soft riverbed. On the morning of 21 July 1880, assistant engineer Pete Woodland and his men found the tunnel to be very 'soft.' Woodland saw a trickle of water, sounded the alarm, ran to the air lock and held the door open for his men. Eight men had rushed into the airlock when the river burst into the tunnel. Woodland slammed the door, saving the men in the lock from the death that he and 19 others suffered in that tragedy.

In 1892, Pennsy official Samuel Rea went to London to study their 'tube' system. Nine years later, Rea told Cassatt that the time had come to tunnel under the Hudson. Due to Cassatt's great concern with safety, Pennsy's hand-

Above: Pennsy No 420 was a 4-4-0 American, a popular type of steam locomotive in the nineteenth century.

Right, above: These men were the first to pass through the Pennsylvania Railroad tunnels under the Hudson River. The photograph was taken at the Manhattan Shaft on 9 October 1906.

Right, below: This passenger train at the Manhattan transfer represented the latest in 1928 railroad technology: electrification.

Left: The main waiting room of New York City's Pennsylvania Station facing one of the two side entrances. In true Roman style, there were no seats in this vast waiting room.

At top: Travelers wait to meet some of the 109 million people who passed through there in 1945 alone.

Above: The station's spacious lunch counter served many rushed meals in an elegant setting.

The tunnels under the Hudson were first contracted in 1904. On 12 September 1906, several 'sandhogs'—the tunnel worker's popular appellation—from the New York end of a Hudson tube passed cigars to their New Jersey colleagues through a small hole in their respective shields. On 27 November 1910, the station was in full service.

The style of the building partook of the Crystal Palace, with its airy traceries of iron and glass. Both Cassatt and McKim were inspired by the monumental, yet elegant, Roman baths at Caracalla. The magnificent building, when finished, was composed of 15 million bricks, 27,000 tons of steel, and 150,000 cubic yards of concrete, in addition to 550,000 cubic feet of Milford pink granite for ornamentation. The granite was shipped in 1140 freight cars from Massachusetts quarries.

Neither Cassatt nor McKim lived to see the completion of Pennsylvania Station. Cassatt, struggling with failing health, was suddenly confronted with accusations that Pennsy officials were accepting graft money. Cassatt himself was fighting graft in his quest for permits to build the station. On 28 December 1906, Cassatt died, at age 67. McKim died, like so many men of those exciting times, of heart failure, on 14 September 1909.

From 1925 to 1929, passenger revenues fell by some $15 million. Other modes of transportation were making themselves felt, especially the automobile. Pennsy joined forces with the Wright Aeronautical Company, the Curtis Aeroplane and Motor Company, National Aviation Corporation and a banking investment group in New York. Together, they incorporated Transcontinental Air Transport, Inc. By the end of 1932, airplanes were flying 24 hours coast to coast, and the powerful locomotives were suddenly too slow.

Motor trucks were competing for small loads, so Pennsy invested in numerous trucking companies. In 1928, Pennsy bought into several bus companies, among them the future Greyhound Corporation.

When war raged in Europe in 1939, the Pennsy ordered 7000 more freight cars and 80,000 tons of rail. Equipment and road improvements cost the Pennsy almost $235 million. But even these preparations left the railroad unready for the heavy wartime traffic. The federal authorities forbade the building of any passenger cars, yet passenger travel had increased fourfold during the war. Afterward, the improvements made for the contigency of war proved cumbersome. In 1946, the company operated at a deficit for the first time in its 100 year history.

A severe recession in 1957 caused the ailing Pennsy to consider a consolidation with its biggest competitor, the similarly weakened New York Central. It took eleven years for the

picked engineers studied the feasibility of such a plan. Cassatt wanted no repeats of the 1880 disaster.

On 24 April 1902, Cassatt interviewed Charles F McKim, the senior partner of McKim, Mead and White, and accepted his bid of $250,000 to design and oversee construction of the $50 million station. Pennsylvania Station would be nearly twice as big as the Hamburg terminal, then the world's largest, and encompass six city blocks.

Thirty-Second Street between 7th and 10th looked, as one account put it, like the Panama Canal under construction. Twenty-eight acres had been cleared and over 500 buildings had been bought and razed. The excavation went down 58 feet through granite-like gneiss; a coal cart sank into the street in front of the Waldorf Astoria hotel.

Left: The 4-4-4-4 Class T1 locomotive could haul the heaviest passenger trains at over 100 mph, but it came late in the age of steam.

Below: This Pennsy steamer saved time by scooping water on the run from the Pennsy between-rails 'track tanks.'

Right: The great GG-1, a 4-6-2 has been in service from the 1930s until the present decade.

Left: A later model Pennsy passenger electric.

Right: This 1953 Electro-Motive E8 2250 hp diesel wore the keystone logo, the Pennsy's famous Tuscan red paint, and had natty pinstriping.

Below: One of the last locomotives built by Baldwin for the Pennsy—a 2400 hp RT-624 center cab diesel freight engine. Baldwin stopped building locomotives in the mid-1950s.

two giants to combine operations, partially because Pennsy chairman JM Symes couldn't bear to lay to rest the world's most important railroad. Symes had started out as a ticket agent and had always hoped to pass the baton to another true Pennsy man, not throw it in with his railroad's most hated enemy.

The New York Central's chairman, Alfred Perlman, shared Symes' lack of enthusiasm. Afraid that the NYC would be swallowed up by the asset-heavy Pennsy, Perlman postponed negotiations.

In 1962, the Pennsy announced plans to raze Pennsylvania Station in Manhattan, keeping a relatively cheap station underneath and selling the property above for the construction of Madison Square Garden. Symes then announced his retirement, and Stuart Saunders took his place.

Saunders and Perlman could not agree on strategy, tactics or even what this new company would actually be. Besides, they sincerely disliked each other. But in 1968, they reached an uneasy settlement and the Penn Central was given its unfortuitous birth.

The few years of Penn Central's existence was snafu-ridden. After losing $325.8 million in 1970, the Penn Central entered bankruptcy proceedings. Amtrak took over the passenger operations in 1971. The Penn Central exists now solely as an organization dedicated to unsnarling the immense legal tangle produced by its own collapse.

The property was then turned over to a new rail organization, a privately owned company, which would be known as Consolidated Rail Corporation—Conrail.

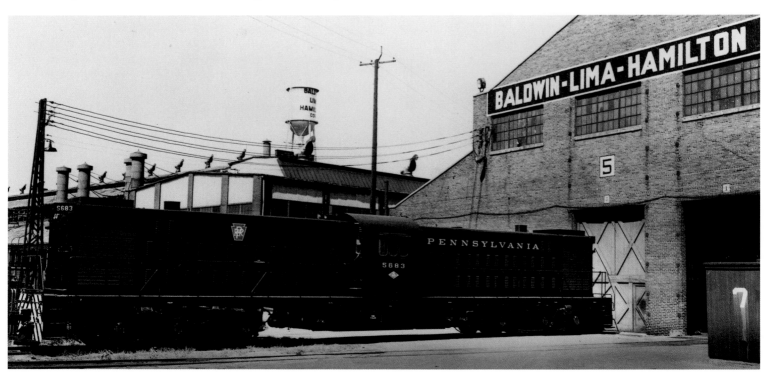

THE ST LOUIS-SAN FRANCISCO

By Bill Yenne

*A*lthough it was known as the 'Frisco,' the St Louis-San Francisco never actually reached its namesake city—San Francisco. In fact, it didn't actually serve St Louis until seven years after it was formed. Its name, however, represented the dreams of its founders, who envisioned it as a link between the mid-South and the Pacific coast.

The story begins—as do most stories involving San Francisco—with the Gold Rush of 1849. Gold was discovered at Sutter's Mill in the Sierra foothills of California in such immense quantity, it caused the greatest internal migration that the United States had yet experienced.

Eager to reach out and touch those gold fields, the Missouri state legislature chartered the Pacific Railroad of Missouri to build a line from St Louis almost due west to the Missouri-Kansas border. At a time when there were no railroads west of the Mississippi, and none had reached it from the east, and despite the avid interest of the legislature, it was July 1851 before work actually began on the Pacific.

Even before the first 37-mile stretch of the Pacific Railroad of Missouri was completed in 1852, the legislature had authorized construction of a branch line to leave the main line at Franklin (now Pacific) and run southwest to Springfield to the border of the Indian Territory (later eastern Oklahoma). The supporters of this line—known as the South-West Branch—believed it would be extended into Indian Territory to the 35th parallel, along which a railroad route to San Francisco was then being surveyed at the behest of Congress, which also had commissioned several other surveys of potential transcontinental routes. However, financial problems that had delayed the start of construction on the Pacific Railroad of Missouri caused a similar delay for the South-West Branch, and it would be June 1855 before construction began on what would become the

nucleus of the Frisco system. Once initiated, work proceeded rapidly, and the onset of the Civil War found the railroad completed to Rolla, about 75 miles southwest of Franklin, but the terminus remained there throughout the war, despite President Abraham Lincoln's interest in further extending the line.

By 1865 both roads were bankrupt, and both were sold to General John C Fremont, the noted California explorer and son-in-law of Missouri Senator Thomas Hart Benton. Benton had been one of the driving forces behind the idea of a transcontinental railroad in general, and specifically behind the projects in which the state of Missouri was interested. With his Washington influence, Fremont was able to obtain a federal franchise and land grant, in the name of his own Atlantic & Pacific Railroad, for extension of the South-West Branch to San Francisco along the 35th parallel survey route.

However, Fremont was considerably less successful in actually laying track, and in 1868, the South Pacific Railroad Company acquired the line from the state of Missouri after Fremont failed to make the first installment of the branch's purchase price. The South Pacific extended the former South-West Branch line to Lebanon in 1869 and through Springfield to Pierce City in 1870. By this time grading was also completed to Seneca on the Indian Territory border.

In 1870 the South Pacific's line came once more under the control of the Atlantic & Pacific, which had retained control of Fremont's St Louis-San Francisco franchise and his land grant, as well as control of the Pacific Railroad of Missouri. Construction then proceeded rapidly. In 1871 the line was completed

Below: This 4-4-0 American was built in 1882 and operated by the St Louis & San Francisco Railway.

beyond Seneca to a junction with the Missouri, Kansas & Texas Railroad's north-south line at Vinita in Indian Territory. However, construction stalled at Vinita as Atlantic & Pacific officers tried to persuade federal officials to abrogate a treaty with the Indians and give the railroad its land grant through the Cherokee Nation. The government sided with the Cherokees in the dispute, and the Atlantic & Pacific's track remained at Vinita until the Panic of 1873 drove the company into bankruptcy in 1875 and postponed resolution of the dispute.

September 1876 saw the final separation of the Pacific Railroad of Missouri from its southwest branch after it was purchased by the newly organized St Louis & San Francisco Railway Company. It was soon permanently nicknamed the 'Frisco.'

Along with the track to Vinita, the Frisco acquired the Atlantic & Pacific's franchise and land grant, and, for a short time, the Golden Gate seemed in sight. The dream might actually have come true, had it not been for the Cherokee tribe, who successfully continued to block survey and construction work on the line.

In 1879 the Atchinson, Topeka & Santa Fe Railway acquired control of the Frisco. Without the hurdle of Indian Territory to overcome, the Santa Fe was able to use the Atlantic & Pacific franchise and most of its land grant to build its own line from Albuquerque to southern California. Indeed, construction of the Santa Fe line in New Mexico and Arizona was paid for in part by the Frisco, and although that effort—useless to the Frisco—drained the Mis-

souri line's finances somewhat, it did provide several extensions in the late 1870s and 1880s to improve its fit into the Santa Fe system.

In the late 1870s the Frisco built a line westward from Pierce City to Wichita to connect with the Santa Fe's main line. During the same period, a number of branches were added in the tri-state lead mining district where Missouri, Kansas and Oklahoma meet. The early 1880s saw the Frisco headed south from Monett, Missouri, with a line through the Boston Mountains of Arkansas to Fort Smith, and thence through the Choctaw Nation to Paris, Texas, where the road connected with the Santa Fe's line to Dallas and Fort Worth.

Numerous other branch lines in Missouri, Oklahoma, Kansas and Arkansas were completed in the 1880s, as well as the 1883 addition of the Frisco's own line from Pacific into St Louis, eliminating the need for trackage rights payments to the Missouri Pacific. Though it would never reach San Francisco, the St Louis-San Francisco finally did reach St Louis—seven years after it was founded!

Although it remained unable to complete its line through Indian Territory, the Frisco was able to extend its trackage from Vinita to Sapulpa, just west of Tulsa, in the early 1880s. The dream of a St Louis-San Francisco transcontinental line had been dashed, but the Frisco had begun developing the western reaches of its system into their final form. Expansion of the Frisco system ground to a halt in the late 1880s, however, and the Frisco was finally swept into bankruptcy along with the Santa Fe in the mid-1890s, and it was reorganized in 1896 as the St Louis & San Francisco Railroad Company.

With reorganization came General BF Yoakum as general manager. He was to serve the Frisco over the next 20 years as general manager, president and chairman of the board, during which time the Frisco would double in size and turn its eyes from the West Coast to the South. Yoakum envisioned a system that would span the central section of the country from Chicago and the Twin Cities to the Gulf of Mexico, and connect the upper Midwest with the Mexican railroad system at the Texas border.

Frisco extended its Oklahoma line from Sapulpa through Oklahoma City to Lawton in the late 1890s, but the real expansion of Yoakum's Frisco came after the turn of the century.

Having turned South, General Yoakum set about building what he hoped would be the region's most comprehensive system. Construction of the Frisco northwest from Wichita to Ellsworth, Kansas came in 1900. So did a connection with the Union Pacific. The same year the Frisco acquired the 147-mile Kansas, Osceola & Southern Railway to provide a link between Kansas City and Springfield. Frisco completed its own line to the Dallas-Fort Worth area in 1901 through construction south from Sapulpa, Oklahoma to Denison, Texas,

and the purchase of a 58-mile line from Sherman to Carrolton, Texas, near Fort Worth. Also added was a 146-mile railroad south from Fort Worth to Brownwood.

Perhaps the key addition of 1901, however, was the long-term lease by the Frisco of the Kansas City, Fort Scott & Memphis Railway Company's line from Kansas City Southeast through Springfield and Memphis to Birmingham, Alabama. Work on this line had begun shortly after the Civil War by the Kansas & Neosho Valley Railroad, which planned a line south from Kansas City through Kansas Indian Territory to the Gulf of Mexico in Texas. Construction had proceeded slowly until 1868, when the Kansas & Neosho Valley's assets (consisting mostly of rather poor grading for a few miles out of Kansas City) were acquired by the Missouri River, Ft Scott & Gulf Railroad.

Octave Chanute, builder of the Hannibal Bridge across the Missouri at Kansas City, became the Kansas & Neosho Valley's chief engineer. Under Chanute, tracks were laid southward rapidly to Oathe in 1868, to Ft Scott in 1869 and to Baxter Springs, on the Indian Territory border, in 1870. However, the Missouri River, Ft Scott & Gulf arrived too late at the border. The Missouri, Kansas & Texas Railroad's line from Kansas City had entered the

ST. Louis & San Francisco Railway.

Territory a few months before, thus winning sole rights as the only north-south railroad permitted across Indian lands.

The Missouri River, Ft Scott & Gulf licked its wounds through the Panic of 1873, until General George H Nettleton arrived to take charge in 1874. Its race for Indian Territory lost, the Missouri River, Ft Scott & Gulf turned southeast and became the Kansas City, Fort Scott & Memphis Railroad.

The Kansas City, Fort Scott & Memphis completed its line to Springfield in 1881 and was operating through trains from Kansas City to Memphis just two years later. After a two-year hiatus at Memphis, the Kansas City, Fort Scott & Memphis finished its line to Birmingham, Alabama in 1887 and built a great bridge, which replaced ferry service, at Memphis in 1892.

General Nettleton died in 1896, his plans for further extension of trackage to the Gulf of Mexico frustrated by the Depression of 1893. Yet the railroad he built fit well into the Frisco system as it began looking south during the Yoakum years.

General Yoakum continued to pursue his vision through the first decade of the twentieth century. The Chicago & Eastern Illinois Railroad was added to the Frisco system, and both were combined with the Rock Island Railroad to form what one writer called 'a railroad principality.' In 1902 Yoakum added the St Louis,

Memphis & Southeastern Railroad's line down the west bank of the Mississippi from St Louis to Memphis, planning to extend that line down the west bank all the way to New Orleans. In 1904 he added a 233-mile line from Ardmore, Oklahoma to Hope, Arkansas, with the ultimately unfulfilled expectation of extending it west to Colorado and east to connect with the west-bank line somewhere south of Memphis.

Throughout this decade of rapid expansion through acquisition, Yoakum collected short feeder lines the way some people collect bottle caps. These included networks of branches in southeastern Missouri and northeastern Arkansas, addditonal branches in Oklahoma and Missouri, as well as longer feeder lines from Salpulpa through Enid to Avard, Oklahoma, and south from Blackwell, Oklahoma to Vernon, Texas.

Although his tracks along the west bank had yet to be built, General Yoakum added, through construction or control, other trackage from New Orleans west along the Gulf Coast to Mexico, and in central Texas between Dallas-Fort Worth and the Gulf Coast lines.

Railroad track was not the only thing built under Yoakum. A new 13-story headquarters office building went up at the corner of Ninth and Olive streets in downtown St Louis, and the largest railroad shop complex west of the Mis-

Above: A Rogers 4-6-0 Ten-Wheeler of the St Louis & San Francisco Railway built in the 1880s.

under federal government control. This disasterous experiment with nationalization came to an end in 1920, and the Frisco was returned to private ownership.

The post-war boom years saw more rebuilding of the Frisco under president JM Kum. New locomotives were purchased, passenger and freight car fleets were upgraded and new train schedules were established.

However, the most ambitious undertaking of the 1920s was construction of a link near Amory, Mississippi on Frisco's Memphis-Birmingham main line, to the Gulf of Mexico at Pensacola, Florida, at last fulfilling the dream of General Nettleton by linking his road to tidewater. It began in 1925 with the purchase of 155 miles of track between Pensacola and Kimbrough, Alabama from the Muscle Shoals, Birmingham & Pensacola Railroad. The Frisco filled in the gap between Kimbrough and its main line with new construction in 1927 and 1928, and the new line was opened with a grand excursion in the summer of 1928. In 1929, on the eve of the Great Depression, the Frisco had 880 locomotives, 669 passenger cars and 34,009 freight cars operating over 5735 miles of main line.

Elation at the Pensacola extension was short-lived, as the Frisco plunged into bankruptcy in 1933, after being hard hit by the Great Depression. No stranger to hard times, the Frisco struggled through the grim years of the Depression by constant economy measures, including abandonment of many of the unnecessary miles of branch lines built during the country's earlier bout of 'railroad fever.'

Survive it did, and the Frisco was there when the nation called again at the beginning of World War II. The closing of the East Coast sea lanes by German U-boats put oceans of Texas and Oklahoma oil onto Frisco rails for movement eastward. The Frisco responded to the challenge by ordering its first new locomotives since the onset of the Depression, and by rebuilding a number of slow freight locomotives into powerful ones fast enough to handle the demands of wartime traffic.

The railroad completed its 14-year reorganization in 1947 and Clark Hungerford was elected president of the Frisco. Under his direction, a railroad battered by the Depression and strained by wartime traffic began rebuilding itself, while setting new traffic records. With a flourish, the Frisco unveiled streamlined, diesel-powered versions of its *Texas Special* and *Meteor* passenger trains in 1947, and it began ordering diesel freight locomotives the next year.

Near the end of 1948 Frisco acquired control of the Alabama, Tennessee & Northern Railroad. Its line from Reform to Mobile, Alabama gave the Frisco access to its second Gulf port, connecting with the rest of the Frisco system at

sissippi was built at Springfield to care for the locomotives, and the freight and passenger cars of the expanding Frisco system.

General Yoakum's dream was well on its way to becoming reality when the Depression of 1913 turned it into a nightmare. The Frisco and Rock Island went into bankruptcy, and their relationship was dissolved. The Chicago & Eastern Illinois was disengaged from the Frisco to go its own way, and the Gulf Coast trackage and the Texas lines south of Fort Worth also were split from the Frisco system. The west-bank line would never be extended south of Memphis.

The Frisco came out of reorganization with its final corporate name—the St Louis-San Francisco Railway Company—and a new president, WC Nixon.

WC Nixon's strategy for the St Louis-San Francisco Railway Company was to develop the assets that it had rather than to indulge in the feverish empire-building of the Yoakum years. He also worked hard with the remnants of Yoakum's dream by sprucing up passenger service. In 1917, for example, the Frisco joined with the Missouri-Kansas-Texas (Katy) line to operate the great *Texas Special* passenger liner.

Nixon's plans to create a leaner, more solvent Frisco were delayed when the United States entered World War I and the Frisco, along with the rest of the United States rail system, came

Aliceville. The Frisco also built a new freight yard and diesel shop at Springfield, the hub of its system. Once begun, dieselization continued rapidly. The last steam locomotive was operated on 28 February 1952, making the Frisco the first major American railroad to become exclusively diesel-powered. In 1956 the Frisco acquired Central Railway of Georgia, but the ICC compelled it to sell out to the Southern Railway in 1961.

Modernization of the Frisco continued throughout the 1950s. Electronic hump yards were opened at Memphis in 1957 and at Tulsa in 1960. The Frisco also began work on a way to recapture automobile traffic from the trucking industry. That work resulted in the development of the tri-level auto rack car. Now used by railroads nationwide, it was responsible for the rail industry's recapturing a share of the burgeoning automobile and truck transportation market.

Clark Hungerford was succeeded as president by Louis W Menk in 1962. Menk relocated the bulk of the railroad's offices from St Louis to Springfield in 1964 and laid the groundwork for the consolidation of all Frisco train dispatching from one suite of offices at Springfield in 1965. It was the first—and remains the largest—such installation in the country.

Louis Menk moved to head the Northern Pacific, and JE Gilliand was elected president in 1965. The following year the Chicago, Burlington & Quincy acquired a large block of Frisco stock. This block was inherited by Burlington Northern in 1970 and eventually led to Burlington Northern's acquisiton of the Frisco. Meanwhile, Menk presided over the first new construction by the Frisco since the 1920s, which involved the 32.7-mile Lead Belt Line from Keyesville on the Salem Branch to Buick, Missouri, to serve a newly opened lead-mining area in south central Missouri.

Below: *No 1062 is a Bald-win 4-6-4 Hudson built in the 1920s.*

Above: *The* Firefly, *one of the Frisco's streamlined passenger trains.*

Above, left: Frisco No 290, an ALCO switcher.

Above: This GE U30B XR (Extra Reliability) series road switcher has a 3000 hp, 16-cylinder engine.

Left: Four new GE U25B heavy locomotives. The U25B was a 2500-hp road switcher with a number of significant design innovations which led GE to capture ALCO's number two market spot. GM-EMD holds the top position.

By the mid-1960s the Frisco, like all other American railroads, was suffering from lack of passenger business, which had begun to taper off two decades before. Gone was the great *Texas Special*, gone was the *Meteor* and gone were the great streamliners. In September 1965 the Frisco sharply reduced its passenger service, and two years later ended it altogether, on 8 December 1967, when trains 101 and 102 completed their runs between Kansas City and Birmingham.

By the time Richard C Grayson succeeded Gilliand as president in 1969, the Frisco was gaining a reputation as a leader in the development of new shipping techniques. In the 1970s the Frisco went through yet another period of rebuilding and modernization of its plant and equipment.

In 1977, the Frisco applied to the Interstate Commerce Commission for a merger with the Chicago, Burlington & Quincy, which was now a major component of the Burlington Northern. At the time of the merger, the Frisco was operating 431 locomotives and 17,392 freight cars, half of what it had in 1929, over 4653 miles of main line, which was 81 percent of its 1929 total. The merger went into effect on 21 November 1980, adding to the Burlington Northern system not only a strategically located railroad, but a long and proud tradition as well.

THE SOUTHERN PACIFIC

By Bill Yenne

During the 1860s, the building of the transcontinental railroad consumed most of the attention of the Big Four—Leland Stanford, Mark Hopkins, Collis Huntington and Charles Crocker. However, they were also busy putting together an empire within California. The Sacramento Valley Rail Road that Theodore Judah completed in 1856 was only the first of many. A number of other railroads were chartered in California in the decade following the start-up of the SVRR, and many of these were actually built. It was toward these that the Big Four turned when their vision shifted to expansion.

One of the major railroads in the state eyed covetously by the Big Four was the San Francisco & San Jose, which had begun service between the two cities in 1864. Because San Francisco is located at the northern end of a peninsula, any attempt to link it by rail to Sacramento in the northeast (and hence to the nation) would necessarily have to be via San Jose to the south.

Another road of interest to the four associates in Sacramento existed largely on paper, but owned the land grants to build south from San Francisco and San Jose to Los Angeles and San Diego. This road, which had been organized in 1865 by some of the same San Francisco financiers who had earlier turned down participation in the Central Pacific, was the original Southern Pacific Railroad.

The Southern Pacific received notice from Congress on 27 July 1866 that it would be the western link of a second transcontinental line then under consideration. On 4 February 1868, the Southern Pacific bought the San Francisco & San Jose Railroad coveted by the Big Four, and in August 1868, Southern Pacific president Timothy Guy Phelps announced his intention to start building a line south to San Diego, where it would then turn east to the California line and on to the Mississippi River.

On 25 September 1869, the Big Four purchased the Southern Pacific. The following year, the Central and Southern Pacific operations were merged, although a full merger did not take place for another 15 years, at which time the operations of the entire network came under the Southern Pacific name.

As the decade of the 1860s ended and the 1870s began, the Big Four owned the beginnings of the network of steel that would ultimately turn California into an economic powerhouse. They owned the Central Pacific, that crossed the state at its midsection. They owned the Yuba Railroad, that ran into northern California from Sacramento, and their Central Pacific spur was being built south from Sacramento into the rich San Joaquin Valley. The four owned a San Francisco connection, with lines of the Southern Pacific, which they built to the south as originally planned. It was the start of what Frank Norris would call 'the octopus' in his less than complimentary 1901 novel of the same name.

While some saw the empire built by the Big Four as a vicious 'iron-hearted' monster that stifled economic development and political reform in California through graft and corruption, it was also a creator of jobs and a provider of the transportation needed to develop the state's awesome agricultural potential. By 1870, after two decades of gold rush, the mining industry dissipated. The boom towns became ghost towns as family farms replaced miners' dreams of finding the mother lode.

The railroads helped to create the potential for basic changes in the fabric of life. Just a few years earlier, a man coming to California faced months of hardship just getting there, and he almost certainly left his family behind. In 1870, he could bring his family to the Golden State in less than a week. The Central Pacific encouraged such immigration by offering low passenger fares and by selling off parts of its

government land grants at reasonable rates to settlers. The Central Pacific/Southern Pacific also developed marketing programs and devoted their resources to encourage immigration. The men picked to head these programs clearly had the state's best interests at heart. Southern Pacific's first chief land agent, Benjamin Redding, was a former Secretary of State, a patron of the Academy of Sciences and regent of the University of California. His successor, William Mills, who served from 1883 to 1907, was an agriculture reformer, a leader of the antihydraulic mining movement and served on the Yosemite Park Commission. In fact, the Southern Pacific was one of the biggest promoters of bringing Sequoia and Yosemite into the national park system.

Land agent Mills was also a leading proponent of agricultural diversity. With the support of the Big Four, he promoted the use of a variety of specialty crops to maximize the advantage of California's many climatic regions. As a result, the San Joaquin Valley became one of the rich-

est agricultural areas in the world. As C P Huntington observed, 'The many advantages of climate and soil which the state of California offers settlers are becoming better known each year.'

Popular notion has it that the railroads of the West, particularly the Southern Pacific, held on to their government land grants for the purpose of speculation. Generally speaking, the opposite was true. The Big Four could see more value in allowing the land to be owned at reasonable cost by people who would settle it and ultimately use the Southern Pacific to transport their products.

With their base firmly grounded in San Francisco, the Big Four spread their empire throughout the state. By 1873, the year that Southern Pacific headquarters were established in San Francisco, rails had been laid as far north as Redding. Construction of the Central Pacific's San Joaquin Valley Line (originally the San Joaquin Valley Rail Road) had laid out such cities as Fresno and had pushed as far south as

Previous page: Three road switchers pull a piggyback freight train.

Above: A 4-4-0 American locomotive, No 10, of Southern Pacific at Monterey, California.

Below: Section men turning out for work on the building of the Southern Pacific line in the Tehachapi Mountains just north of Los Angeles during 1875.

At bottom: A stage coach of the old 'Pioneer Line' meeting a passenger train of the Southern Pacific.

Delano, while Southern Pacific's Coast Line had reached Soledad.

In November 1874, Southern Pacific reached Bakersfield, and its engineers, under chief engineer Bill Hood, designed the Tehachapi Loop to conquer the last mountainous obstacle on the route south to Los Angeles, the City of the Angels. As crews attacked the Tehachapi Mountains from the north, other crews were building the Southern Pacific line out of Los Angeles. On 5 September 1876 at Palmdale, in a scene reminiscent of the one at Promontory, Utah, five years before, Charlie Crocker drove a golden spike, and the Golden State was

united from north to south. A Southern Pacific train, bound from San Francisco, reached Los Angeles the same day. Fulfilling the dream of Southern Pacific's original founders, the Big Four immediately turned east from Los Angeles, reaching the Colorado River across from Fort Yuma, Arizona in May 1877. Yuma was an important linchpin in their grand design to defeat Tom Scott's Texas Pacific Railroad in the race for the domination of the Southwest. The Big Four also continued to expand their empire by purchasing smaller railroads. In 1876, they bought the California Pacific, which had been operating a line between Sacramento and Benicia, a city near the point where the Sacramento River enters the San Francisco Bay. The line was particularly valuable because it was level, without complicating hills or grades. The California Pacific also operated a ferry from South Vallejo near Benicia down to Oakland, where the Big Four already dominated ferry service across the bay to San Francisco.

By 1884, the empire consisted of no less than every mile of standard-gauge railroad in the state of California, a 4711-mile system radiating from the bustling San Francisco yards to the far corners of the state, and 800 miles beyond. By the same year, the Central Pacific itself, nearly broke when the last spike was driven at Promontory, had grossed $277 million, with a profit of roughly $37 million.

The Golden State of California may have been the keystone of the Southern Pacific, but it was only part of the empire, an empire that stretched from the Pacific to the southwestern deserts of Arizona and New Mexico, across the great state of Texas, and all the way to New

Orleans and the mouth of the Mississippi. To the north, the empire extended into Oregon and came to dominate the rails of that state. The first company steel reached the Colorado River leading eastward toward Texas in 1877, but Texas already had a railroad infrastructure with a history predating the rails in California.

In 1877, Yuma was nothing more than a dusty, little desert town in Arizona, adjacent to the US Cavalry's Fort Yuma. But to the great railroad barons, it was much more; it was Waterloo, and Huntington was Wellington. Due to a series of events, Yuma was lifted from obscurity to become the site of a turning point in railroad history that allowed western railroads to expand as they did.

It was the cornerstone of Tom Scott's dream for his Texas Pacific, but he was still 1200 miles away in May 1877 when the Southern Pacific arrived on the western banks of the Colorado River. Some of the Southern Pacific men crossed the river to Yuma on the Arizona side, armed with a generous supply of whiskey which they proposed to share with the cavalry troopers at Fort Yuma. The cavalry's job was to protect Arizona from the Apaches—and from incursions by railroad companies that did not have a land grant to build a railroad into Arizona.

The initial toasts turned into a bout of merrymaking that lasted nearly a week. By that time, a wooden bridge spanned the Colorado. Southern Pacific was already laying rails when the cavalry troops were finally able to shake off enough of the whiskey to stop the railroad

men. Popular opinion in southwest Arizona, however, was vociferously supportive of having a railroad service the area. The Arizona Legislature backed the populace, as did Army Chief of Staff General William Tecumseh Sherman in Washington. Huntington went to work on President Rutherford B Hayes, who was at last persuaded to sign an executive order on 9 October 1877, authorizing Southern Pacific access to Arizona. The battle of Yuma had been won without firing a shot.

By the time Mark Hopkins died in his private car outside Yuma in March 1878, Southern Pacific tracks had been laid across the Arizona desert for nearly nine months. The second transcontinental line was called the Sunset route; it was all Southern Pacific, from the Mississippi delta to the Pacific coast. Building east from Yuma, Southern Pacific crews arrived in Tucson on 20 March 1880. By 19 May 1891, the railroad had crossed both Arizona and New Mexico and had reached El Paso, Texas. At the same time, the Southern Pacific's Galveston, Harrisburg & San Antonio subsidiary began building westward from San Antonio.

On 12 January 1883, the two lines met on the west bank of the Pecos River, 227 miles from San Antonio, and the last spike was driven by Colonel Tom Pierce, the GH&SA president. The first train from New Orleans arrived in San Antonio on 6 February, and the first train from Los Angeles the next day. CP Huntington, in the meantime, had acquired the Louisiana & Texas Railroad & Steamship Company from

Left: Southern Pacific's No 49 in the Monterey yard, 1881.

Right: Built in 1884 at the request of Leland Stanford, **El Gobernador** *was the largest locomotive in the world, weighing in at 73 tons unloaded.*

Below: The CP Huntington, *Central Pacific's third locomotive, was later renumbered as Southern Pacific No 1 and is now preserved in the California State Railroad Museum.*

Charles Morgan. This not only provided the last link in the Southern Pacific line, connecting Los Angeles to new Orleans, but it gave the company access to eastern ports by means of Morgan steamships. Sunset Route passengers were then able to travel from Los Angeles to New Orleans by rail and on to New York, enjoying '100 golden hours at sea,' as the advertising copy read. The steamship link continued to be an important adjunct to the Sunset Route for more than half a century, until it was permanently discontinued during World War II.

Oregon Territory became the state of Oregon in 1859, making it the second state after California to be established in the Far West. It was only natural, some thought, that the two states should be connected by rail. The Central Pacific was in its fourth year of operation in 1865 when citizens of the city of Marysville, 52 miles north of Sacramento, founded the California & Oregon Railroad to build a line north to Portland, Oregon. Construction began, but the company experienced difficulties, and it was sold and resold several times before being incorporated into the Central Pacific network in 1870.

In Oregon, Ben Holladay, who had made a fortune in the stagecoach business before selling out to Wells Fargo in 1866, became involved in a scheme to build a railroad south from Portland. The Oregon Central Railroad Company was formed, and on 26 October 1869 construction began. By completing 20 miles before Christmas, the line qualified for a federal subsidy, which allowed it to forge southward through the Willamette Valley. The

Oregon Central reached Oregon's capital, Salem, on 29 September 1870, in time to carry visitors to the state fair. The railroad arrived in Eugene a year later and in Roseburg by the end of 1872.

As Holladay pushed his railroad through the Oregon backwoods, he continued to sell bonds to supplement his federal aid and to hope that demand would arise for the service he had established. The demand for a railroad in this remote part of Oregon simply didn't materialize, and Holladay's bondholders, mostly German industrialists, seized the company. They turned it over to Henry Villard, who had a proven record of service with the Oregon Railway & Navigation Company. Villard's first move

Below: Built by the Vulcan Iron Works in San Francisco in 1862, the Cascade Railroad's Ann *is shown at Scio, Oregon, working for the Oregon & California. The engine saw later use by the Southern Pacific during branch line construction in Oregon.*

Below, left: Main and Front streets in Medford, Oregon, during the 1880s. The structure to the left is the first SP station.

Above: An early 4-4-0 locomotive built for the Oregon & California Railroad.

Right: One of the first locomotives on the railroad between Cascade Locks and Bonneville, this engine was built in 1862 and was the same type as the Oregon Pony with a flat car body cab and a rear truck.

was to suggest to the Big Four in 1876 that they merge their California & Oregon with his Oregon Central (then Oregon & California). The four were interested, but feigned disinterest, waiting for Villard's next move. Having achieved nothing, Villard began building south from Roseburg in 1881, nine years after Holladay halted construction. He reached Ashland, just short of the California border, in 1884. However, the railroad, its financing exhausted, went bankrupt the same year.

To the south, the Big Four had constructed no new California & Oregon tracks since the line had reached Redding in 1872. In 1887, three years after it failed, the Oregon & California finally joined the California & Oregon as part of the Southern Pacific system. Construction resumed immediately on the tracks across the Siskiyou Mountains north of Redding. They reached Ashland by year's end, and on 17 December 1887, Charles Crocker came north from San Francisco to drive the last spike of Southern Pacific's new Siskiyou line. The company thus had a continuous arc of steel linking Oregon, California, Arizona, New Mexico, Texas and Louisiana. A traveler could buy a ticket from a single company and travel from the mouth of the Columbia to the mouth of the Mississippi.

In 1888, Southern Pacific consolidated the railroad shops of two of its Texas subsidiaries, the GH&SA and the Texas & New Orleans Rail-

Below: The first train into Santa Barbara, California, on 19 August 1887 was the occasion for a big civic celebration. Most of the town's population was on hand to greet the train.

Right: This old 4-4-0 SP locomotive was built in 1888 and was scrapped in 1912.

Below, right: A group of Southern Pacific workers assemble outside the Sacramento Shops in 1889.

road. The resulting facility at Houston employed 5000 people and constituted the largest such facility in the entire Southwest, indicative of the enormous proportions to which the Southern Pacific had grown.

In the 20 years leading up to CP Huntington's 1890 ascendancy within Southern Pacific, the company had grown from a mere component of the first transcontinental line, with a nearly empty bank box, to a giant network that dominated California and covered more territory than any other railroad on the continent.

Within California, the company's power was so great that its offices in San Francisco had become the de facto capital of the state. Because it controlled California's transportation network, many perceived it as controlling the state itself. The phrase, 'The Southern Pacific is the state of California,' was coined. The state's people and her politicians lined up on either side of the issue of whether or not this power was wielded in the best interests of the state. While some saw the company as an important element of agricultural and industrial development, others saw it only as a greedy monster, exploiting rather than developing California's resources. Some politicians ran on platforms built on the latter idea, and others were willing to support the Southern Pacific with or without renumeration. There is little doubt that the Big Four bought the services of judges and legislators during the final

quarter of the nineteenth century, but this would not have happened were those services not for sale.

Collis Huntington assumed Southern Pacific's presidency in 1890 after 29 years as vice president and at least five years as the company's de facto president. He had spent most of those years in New York, where he made the deals and arranged the financing that kept the Southern Pacific afloat in its early days and made it vastly wealthy in later years. During that time, his personal fortune did not suffer either. In the year that he took over the presidency, the *New York World* reckoned him to be the sixth wealthiest man in the United States after John D Rockefeller, William Astor, Cornelius and William Vanderbilt and his archrival, Jay Gould.

Estimated at $40 million, the fortune Huntington controlled from his small office at 23 Broad Street included his interest not only in the Southern Pacific, but in a number of other endeavors as well. He had taken control of the Chesapeake & Ohio Railroad and several lesser railroads from Kentucky to Mexico. He owned the Newport News Shipbuilding Company at the mouth of Chesapeake Bay, and the Pacific Mail Steamship Company, that sailed from San Francisco Bay.

Collis Huntington, the last surviving member of the Big Four, died at Raquette Lake, New York, on 13 August 1900, having seen in a new century and succeeded during his final years in

forestalling repayment of the Central Pacific's original federal construction loan. His fortune went to his widow and nephew (who eventually married one another), his fabulous art collection went to the Metropolitan Museum in New York, his effects went to the Huntington Library in Southern California and the presidency of Southern Pacific went to Edward Henry Harriman.

The man who took control of the Southern Pacific a year after Huntington's death proved to be as competent a railroad man as he was a financier. Edward Henry Harriman had been buying and selling railroads since 1884, but had risen to prominence in 1897 when he took over the bankrupt Union Pacific and turned a profit in less than three years.

When Huntington died, he was temporarily succeeded as president by Charles Hays, but Harriman's eye was on the chair. Having just restored the Union Pacific to health, Harriman mortgaged it for $100 million and began buying Southern Pacific stock. In a year's time, he owned 45 percent of railroad, and a month later, in September 1901, he assumed the presidency. Unlike many of the railroad barons of the era who bought and sold railroads as though they were any other type of bauble, Harriman had a distinct interest in, and understanding of, railroading.

Harriman ordered an extensive refurbishment of the Southern Pacific. The improvements included straightening curves and rebuilding worn sections of track, such as the entire section of the transcontinental across Nevada that was replaced in 1902. The most spectacular bit of curve-straightening undertaken during this era was the construction of the Lucin Cutoff, a 16-mile, rock-filled causeway and 12-mile wooden trestle across the northern end of the Great Salt Lake. When the original tracks were laid in 1869, the company was in a race with the Union Pacific and had detoured around the northern perimeter of the lake. The Lucin Cutoff, completed in 1903, reduced the distance from California to Ogden by 44 miles. Ironically, the section north of the lake, which was then just a siding, included Promontory, the site of the original golden spike ceremony. Thus the site that had seen the historic meeting of the Central Pacific and the Union Pacific was deleted from the main line.

The years between 1900 and 1917 saw tremendous growth in the West. The infrastructure laid down by the Southern Pacific and other railroads in the preceding years provided a framework for both agricultural and industrial development. Despite the services it performed and the public support it received, the Southern Pacific became a favorite target of

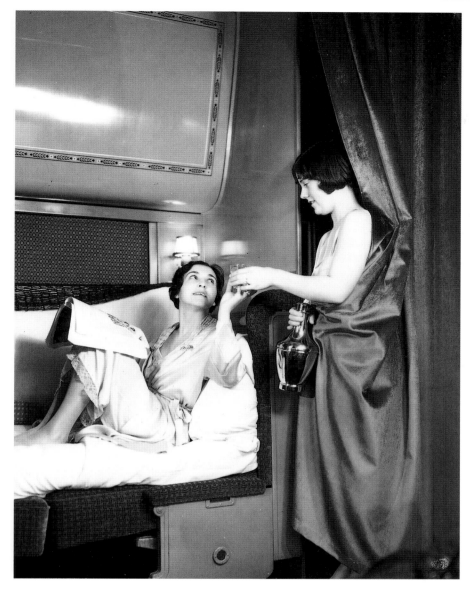

Above, left: In 1930, the Golden State Limited, *one of SP's finest passenger trains, made the Chicago-to-Los Angeles transit in 61 hours. By 1948 the* Golden State, *the* Limited's *successor, would complete the route in 45 hours.*

Left: SP passenger trains offered a special children's menu that allows girls and boys to order meals in a grown-up fashion.

Above: Sleeping compartments such as this one were quite comfortable. The curtain afforded the occupant privacy and minimized external sound and light.

zealous crusaders and issue-hungry politicians. Hiram Johnson was elected Governor of California in 1910 on a platform of driving the company out of state politics. The federal government had asked the Southern Pacific to save the Imperial Valley, and when the task was accomplished, it responded by trying to break up the company. Ultimately, the company survived these adversities while continuing to bring taxpayers into the western states and generating jobs that sparked true economic growth. New tracks were laid on old routes and additional routes enlarged the existing network. New lines were added to the system both north and south of San Francisco.

Edward Harriman died on 9 September 1909 and was succeeded as president by Robert Lovett, who served for two years until he was replaced by William Sproule in 1911. The company's general offices, destroyed in the 1906 earthquake, were re-established on Market Street near Powell, where they remained pending completion of the new Southern Pacific Building at the foot of Market Street overlooking the Ferry Building and San Francisco Bay.

Completion of the huge, red-brick Southern Pacific Building at 65 Market Street in San Francisco in 1917 marked the beginning of a new era in the company's history. The age of the pioneers was gone, as were all the great nineteenth century industrialists who had built the largest spread of railroad trackage in the United States. The business at hand had turned from building an empire to running a railroad. The Southern Pacific had entered the twentieth century.

The grand opening of the new symbol of Southern Pacific's power took place against the backdrop of the twentieth century's first great war, the first major conflict to affect the United States since the Civil War more than half a century earlier. The United States entered World War I in April, and the Southern Pacific was called upon to increase its capacity dramatically almost overnight. The nation's entire rail network was soon doing double duty, transporting men and supplies to embarkation points on the East and Gulf coasts. The problem of integrating the dozens of railroads in the country proved insurmountable for the federal government. Washington decided that Southern Pacific was the best-equipped entity to manage the war effort of the American railroad system, and on 28 December 1971, the railroads were nationalized. For 26 months thereafter, until 1 March 1920, the Southern Pacific was a government employee. Both the government and the railroads learned from the experience—and from the enormous, frustrating rail traffic jams that ensued through 1918. The railroads saw the need for more sidings and larger yards to cope with such an emergency, and the government learned that railroads are best run by railroad companies.

The decade that followed the return of the railroads to private ownership was an era of expansion for the entire American economy, particularly that of the West, where California's population grew by 65 percent. For the Southern Pacific, profits grew steadily. In 1922, the *Prosperity Special*, a train consisting of 20 brand-new Baldwin locomotives, crossed the country to join the Southern Pacific's growing fleet.

The 1920s had been good for Southern Pacific. Net profits had increased 55 percent, from $31.2 million in 1922 to an all-time high of $48.4 million in 1929. With the sudden onset of the Depression, net profits plummeted to $29.8 million in 1930 and to $3.9 million in 1931, just eight percent of the 1929 net. The following year, 1932, was the lowest point of the Depression. Southern Pacific lost money for the first time in its history and missed a dividend for the first time since 1905, the year of the Imperial Valley flood. The railroad's revenue ton-miles had dropped by half since 1929—the greatest decline in company history. The $9.5 million loss in 1932 was followed by a $9.3 million loss in 1933. It was 1936 before the company managed to struggle out of red ink to turn a profit of $11.2 million.

It was in the darkest hour, 1932, that Angus David McDonald came to the helm of Southern Pacific. A quiet, serious, former football player from Notre Dame who had joined the company in 1901, McDonald walked daily from his Nob Hill home down to the company's headquarters at the foot of Market Street. There he grappled with difficult decisions and made the necessary cuts in maintenance and manpower that ultimately saved the company.

As Angus McDonald pulled the company out of the Depression, it regained the vitality of its halcyon days. Profits were low at first, but they began slowly growing at a healthy rate. The cuts that McDonald had been forced to make in 1932 had been deep, but most of the company's muscle was intact. As the Depression waned in late 1937, the company was in an enviable financial position.

Southern Pacific was the third largest industrial corporation in the United States, exceeded by only AT&T and the then-gargantuan Pennsylvania Railroad. The San Francisco-based corpora-

tion exceeded in size such giants as General Motors, US Steel, all of the Standard Oil companies and the New York Central Railroad. Its 16,000 miles of track spread farther and wider than those of any other railroad in the United States. By virtue of owning the Morgan Steamship Line out of New Orleans, Southern Pacific was the nation's only coast-to-coast system.

In terms of passenger revenue, the company was by far the West's largest railroad in 1937, and was nearly tied for third place nationally. Passenger miles, however, accounted for only 12 percent of the company's revenues; freight was king. Southern Pacific carried 65 percent of the nation's copper ore, 33 percent of its watermelons and 22 percent of its logs. By 1937, the company operated 36,646 refrigerator cars, which were monitored by telegraph so that they could be diverted en route if the owner of their contents found a better market for his produce.

Another jewel in the Southern Pacific crown was an 87 percent controlling interest in a new subsidiary, the St Louis Southwestern Railroad, or Cotton Belt, which Southern Pacific acquired in 1932 during the depths of the Depression. The Cotton Belt was an elaborate

Right: This photo from 29 September 1924 shows a 200-ton crane lifting a 2-10-0 Decapod locomotive in SP's Los Angeles repair shops.

Below: The men perched on top of this engine reveal the true size of a powerful steam locomotive. It is not unusual for an engine to weigh 315,000 pounds.

network of lines that extended from Missouri to Texas and Louisiana, where it intersected the tentacles of Southern Pacific's Sunset Route. Begun in the heart of the cotton country a half century before, the Cotton Belt had finally reached St Louis in 1903 (in time for the World's Fair), and crossed the Mississippi River into Memphis in 1912.

The first scheduled ferry service on San Francisco Bay began in 1850. Within a few years of its inception, the ferryboat activity on the Bay—almost entirely between San Francisco and Oakland—had become a competition largely between James Larue and Charles Minturn. In 1865, Larue sold his boats to Central Pacific, which continued to compete with Minturn between San Francisco and Oakland. In 1866, Minturn moved his operation to the north end of the Bay, where he began what eventually became the ferry portion of the Northwestern Pacific, a line which in turn became a Southern Pacific subsidiary in 1929. By 1930, under Southern Pacific control, the ferryboat system on the Bay was the largest in the world, with 43 Southern Pacific ferries carrying 40 million passengers and 60 million automobiles annually.

The Central Pacific, and later the Southern Pacific, operated the ferryboat fleets from San Francisco's Ferry Building, whose clock tower is still a major landmark at the foot of Market Street. From Market Street, the ferries crossed to the city of Alameda, adjacent to Oakland, where passengers boarded trains for points east and south. Travelers from Sacramento boarded ferryboats at Benicia for the final leg of their trip to Oakland or San Francisco. On 28 December 1879, the company began service from Benicia with the huge ferry *Solano*, a boat large enough to carry an entire train.

The year 1936 was Southern Pacific's first profitable year since the onset of the Depression, but for the ferry system it was the beginning of the end: the year the San Francisco-Oakland Bay Bridge was opened to automobile traffic. The Bay Bridge proved to be a fast, convenient alternative to the ferry. A year later, the Golden Gate Bridge was completed, linking San Francisco to Marin County to the north. While the service to the east side of the Bay continued on a smaller scale until 1958, service to Marin County ended on 28 February 1941 with the last run of the *Eureka* from Sausalito to San Francisco.

Left: A cab-ahead 2-8-8-2 Mallet No 4034 with the smaller CP Huntington. The wood burner was Central Pacific's third locomotive and later was renumbered as SP's No 1.

Below: Engine 5000 is a 4-10-2 Overland-type locomotive, typical of the SP's motive power in the late 1930s.

In anticipation of the Bay Bridge's construction, Southern Pacific had arranged during the 1930s to operate an electric commuter train line between San Francisco and Oakland via the bridge's lower deck. The Southern Pacific Interurban Electric Railway Company began service from a terminal at Mission and Fremont streets in San Francisco when the bridge opened in 1936. This subsidiary did not live up to the expectations of Southern Pacific, and in July 1941 the Interurban Electric was sold to the Key Route—ironically, a former rival in the ferryboat business. The Key Route rails were eventually removed from the lower deck, which was then modified for use by automobiles.

By 1951, only six of the one-time 43-ship fleet of ferryboats remained in service on San Francisco Bay. The automobile ferries *El Paso*, *Klamath* and *Russian River* operated between Richmond and San Rafael at the north and over the Bay, while *Berkeley*, *Eureka* and *Sacramento* operated between the San Francisco Ferry Building and Oakland. *Stockton* and *Fresno* were sold to the Washington State ferry system as *Klickatat* and *Willapa*, while

Yosemite sailed 9000 miles to Buenos Aires to become *Argentine*, in service between Argentina and Uruguay. The six boats still in service on the Bay became four, then two; after 1958, there were none.

As the major railroad over most of the Far West, the Southern Pacific developed many pieces of specialized equipment to meet its unique requirements on its vast and varied rail network.

Among the most important of these were the cab-ahead (also called cab-forward or cab-in-front) locomotives. They had their genesis in two enormous 2-8-8-2 Class MC-1 (Mallet Consolidated) steam locomotives delivered to the Southern Pacific by the Baldwin Locomotive Works in 1909. These locomotives (serial numbers *4000* and *4001*) weighed 197 tons on 16 huge driving wheels, and were powered by two 26-inch, high-pressure cylinders that received steam directly from a single oil-fired boiler and exhausted it directly into two 40-inch, low-pressure cylinders. The engines of these articulated locomotives were designed by Samuel Vauclain at the Baldwin Works, and were based on the articulated compound

Above, left: Southern Pacific's most famous passenger train, the Coast Daylight. *One of the general service locomotives (class GS-2 through GS-4), the* Daylight *ran between San Francisco and Los Angeles.*

Above: The last Daylight *in existence, No 4449, was repainted in its authentic color scheme for a ceremonial run between Portland, Oregon and New Orleans in honor of the 1984 World's Fair.*

Left: During World War II, the SP serviced more military installations and embarkation points than any other road in the United States.

expansion engines developed in France by Anatole Mallet (1837-1919). The Mallet-type locomotives had been in use all over the world, and Southern Pacific's first Mallets were the first 2-8-8-2s to be built in the United States.

Engines *4000* and *4001*, articulated to handle curves better, exceeded expectations, handling 1200 tons over the Sierra at 10 mph, while using less fuel and water than earlier locomotives. The major drawback to these incredibly powerful machines, however, was the tremendous heat and concentration of foul gases pulled back into the cab by the 100-foot engine. Ventilation was a problem in the miles of tunnels and snowsheds on the Sierra line, so air was pumped into the cab from the air brakes. Although the engineer could then breathe, he still had the 750-degree F exhaust temperatures to deal with.

The idea that evolved was to turn the locomotive around; the cab, which was normally at the rear, would point ahead. The tender was then moved to the rear, and the cab-ahead locomotive was born. Southern Pacific was the first and only major user of cab-aheads, and they were immensely successful. One factor that made them practical for Southern Pacific as

early as 1901 was that oil-powered engines were required because of the position of the tender, and Southern Pacific had been one of the first American railroads to convert its entire locomotive fleet from coal to oil.

The American entry into World War II in 1941 came at the end of Angus McDonald's $100 million investment program aimed at upgrading Southern Pacific's plant and equipment. The new switches, rails, boxcars and articulated locomotives put the railroad in a much better position to handle the challenge that was to come. The war, which had already been raging in Europe for two years, came as a surprise to few. Defense had been a national priority for over a year when the Japanese bombed Pearl Harbor. Southern Pacific had even participated, in August 1940, in the biggest mass railroad transportation exercise since World War I. Southern Pacific lines, including the Texas & New Orleans subsidiary, had cooperated with the US Army to move troops aboard 119 special military trains, meeting precise schedules. Even this massive exercise would be dwarfed by the actual wartime operations. By the end of January 1942, seven weeks after the United States entered the war,

Left: In 1948 SP took delivery of its first 6000 hp ALCO passenger diesels.

Below, left: Trapped by blizzard conditions for several days in the Sierra in January 1952, the City of San Francisco *was kept supplied by airplanes.*

Below: The City of San Francisco *prepares for boarding at the Oakland pier in 1938.*

670 special military trains had been pulled over Southern Pacific lines. By the end of hostilities, the total had risen to 28,349—enough trains to move 436 infantry divisions.

The years just after the end of World War II were a time of bright hopes and golden dreams for the Southern Pacific. In 1945, president Armand Mercier (1941-51) kicked off a $2 billion expansion program the likes of which hadn't been seen since the days of president Edward Henry Harriman (1901-09). New streamliners were introduced to take advantage of the surge in train travel that the company was sure would accompany postwar prosperity. Introduced in 1948, the *Golden State* reached Tucson from Chicago in 34 hours, and Los Angeles only 11 hours later. The *Daylight*s that had served the San Francisco-Los Angeles Coast Route since the 1930s were augmented by the *Shasta Daylight* and *Shasta Starlight*, connecting the San Francisco Bay Area with Portland. In 1950, an all-streamlined *Cascade* overnight train was added, which made the Portland-San Francisco run in 16.5

hours. Also in 1950, the new streamlined *Sunset Limited* went into service on the Sunset Route between New Orleans and Los Angeles. Described as 'the loveliest train on wheels,' the *Sunset Limited* made the trip in 42 hours, five hours less than previous trains.

Diesel locomotives became common on Southern Pacific's system by the early 1950s, though the company's lines were not fully dieselized until 1957. By the end of 1951, diesels were in use on such passenger routes as the crack *City of San Francisco*, operating over the old Central Pacific lines between Ogden and San Francisco. In January 1952, the *City of San Francisco* was trapped in the Sierra by a blizzard reminiscent of those encountered by Crocker and Strobridge when they built the original Sierra line nearly a century before. However, the availability of airplanes to drop supplies and of modern communications made the several days that the train spent marooned in a snowdrift more of an inconvenience than a life-threatening hardship. The episode did serve to illustrate that an end to the era of mass

train travel in the United States was at hand. Although air travel had not yet eclipsed the steel rail as the major means of long-distance passenger transportation, it was gaining fast. The era of the grand streamliners would soon be a fading memory.

By 1954, Southern Pacific passenger operations lost $58 million to competition with airlines and freeways. Emphasis in the company's rail operations shifted heavily toward freight. As the company's freight operations increased, passenger operations dwindled. On 1 May 1971, the federal government's passenger rail service, Amtrak, took over operation of the last of Southern Pacific's intercity passenger routes, with the exception of the commuter line between San Francisco and the suburban peninsula to the south. These routes, to which the company had added 15 new double-decked passenger cars in 1968, were operated at a loss by Southern Pacific until 1980. In that year, part of the financial burden was taken over by the California Department of Transportation, which considered the low-cost peninsula commuter route necessary to serve a public need.

With the exception of the Cotton Belt (acquired in 1932) and the Southern Pacific de Mexico lines (added in 1919, extended in 1927 and sold off in 1951), the overall Southern Pacific railroad map of 1980 was essentially identical to the Southern Pacific Railroad map of 1890. Some sidetracks were added or deleted, including the Lucin Cutoff and the 78-mile Palmdale-Colton Cutoff, but these changes entailed bypasses and track-straightening and did not really integrate any new territory into the system. One branch of the Sunset Route was completed in 1902 between El Paso and Tucumcari, New Mexico, but this was insignificant compared with the empire-building of the 1870s and 1880s. The significance of the tracks up to Tucumcari, where they met the lines of the Chicago, Rock Island & Pacific Railroad (Rock Island Line), increased as the twentieth century progressed.

Southern Pacific's Cotton Belt had been in St Louis since 1904, where it met the Rock Island Line coming south from Chicago. The Rock Island then turned west to Kansas City and southwest to Tucumcari. In 1963, Southern Pacific expressed an interest in buying this segment of the Rock Island, because the distance between Los Angeles and St Louis would be much shorter by way of Tucumcari than by way of Southern Pacific's Texas and Louisiana lines. Agreement on the sale was not reached until 1978, after Rock Island went bankrupt. On 24 March 1980, Southern Pacific began operating on the new 992-mile line under temporary operating authority, until the $57 million deal closed in October 1980.

In 1980, as Southern Pacific trains first rolled north out of Tucumcari, the company entered into serious negotiations with Santa Fe Industries regarding a merger. Negotiations continued off and on for the next three years, and on 27 September 1983 a press release was issued jointly by Southern Pacific headquarters in San Francisco and Santa Fe headquarters in Chicago stating that the two companies had agreed in principle to 'enter into a business combination.' The statement went on to say that 'Under the agreement each company would become a subsidiary of a newly formed

Previous pages: The restored Coast Daylight *works up a big head of steam as it rounds a bend in the Siskiyou Mountains on its historic run to the 1984 World's Fair.*

Below: A Southern Pacific road switcher, No 5203.

Above, right: Factory-fresh, Nos 6370 and 6371 are ready to roll.

Right: Sharing the road with Santa Fe locomotives, No 8270 emerges from the tunnel section of the Tehachepi Loop in Southern California.

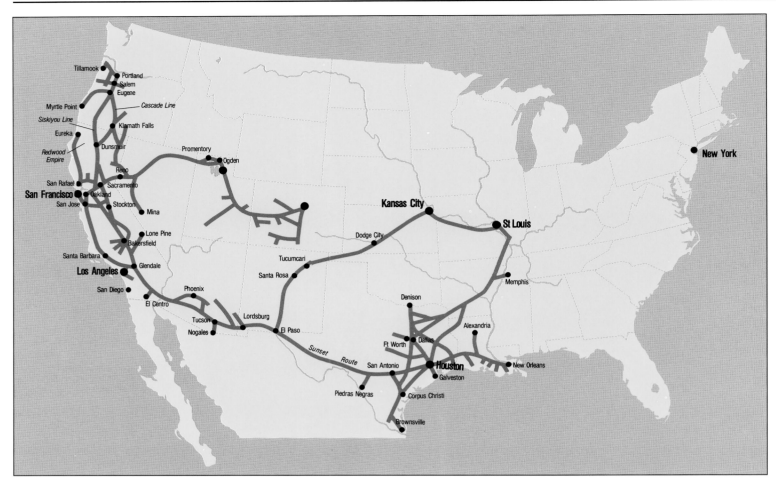

Above, left: This map shows the SP roads that together form the United States' fifth largest rail network, including SP's recent merger in 1988 with the Denver, Rio Grande & Western.

Left: No 7672 circles in an SP intermodal freight depot, ready to make the return trip with a new freight load.

Above: SP diesels Nos 8594 and 7900 snake their way along the cliffs, pulling piggyback freight cars.

holding company to be called Santa Fe Southern Pacific Corporation.'

However, in 1987, the Interstate Commerce Commission overruled the merger of the two roads. Then, on 13 October 1988, the Southern Pacific merged with the Denver & Rio Grande Western Railroad to form the nation's fifth largest rail network, with 15,000 miles of track in 15 states, connecting the mouth of the Columbia in the Pacific Northwest to the mouth of the Mississippi on the Gulf of Mexico. The combined services of the two railroads will be marketed under the southern Pacifc Lines banner, with headquarters in San Francisco.

Southern Pacific is the largest and busiest transportation system in Oregon, California, Nevada, Colorado, Arizona and Texas. It serves 15 Pacific Ocean ports, seven ports of entry into Mexico and 10 ports on the Gulf Coast.

Built a century ago on the dreams of four men, the Southern Pacific grew from a tenuous steel track across hostile plains into one of the largest, privately owned rail transportation companies in the world. But the Southern Pacific is more than a railroad; it is a diversified transportation and land development company with holdings in pipelines and of telecommunications.

Southern Pacific is a vast network of steel and microwave that spans what the company calls 'The Golden Empire,' and what the commentators call 'The Sun Belt.' It is an enormous marketplace of over 70 million people — representing nearly a third of the nation's population and gross national product. The gross national product of the Golden Empire exceeds that of the rest of the nation in per capita terms, and that of nearly every nation on earth in absolute terms. From this empire comes 97 percent of the nation's rice crop, 88 percent of its copper ore, 85 percent of its lettuce and grapes, 83 percent of its natural gas, 75 percent of its oil, 65 percent of its cotton and 40 percent of its lumber. It is a land of shimmering natural beauty and bountiful farms, the fastest-growing region in the country and the one with the most modern industrial base.

Southern Pacific began as a golden dream to bind a continent with tracks of steel and to develop the rich resources of California and the West. In so doing, it helped bring to fruition the dreams of the millions who rode its rails to begin new lives in the West. Southern Pacific is today the legacy of the men who tamed the Sierra, saved the Imperial Valley and united California with Texas and Oregon. Southern Pacific is the men and women who built the empire of steel so that others could build their futures in the Golden Empire.

THE UNION PACIFIC

Edited by Marie Cahill & Lynne Piade

As the American frontier expanded across the continent, settlers bravely journeyed across the great American desert in search of a better life on the West Coast. The journey was long and arduous, and the wagon trains that carried those first settlers across the nation inspired a vision of a great railroad spanning the continent. For the country to survive and prosper, its borders had to be linked, and thus was born the dream of the Union Pacific Railroad.

The seeds for a railroad to the Pacific were first planted in the 1840s, when the demand for goods from the Far East and exotic ports around the world inspired merchants and explorers to lobby Congress for funding to survey new routes to the Orient. By providing an alternate route, a transcontinental railroad would immensely reduce the time it took to sail around Cape Horn. By sea the trip took a hundred days or more, whereas by train it would take just over a week. It would encourage settlement across the new territories in the West and would link California to the East Coast, thus serving as insurance against the state's secession from the Union.

Debate continued with much talk and little action until 1853, when Congress instructed the War Department to determine the best and least costly route from the Mississippi River to the Pacific coast. Congress gave Secretary of War Jefferson Davis (who later became the president of the Confederacy) $340,000 to conduct the survey. Five possible routes were chosen and presented to Congress.

The first—the Northern Route—ran between the 47th and 48th parallels, stretching a distance of 2025 miles from St Paul, Minnesota to Seattle, Washington. The cost was estimated at $141 million. Today, this route is one of the main lines of the Burlington Northern.

The second, known as the Central or Overland Route, extended for a distance of 2032 miles along the 41st and 42d parallels from Council Bluffs, Iowa to Benicia, California. The price for this route was set at $131 million and parts of it would form the Union Pacific and the Central Pacific.

The third route, called the Buffalo Trail, followed the 38th and 39th parallels, beginning at what is now Kansas City, Missouri and ending at San Francisco, a distance of 2080 miles. The cost was never determined because the survey party was massacred by Indians before they could complete the survey. An added deterrent was that this route reached elevations more than 10,000 feet in the Rocky Mountains, making construction difficult if not impossible. Today, however, sections of this route are followed by the Denver & Rio Grande Western Railroad.

The fourth route, known as the Santa Fe Trail, covered a distance of 2096 miles from Fort Smith, Arkansas through Santa Fe, New Mexico. Estimated at a cost of more than $106 million, it was the route eventually followed by the Atchison, Topeka & Santa Fe Railroad.

The fifth, known as the Southern Route, ran for a distance of 2024 miles along the 32d parallel from Fulton near Texarkana on the Arkansas-Texas border to San Francisco via El Paso, Fort Yuma and Los Angeles.

The Southern Route was favored by Davis and other southerners in government who naturally wanted the South to benefit from the construction of a transcontinental railroad. The US did make plans to build a southern railroad and purchased land along the US-Mexico border from Mexico for that purpose, but the Civil War altered those plans. Jefferson Davis hastened south to serve as president of the secessionist states and Congress fixed the route for a transcontinental railroad north of the Mason-Dixon Line.

The route that was chosen for the Pacific Railroad was the one laid out by Theodore D

Judah, a civil engineer who had written a pamphlet on the subject and distributed it to the lawmakers in Washington. At the time, however, the lawmakers were more concerned with the threat of civil war and Judah returned home to California, where he found four Sacramento merchants—Collis Huntington, Leland Stanford, Mark Hopkins and Charles Crocker—who joined him in his quest for a Pacific railroad. The 'Big Four,' as they were known, formed the Central Pacific, the road that would form the western portion of the transcontinental railroad.

In 1862, President Abraham Lincoln signed the Pacific Railroad Act into law. This act granted a charter to the Union Pacific Railroad Company to begin building a railroad west from Omaha, Nebraska to Promontory, Utah, where it would connect with the Central Pacific, which had come from Sacramento, California under the management of Huntington, Stanford, Hopkins and Crocker—the Big Four. General John A Dix of New York City was the appointed president of the Union Pacific, but his involvement in army affairs kept him so busy that he passed the baton of leadership to Dr Thomas C Durant.

Under the terms of the Pacific Railroad Act, the UP was to be awarded land grants and cash from the sale of 30-year US bonds to subsidize the cost of materials and construction. For each mile of track completed the railroads would be awarded one section of land 10 miles square in alternative sections on each side of the right-of-way. They would also receive a loan of $16,000 for each mile completed on the flat terrain, $32,000 for each mile in more difficult terrain and $48,000 across the mountains.

Despite the promise of government land grants and cheap loans, the two railroads had to struggle to get under way. Disruptions resulting from the Civil War prevented the UP from breaking ground until December 1863 and actual work did not begin for another year. The UP's charter required raising $2 million in stock before beginning construction, but there were few takers. Within two years, it was clear that the concessions granted to the two railroads would not be sufficient. Thomas Durant of the UP and Collis Huntington representing the Central Pacific persuaded Congress to amend the Railroad Act of 1863, which had called for loans to be held up until track could be completed.

Previous page: UP 6018 proudly wends its way through the forests of California.

Below: The excavation of this grade in Echo, Utah, proved to be one of the most difficult tasks faced by UP work crews.

Right: The engine McQueen, stopping here on the main track at Wyoming Station, was built by Schenectady in 1868. Antlers adorn No 23's headlight.

Right, below: A UP train pauses in 1868 on the bridge beside Citadel Rock.

While the Central Pacific had its Big Four, the Union Pacific had Thomas Durant. A native of Massachusetts, Durant attended medical school in New York, where he graduated with a degree in surgery. He soon abandoned medicine in favor of working for an uncle who exported grain and flour in New York City and began to speculate in railroad stocks. Discovering how profitable railroads could be, he moved from stock speculation to participation and became one of the builders of the Chicago & Rock Island Railroad.

To assist him with the construction of the Union Pacific, Durant hired Major Grenville Dodge, one of the most knowledgeable railroad engineers in the nation. Dodge had studied civil engineering in Vermont with aspirations of one day building a railroad across the continent. After graduation, he took a job as a sur-

veyor with the Illinois Central Railroad, where he met Durant.

As soon as he arrived in Omaha to begin work on the UP, Dodge ran into problems with Durant. Durant and other investors wanted the railroad to take the least direct route west so that they could collect as much money as possible from land grants and bond sales. Dodge, however, won the argument for the most direct route possible by calling in Ulysses Grant to settle the dispute. With the Civil War over and with capital and materials once again available, work began to pick up. By September 1866, more than 180 miles had been laid west of Omaha. After fours years of struggle, the Pacific Railroad was gathering steam.

Although Grenville Dodge was the chief engineer, the actual track work was carried out under the supervision of the Casement brothers, Daniel and Jack. Both were short, wiry men, who, between them, had garnered 13 years' experience in railroad construction.

Before UP construction began in earnest in 1865, just 250 men worked on the project. Within a year of their arrival Dodge and the Casement brothers had 10,000 men on the job, living in boarding cars and tents kept at the back of track construction, moving everything forward every few days as construction on the track advanced.

At first, the gangs could lay only three miles of rail each day. Later, when they had been on the job for a number of years, they could build as many as eight or nine miles of track in one

Above: The driving of the golden spike at Promontory, Utah on 10 May 1869.

Left: A great deal of excitement surrounded the opening of a new line, as illustrated by this poster announcing the inauguration run of the Omaha to San Francisco route.

Right: A reproduction of UP No 119 was built for a reenactment of the historic meeting of the Central Pacific and the Union Pacific at Promontory, Utah on 10 May 1869.

day. The men were organized according to jobs performed. One gang first graded the track bed, while other gangs followed to put down ties, ballast and rail.

It was hard, heavy work requiring muscle and stamina. Crews rolled flat cars—each carrying a set number of rails along with the exact numbers of spikes to hold them down—up the railhead. As soon as the ties were dropped into place, a dozen men hauled two rails from the car and dropped them onto the ties. Another crew then gauged and hammered down the rails while the rail gangs pulled the cars forward to begin the process again.

Work proceeded as fast as a man could walk, with 30 to 40 men hammering in spikes behind the rolling flatcar. It took 30 seconds to lay a rail. With two crews working side-by-side, four rails could be thrown down in a minute. Close behind came the gaugers, spikers and bolters, who finished up by hammering spikes—10 spikes to a rail, 400 rails to a mile—to hold the work in place. The iron rails used in construction of the transcontinental project were shipped in from Pittsburgh and other eastern steel mills and were half the weight and size of today's steel rails.

Bases for handling the materials were organized from 100 to 200 miles from the construction site. Many of those bases remain today as the towns and cities of Fremont, Fort Kearny, North Platte, Julesburg, Sidney, Cheyenne, Laramie, Benton, Green River, Evanston and Ogden.

The workmen included many Irish and Civil War veterans from both the North and the

South who labored for $3 a day—good money for those times. Working conditions were primitive. Small bands of Indians would attack the crews and burn the tracks to avenge the trespassing of their hunting territories. The workers gave them whiskey to keep them away, but sometimes had to fight them off with handguns and rifles.

By the end of 1868, UP crews had completed 450 miles of track westward from Omaha, By the next spring, construction crews were racing through Wyoming and Utah to earn UP its share of entitlements to the government land

Above: This old-time train, assembled by UP for exhibition purposes, closely resembles the first passenger train to run west from the Missouri River on the UP line.

Below, left: An American-type 4-4-0 locomotive, the most common locomotive of its day, near Columbus, Nebraska in 1892.

Right: This Union Pacific 4-4-0 Camelback locomotive was built by Rogers of Paterson, New Jersey in 1887. Notice that the engineer's cab sits astride the boiler like a camel's hump, hence the 'Camelback' appellation.

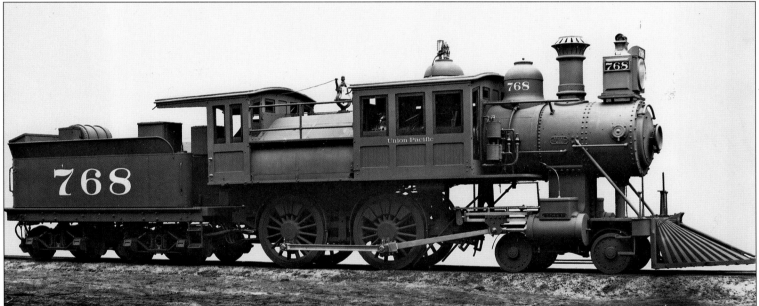

grants before meeting up with the competing Central Pacific crews.

The CP and UP became so intent on getting as much government land as possible that in the spring of 1869, they were even constructing parallel lines. Finally, Congress designated Promontory, Utah as the meeting point. On 10 May 1869, as UP's No 119 and CP's *Jupiter* came to a shuddering halt within a few feet of each other, the last rails were laid and the ceremonies began. Leland Stanford, wielding a sledgehammer, took a swing at the golden spike — and missed. Finally, Jack Casement stepped up, replaced the golden spike with an ordinary one and drove it home. The two locomotives then rolled slowly together, signifying the end of the ambitious project.

Unfortunately, successful completion of the transcontinental railroad did not prevent finan-cial problems from pulling it into receivership, and during the Panic of 1873 the UP declared bankruptcy. Like other railroads, the UP had been undercapitalized, leaving it in weak financial condition. When business was good, the UP barely generated revenues sufficient to cover operating costs and return a profit to investors. When the economy dipped, as it did often in the turbulent latter half of the nineteenth century, the UP was a losing endeavor.

After reorganization, however, the railroad expanded from its single line across the continent. In 1880, the Kansas Pacific and Denver railroads, and the cities of Kansas City and Denver were added. At the western end of the railroad, branch lines were built into Idaho and Oregon and, later, into Seattle. The discovery of gold, silver and copper spurred the construction of another line into western Montana.

The UP again fell into bankruptcy during the Panic of 1893 and was auctioned in Omaha on November 1897 to a group of investors headed by financier Edward H Harriman, who recognized the need to provide UP with the best he could afford. He set about inspecting almost every mile of track and, upon returning to New York, ordered a substantial rebuilding, including extensions of the Union Pacific into Utah. The cost was more than $25 million, and by the turn of the century Harriman announced that the rebuilding was complete. Within two years, despite the fact that loadings had declined 15 percent, he had doubled earnings.

Harriman took over the Southern Pacific in 1900 and merged the two giant railroads, but in 1913 the Supreme Court ruled that the Union Pacific had to divest itself of SP stock, and the two railroads separated.

When World War I broke out, the Union Pacific was ready to serve the nation. Unlike other railroads that struggled to meet the demands imposed by the war—antiquated locomotives and rolling stock, broken down yards and trackage—Union Pacific trains and equipment, operating under the wartime command of the US Railroad Administration, performed without problems.

In 1934, in the midst of the Great Depression, the Union Pacific introduced the nation's first streamlined diesel passenger train, *The City of Salina*, which toured the country on a grand publicity tour. It could speed along at 110 miles per hour on straight sections of track, and it hastened the arrival of diesel locomotives for passenger and freight service.

However, the Union Pacific was not quite finished with steam. In 1941, Union Pacific received the first *Big Boy* locomotive, at the time the world's most powerful steam locomotive. One of the largest ever made, the *Big Boy* could consume 22 tons of coal and 22,000 gallons of water in an hour.

When World War II began, millions of tons of materials and hundreds of thousands of troops had to be moved in short order. Increases in freight loadings were staggering, but the UP handled it without major problems and set records in the process.

On October 1980, the Interstate Commerce Commission approved the application for the merger of the Union Pacific, Missouri Pacific and Western Pacific railroads. The Missouri Pacific, like the Union Pacific, had played an important role in the development of western railroading. The Missouri Pacific can trace its roots back to 4 July 1851, and the groundbreaking at St Louis for a Pacific railroad. A year later the line's first locomotive, *The Pacific*, became the first train to operate west of the Mississippi.

About the same time, track was being laid for the Iron Mountain Railroad, another Missouri

Previous pages: A 2400 hp EMD passenger diesel (left), one of 144 E9s built from 1954 to 1963. Acquired in 1944, No 8444 (right) was UP's last steam engine. One of 45 4-8-4 Northerns, originally designated No 844, No 8444 was retired to special service in 1960.

Below: The Union Pacific terminal in Los Angeles in the late 1920s.

Right: UP X 4019 Big Boy was among the world's largest steam locomotives ever built.

Right, below: These streamliners headed the City of San Francisco (left) and the City of Portland (right).

Pacific predecessor, and in Texas and Missouri, other lines that would one day be part of the Missouri Pacific were under way. After the Civil War, the Pacific Railroad completed its line from St Louis to Kansas City, and daily service began between the two cities. Other railroad construction began, but despite ambitions of building to the Pacific, the Missouri Pacific never received grant aid from Congress as other railroads had.

In 1879, New York financier and notorious 'robber baron' Jay Gould purchased controlling interest in the Missouri Pacific and gave himself the title of president. Using the Missouri Pacific as a foundation, he forged a network of rail lines in the Midwest, merging five smaller railroads into the Missouri Pacific.

Gould did not retain control of his new system for long. In 1885, he broke off the Texas & Pacific from the Missouri Pacific, and in 1888, allowed the Missouri-Kansas-Texas railroad properties to slip from his control. Of all the roads he had acquired, only the Iron Mountain remained under his control.

However, between 1885 and 1892, Missouri Pacific mileage increased through construc-

tion of subsidiary lines, including extensions to Colorado and Louisiana. When Jay Gould died in December 1892, control of the company passed to his son, George J Gould. Between 1909 and 1923, smaller subsidiaries merged with the railroad.

Like most other railroads, the Missouri Pacific experienced hard times during the Great Depression. In 1933, it went into receivership for 23 years. After its reorganization, the Missouri Pacific vigorously went after new business. It modernized its equipment, constructed new classification yards and became the first railroad to acquire a solid state computer. Expansion by acquisition was the rule through the late 1960s. In the 1970s, the system took over the Chicago-based Chicago & Eastern Illinois Railroad and later the Texas & Pacific Railway. In 1980, the Missouri Pacific became a subsidiary of the Union Pacific when stockholders voted to approve a merger of the two lines.

The Western Pacific was organized in 1903 by George Gould, Jay Gould's son and successor, to run from San Francisco through California's Feather River Canyon and Beckworth

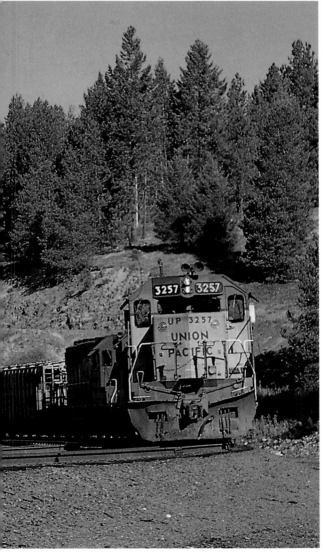

Above: *It takes three loco-motives to keep this UP freight train on time.*

Left: *The Union Pacific system includes Union Pacific, Missouri Pacific, Western Pacific and the Katy lines. Powerful MoPac and UP road switchers lead trains through the mountains of the West.*

Pass to Salt Lake City, Utah, where it would connect with the Rio Grande-Missouri Pacific system. Operations finally began in 1910. Because the railroad had no branches to feed it, revenue failed to cover operating expenses. In 1915 Rio Grande defaulted on its obligations and the Western Pacific went into receivership.

After reorganization, the company expanded and prospered until the 1930s, when it again was placed in receivership. The Western Pacific emerged from bankruptcy in 1945 and operated independently until 1980, when Union Pacific acquired the line.

The Union Pacific's most recent merger was with the Missouri-Kansas-Texas Railroad, the KT line, or simply the Katy. Originally a line between New Orleans and Northern Kansas, the Katy today operates primarily between the Gulf Coast at Galveston and Omaha/Council Bluffs. UP executives have long considered the Katy a vital part of the Union Pacific's main route between Kansas and Texas because of trackage rights agreements. Because the sound welfare of the Katy has always been of vital importance to the Union Pacific, the UP merged with the Katy in 1988, when the smaller line was beset with severe financial difficulties.

The realization of the nation's dream to span the continent, the Union Pacific today is the third largest railroad system in the United States. Its 24,000 miles of track serve 22 states, with main lines extending from Chicago in the Midwest to Los Angeles, Oakland and Seattle in the West and El Paso, Houston and New Orleans in the South.

INDEX